T0419162

NEW DIRECTIONS IN ASSESSING HISTORICAL THINKING

New technologies have radically transformed our relationship to information in general and to little bits of information in particular. The assessment of history learning, which for a century has valued those little bits as the centerpiece of its practice, now faces not only an unprecedented glut but a disconnect with what is valued in history education. More complex processes—historical thinking, historical consciousness, or historical sense making—demand more complex assessments. At the same time, advances in scholarship on assessment open up new possibilities.

For this volume, Kadriye Ercikan and Peter Seixas have assembled an international array of experts who have, collectively, moved the fields of history education and assessment forward. Their various approaches negotiate the sometimes conflicting demands of theoretical sophistication, empirically demonstrated validity, and practical efficiency. Key issues include articulating the cognitive goals of history education, the relationship between content and procedural knowledge, the impact of students' language literacy on history assessments, and methods of validation in both large-scale and classroom assessments. *New Directions in Assessing Historical Thinking* is a critical, research-oriented resource that will advance the conceptualization, design, and validation of the next generation of history assessments.

Kadriye Ercikan is Professor of Measurement, Evaluation, and Research Methodology, Faculty of Education, University of British Columbia, Canada.

Peter Seixas is Professor of History Education, Faculty of Education, University of British Columbia, Canada.

NEW DIRECTIONS IN ASSESSING HISTORICAL THINKING

Edited by Kadriye Ercikan and Peter Seixas

Routledge
Taylor & Francis Group

NEW YORK AND LONDON

First published 2015
by Routledge
711 Third Avenue, New York, NY 10017

and by Routledge
2 Park Square, Milton Park, Abingdon, Oxon OX14 4RN

Routledge is an imprint of the Taylor & Francis Group, an informa business

© 2015 Taylor & Francis

Library of Congress Cataloging-in-Publication Data
Library of Congress Cataloging in Publication Control Number: 2014035322

ISBN: 978-1-138-01826-6 (hbk)
ISBN: 978-1-138-01827-3 (pbk)
ISBN: 978-1-315-77953-9 (ebk)

Typeset in Bembo
by Apex CoVantage, LLC

CONTENTS

FIGURES

TABLES

PREFACE

New technologies have radically transformed our relationship to information in general and to little bits of factual information in particular. The assessment of history learning, which for a century has valued those little bits as the centerpiece of its practice, now faces an unprecedented glut (Osborne, 2003; Wineburg, 2004). There are ever more assessments, ever easier to access, worth less and less. Mere memorization can no longer be the name of the game. This creates opportunities—indeed, it demands that history education broaden its goals and that history assessments focus on more complex processes.

Internationally, history educators have recently aimed formal curricula towards, variously, advancing sophistication in historical thinking, developing more complex levels of historical consciousness, and teaching more competence in historical sense making, among others. What's more, an exponentially developing field of research on history students and teachers has provided an empirical base for this reform movement (Carretero, Asensio, & Rodriguez-Moneo, 2012; Köster, Thünemann, & Zülsdorf-Kersting, 2014; Monte-Sano & Reisman, forthcoming; Stearns, Seixas & Wineburg, 2000; VanSledright & Limon, 2006; Wineburg, 1996).

Recognition in the public culture of the powerful role of collective memory, awareness of rapid demographic changes, and the ubiquity of conflicts over recognition, reparation, and commemoration of historical injustice: all of these pose new opportunities and new demands on history education in schools. Their impact is magnified in school programs to the degree that education researchers, administrators, and teachers pay attention, both as an issue of fairness and as an issue of pedagogy, to the beliefs, ideas, and capacities with which students arrive on the first day of school. This rethinking of history has obvious implications for history assessment, implications compounded by changes in the field of assessment itself.

Three developments within the field of assessment are particularly relevant in this regard. First, there is a general shift in emphasis towards assessment of complex thinking (Schraw & Robinson, 2011). This is a response to a growing focus across all school subject areas, on the integration of knowledge, inquiry, problem solving, and critical analysis.

Second, different uses of assessment results are changing the make-up of history assessments. International assessments of educational outcomes such as the Programme for International Student Assessment (PISA) and the Trends in International Mathematics and Science Study (TIMSS) have led to comparisons of education systems in dozens of countries, as well as evaluations of the education levels of work forces in these countries. Several countries including the United States (US) and Germany have taken their standing in these international comparisons seriously and have implemented changes in education with the intention of improving the competitiveness of their work force in numeracy and literacy, as well as complex thinking in several areas. The US's "Race to the Top" program, for example, is tied to federal funding, and the associated "Common Core Standards" include literacy in history and social studies (Common Core State Standards Initiative, 2012).

Third, assessment design has been profoundly affected by the considerable consensus among assessment scholars that led to and flowed from the US National Research Council's *Knowing What Students Know: The Science and Design of Educational Assessment* (2001). That consensus was embodied in the "assessment triangle" of three interacting components: cognition, observation, and interpretation. The Council's work also contributed to the widespread recognition of the interplay among teaching, learning, and assessment. This interplay had implications not only for classroom-based assessments and the professional development they required, but also for large-scale assessments to focus on valued learning outcomes instead of basic recall of factual knowledge.

This dynamic context calls for, and has generated, new thinking about assessments of historical thinking. The chapters in this volume provide a clear sense of the directions it is taking.

References

Carretero, M., Asensio, M., & Rodriguez-Moneo, M. (Eds.). (2012). *History Education and the Construction of National Identities*. Charlotte, NC: Information Age.

Köster, M., Thünemann, H., & Zülsdorf-Kersting, M. (Eds.). (2014). *Researching History Education: International Perspectives and Disciplinary Traditions*. Schwalbach/Ts: Wochenschau Verlag.

Monte-Sano, C., & Reisman, A. (forthcoming). Understanding history. In E. M. Anderman & L. Corno (Eds.), *Third Handbook of Educational Psychology*. Mahwah, NJ: Lawrence Erlbaum.

Osborne, K. (2003). Teaching history in schools: A Canadian debate. *Journal of Curriculum Studies, 35*(5), 585–626.

Schraw, G., & Robinson, D. H. (2011). *Assessment of Higher Order Thinking Skills.* Charlotte, NC: Information Age.

Stearns, P., Seixas, P., & Wineburg, S. S. (Eds.). (2000). *Knowing, Teaching, and Learning History: National and International Perspectives.* New York, NY: New York University Press.

VanSledright, B., & Limon, M. (2006). Learning and teaching social studies: A review of cognitive research in history and geography. In P. A. Alexander & P. H. Winne (Eds.), *Handbook of Educational Psychology* (pp. 545–571). Mahwah, NJ: Lawrence Erlbaum.

Wineburg, S. (1996). The psychology of learning and teaching history. In D. C. Berliner & R. C. Calfee (Eds.), *Handbook of Educational Psychology* (pp. 423–437). New York, NY: Macmillan.

Wineburg, S. (2004). Crazy for history. *The Journal of American History, 90*(4), 1401–1414.

ACKNOWLEDGEMENTS

We would like to express our thanks to the numerous contributors for their thoughtful chapters and for working with us. Each of the chapters was reviewed by at least two experts in the field (some of whom also contributed other chapters). We thank this international set of scholars (see below) for their contributions to improving the work:

Sirkka Ahonen, University of Helsinki
Heinrich Ammerer, Salzburg University
Bob Bain, University of Michigan
Keith Barton, Indiana University, Bloomington
Joel Breakstone, Stanford University
Lawrence Charap, College Board
Penney Clark, University of British Columbia
Fred Drake, Illinois State University
Cate Duquette, Université du Québec à Chicoutimi (UQAC)
Per Eliasson, Malmö University
Maureen Ewing, College Board
Joanna Gorin, Educational Testing Service
S. G. Grant, SUNY Binghamton
Maria Grever, Erasmus University, Rotterdam
Kristen Huff, Regents Research Fund
Anders Jönsson, Kristianstad University
Pamela Kaliski, College Board
Andrew Kolstadt, National Center for Education Statistics
Stephen Lazer, Educational Testing Service
Stéphane Lévesque, University of Ottawa

Jan Löfström, University of Helsinki
Chauncey Monte-Sano, University of Michigan
Gabriel Reich, Virginia Commonwealth University
Abby Reisman, University of Pennsylvania
David Rosenlund, Malmö University
Kara Smith, College Board
Mark Smith, Stanford University
Allison Thurber, College Board
Bruce VanSledright, University of North Carolina at Charlotte
Kaat Wils, KU Leuven
Arie Wilschut, Amsterdam University of Applied Sciences

We would like to acknowledge the financial support we received from "Canadians and their Pasts," (Jocelyn Létourneau, P.I.) a project funded by the Social Sciences and Humanities Research Council Canada (SSHRC)'s Community University Research Alliance (CURA) program. We would further like to thank The History Education Network/Histoire et éducation en réseau (THEN-HiER) for including this as Volume IV of its major publication series and for funding the 2012 Historical Thinking Project conference which brought some of the authors together for the first time. We also acknowledge the financial support of the Canada Research Chairs program. The book could not have been completed without the excellent editorial and administrative assistance we have received from Juliette Lyons-Thomas and Ulrike Spitzer. We thank them for their contributions.

CONTRIBUTOR BIOGRAPHIES

Fredrik Alvén, Ph.D. Student in History and History Didactics, Malmö University, Sweden. Fredrik Alvén is a writer of the National Test in History grade 9 with research interests in analyzing how the purpose of history as a school subject is perceived by politicians, teachers, and students, and how these different purposes fit the idea of assessing skills in history.

Robert B. Bain, Associate Professor, University of Michigan. Bob Bain has appointments in both the Departments of History and Education, where he also chairs the Secondary Teacher Education Program. A historian by training, his research centers on the practices involved in teaching and learning history and learning to teach history. He is one of two faculty leaders on the Big History Project, www.bighistoryproject.com.

Joel Breakstone, Stanford University. Joel Breakstone directs the Stanford History Education Group (SHEG). Along with Mark Smith and Sam Wineburg, he led the development of SHEG's assessment website, Beyond the Bubble. He previously taught high school history in Vermont. His research focuses on how teachers use assessment data to inform instruction.

Susan M. Brookhart, Senior Research Associate, Center for Advancing the Study of Teaching and Learning, School of Education, Duquesne University. Susan Brookhart is past editor of *Educational Measurement: Issues and Practice* and has written or co-authored sixteen books and over 60 articles on assessment. Her interests include the role of formative and summative classroom assessment in student motivation and achievement, the connection between classroom assessment and large-scale assessment, and grading.

Lawrence G. Charap, Director of Social Studies Content Advanced Placement Program, The College Board. Lawrence Charap has taught high school and college history and worked on teacher professional development for the University of Pittsburgh. He received a Ph.D. in American History from Johns Hopkins University in 2001.

Catherine Duquette, Professor of Didactics of History, Université du Québec à Chicoutimi (UQAC). Catherine Duquette is a member of the Centre de recherche interuniversitaire sur la formation et la profession enseignante (CRIFPE-UQ) and The History Education Network (THEN-HiER). Her research interests include how students learn historical thinking, the relationship between historical thinking and historical consciousness, and the assessment of historical thinking.

Per Eliasson, Professor of History and History Didactics, Malmö University, Sweden. Per Eliasson is head of teacher training in history at Malmö University; coordinator for the work with a new Swedish history curriculum in compulsory schools and upper secondary schools in 2009–2010; and project leader for the National Test in history grade 9. His research interest is environmental history and history didactics.

Kadriye Ercikan, Professor of Measurement, Evaluation, and Research Methodology, Director of Cross-cultural Assessment and Research Methods in Education, Faculty of Education, University of British Columbia, Canada. Kadriye Ercikan's research focuses on educational assessment and measurement, and making generalizations in educational research. She is the co-editor of *Generalizing from Educational Research: Beyond Qualitative and Quantitative Polarization, Improving Large-Scale Assessment in Education: Theory, Issues, and Practice* and co-author of *Canadians and Their Pasts*.

Lindsay Gibson, Department of Curriculum and Pedagogy, University of British Columbia. Lindsay Gibson recently completed his Ph.D. dissertation on ethical judgments in secondary school history classrooms. He is a member of the Instructional Leadership Team in the Kelowna, British Columbia School District. He also writes and edits for The Critical Thinking Consortium's (TC2) history education projects.

Susan R. Goldman, Distinguished Professor of Liberal Arts and Sciences, Psychology, and Education, University of Illinois at Chicago, Co-director of UIC's Learning Sciences Research Institute. Susan Goldman's research and scholarly interests focus on learning and assessment in subject matter domains such as literacy, mathematics, history, and science.

Maria Grever, Professor of Theory and Methodology of History, Director of the Center for Historical Culture, Erasmus University Rotterdam. Maria Grever has published widely on historical culture, collective memory, and plural identities, among others in *Journal of Curriculum Studies, British Journal of Educational Studies, Paedagogica Historica, Tijdschrift voor geschiedenis,* and *Gender & History.* One of her recent co-edited books is *Beyond the Canon: History for the Twenty-First Century* (2007). (www.eshcc.eur.nl/grever/)

Jan Hodel, Lecturer in History Didactics, Institute for Secondary Education, University of Applied Sciences Northwestern Switzerland (FHNW). Jan Hodel holds a Masters Degree (1995) in history, biology, and geography and a Ph.D. in History (2013) from the University of Basel. From 1996 to 2004 he worked at a communication agency in Basel. From 2004 to 2013 he was a scientific associate at the Institute of Research and Development, FHNW.

Kristen Huff, Senior Fellow for Assessment, Regents Research Fund. Kristen Huff specializes in educational assessment and is responsible for advising New York State education leaders on all aspects of assessment design and validation.

Pamela Kaliski, Associate Psychometrician, The College Board. Pamela Kaliski received her Ph.D. in Assessment and Measurement from James Madison University in 2009, and has been working at the College Board since then. Her areas of expertise and research interests include standard setting, evidence-centered design, and test score validity evidence.

Stephan Klein, Assistant Professor, ICLON, Leiden University Graduate School of Teaching. Stephan Klein was a post-doctoral researcher at the Center for Historical Culture, Erasmus University Rotterdam and project leader of the valorisation program *Dynamic heritage education in the Netherlands*, which resulted in the website *Slave Trade in the Atlantic World.* His research interests include history teaching, heritage education, and early modern political, cultural, and colonial history.

Carlos Kölbl, Professor of Educational Psychology, Kulturwissenschaftliche Fakultät, University of Bayreuth, Germany. Carlos Kölbl worked at the Leibniz Universität Hannover before he became professor of educational psychology at the University of Bayreuth. Currently, in addition to teaching, his major activities are oriented towards a culture-inclusive psychology. His research investigates historical consciousness in children and adolescents, societal understanding, and intercultural learning.

Lisa Konrad, Ph.D. student, Kulturwissenschaftliche Fakultät, University of Bayreuth, Germany. Lisa Konrad worked at the Freie Universität (2010–2011) and Leibniz Universität Hannover (2011–2013) in different research projects. Her research interests are intercultural learning, gender studies, intersectionality studies, and professional competence of teachers.

Andreas Körber, Professor in Education, Didactics of History, and Political Studies, Hamburg University. Andreas Körber was project manager for YOUTH and HISTORY (1993–1997). He wrote his doctoral dissertation on the public remembrance of Gustav Stresemann (1999). He was a teacher at Gymnasium (1999–2005), assistant in History Didactics (2000–2004), and professor since 2004. He has served as Vice Dean for Teaching (2010) and International Coordinator of the TeacMem Project (2009–2012).

Stephen Lazer, Senior Vice President, Student and Teacher Assessment, Educational Testing Service. Stephen Lazer has worked in various roles in large-scale assessment at Educational Testing Service, including as Senior Vice President for Student and Teacher Assessment, Vice President for Assessment Development, and Executive Director of the United States National Assessment of Educational Progress. His areas of expertise include assessment design and instrument development.

Juliette Lyons-Thomas, Post-doctoral Fellow, Columbia University. Juliette Lyons-Thomas is also a Fellow at the Regents Research Fund. Her research interests include the use of think aloud protocols for validation of assessments of complex thinking, equity in education, and issues surrounding cross-cultural assessment.

Johannes Meyer-Hamme, Research Associate, University of Hamburg. Johannes Meyer-Hamme studied history, geography, and education at the Universities of Hamburg and Southampton (UK). He graduated with a qualitative empirical study on intercultural learning in history under the supervision of Bodo von Borries. Currently he is a research associate on the "HiTCH" Project (Historical Thinking—Competencies in History).

James W. Pellegrino, Liberal Arts and Sciences Distinguished Professor, Distinguished Professor of Education, Co-director of *Learning Sciences Research Institute*, University of Illinois at Chicago. James Pellegrino's research and development interests focus on children's and adult's thinking and learning and the implications of cognitive research and theory for assessment and instructional practice.

Josh Radinsky, Associate Professor of Curriculum Studies and the Learning Sciences, University of Illinois at Chicago. Josh Radinsky's research focuses on teaching and learning with graphic and geographic data, in history and the social sciences, and the construction of roles and narratives in classroom discourse.

Gabriel A. Reich, Associate Professor of Secondary History/Social Studies Education, Virginia Commonwealth University. Gabriel A. Reich is a former high school history teacher and current Associate Professor of Secondary History/

Social Studies Education. His research interests include assessment, curriculum, and collective memory. He has published articles in journals such as *Theory and Research in Social Education* and the *Journal of Curriculum Studies.*

Abby Reisman, Assistant Professor of Teacher Education, Graduate School of Education, University of Pennsylvania. Abby Reisman's research focuses on curriculum design and teacher practice in history. She was Project Director for "Reading Like a Historian" in San Francisco, the first extended history curriculum intervention in urban high schools. Her work has appeared in *Cognition and Instruction, Journal of Curriculum Studies*, and *Teachers College Record.*

David Rosenlund, Ph.D. Student in History and History Didactics, Malmö University, Sweden. David Rosenlund is a writer of the National Test in History grade 9, with research interests in the alignment among history curriculum, history teachers' assessment practices, and student perceptions of the subject of history in Swedish upper secondary schools.

Peter Seixas, Professor and Canada Research Chair, Faculty of Education, University of British Columbia. Peter Seixas is the director of the Centre for the Study of Historical Consciousness, editor of *Theorizing Historical Consciousness* (2004), and author, with Tom Morton, of *The Big Six Historical Thinking Concepts* (2013), designed to help teachers incorporate historical thinking into their classes.

Denis Shemilt, Formerly Leeds University and Leeds Trinity University. Denis Shemilt was Evaluator of the Schools Council Project "History 13–16" 1974–78 and Director 1978–82. With Peter Lee, he was Co-Director of the Cambridge A-Level History Project 1984–88. Since retirement in 2007, he has researched impediments to and benefits of teaching and learning "big history."

Kara Smith, Associate Research Scientist, The College Board. Kara Smith works on the Higher Education team in the Research Department of the College Board. Her primary research focus is on examining and understanding factors related to college and career readiness at both two- and four-year institutions. She focuses primarily on retention, graduation, and academic performance at the post-secondary level.

Mark Smith, Researcher, Stanford History Education Group. Mark Smith is a researcher for the Stanford History Education Group and serves as assistant director of the Stanford Teaching with Primary Sources program. His research focuses on history assessment, particularly issues of validity related to the uses of K-12 history assessments to measure historical thinking.

Holger Thünemann, Professor of History Didactics, University of Cologne. Until 2012 Holger Thünemann worked as lecturer at Münster University. In 2012/13 he was professor for history and its didactics at the PH Freiburg. His research interests include teaching, learning, and textbook research in the field of the didactics of history, historical culture, and contemporary history.

Carla van Boxtel, Professor of History Education, Research Institute of Child Development and Education and the Institute of Culture and History, University of Amsterdam. Carla van Boxtel leads the Dutch Center of Social Studies Education. Her main research interests are the learning and teaching of history in schools and museums, and the improvement of students' historical thinking and reasoning. She has received several research grants and has published in international peer reviewed journals and books.

Bruce VanSledright, Professor, Department of Reading and Elementary Education, University of North Carolina at Charlotte. Bruce VanSledright has studied how history teachers prepare their students to cultivate historical understandings. He is interested in how curricula, textbooks, and other texts intersect with teaching strategies to influence student learning. Recently, he authored a book on how assessments can be developed to measure growth in learning.

Monika Waldis, Research Assistant and Teacher Educator, School for Teacher Education FHNW, Center for Democracy, Aarau, Switzerland. Monika Waldis' research focus is educational research and assessment in the field of mathematics, history and citizenship education, and professional development of history teachers. See http://www.fhnw.ch/personen/monika-waldis and www.zdaarau.ch/en/.

Cecilia Axelsson Yngvéus, Assistant Professor of History Didactics, Malmö University, Sweden. Cecilia Axelsson Yngvéus has a Ph.D. in History Didactics, Mediation and Learning in Museums. She is a writer of support material for assessing history in upper secondary schools for the Swedish National Agency for Education and is a team leader in the Agency's project on assessing newcomers' knowledge of history.

Béatrice Ziegler, Professor of History and History Didactics, Head of the Center Civic and History Education, School for Teacher Education FHNW, Center for Democracy, Aarau, Switzerland. Béatrice Ziegler's research foci are public history and citizenship education. See http://www.fhnw.ch/personen/beatrice-ziegler and www.zdaarau.ch/en/. For the project *narratio* see: http://www.fhnw.ch/ppt/content/prj/T999–0373.

Meik Zülsdorf-Kersting, Professor, University of Osnabrück, School of Cultural and Geosciences, History Education. Meik Zülsdorf-Kersting's research fields are history education, historical thinking theory, and public history. Selected publications include Manuel Köster/Holger Thünemann/Meik Zülsdorf-Kersting (Eds.): Researching History Education. International Perspectives and Disciplinary Traditions. Schwalbach/Ts. 2014 (Geschichtsunterricht erforschen, vol. 4); and Meik Zülsdorf-Kersting: Sechzig Jahre danach: Jugendliche und Holocaust. Eine Studie zur geschichtskulturellen Sozialisation (Geschichtskultur und Historisches Lernen, Bd. 2). Berlin 2007.

INTRODUCTION

The New Shape of History Assessments

Peter Seixas and Kadriye Ercikan

Globally, new technologies, new sociocultural contexts, and new understandings of assessment constitute the field upon which new directions in assessing historical thinking are being worked out. While there is considerable variety in the ways educators and researchers handle them, three fundamental sets of problems must be confronted by all. First, what are the goals of history education; how should they be defined in terms of knowledge, skills, concepts, competencies, and/or dispositions; and what are the paths through which students might achieve them? Second, to paraphrase the memorable title of the U.S. National Research Council's (2001) collection, how can educators know what students know; what kinds of tasks and tests will provide this crucial information to those guiding the process of education? And third, how do we know that we have it right? That is, how can we ensure that our interpretations of students' performance are valid indicators of progress or lack thereof in reaching the goals of history education?

To restate these succinctly, history educators, researchers, and practitioners involved in assessment must (1) define models of cognition and learning in historical thinking, (2) design tasks and assessments targeting historical thinking, and (3) validate score meaning in those assessments. In this introductory chapter, we begin with overviews of each set of problems. These three sections are followed by an exploration of the structure of the book and its chapters.

Goals of History Education: Models of Historical Cognition and Learning

In the chapters that follow, readers will find a multiplicity of approaches to history education. Even the names diverge: historical thinking, historical consciousness, narrative competence, heritage education. There is an uneasy tension in the fact that current models are both universal in their claims (i.e., *"this* is what school history should be about") and heterogeneous in their aims. On the other hand, history education and assessment communities might do well to embrace this heterogeneity, as long as they are clear about what pieces of historical thinking/consciousness/competence they are targeting. Precisely because of the broad range of conceptions of history education, clear definitions of *what is being assessed* (that is, the cognition model) are an imperative starting point.

The chapters in this volume present an array of possibilities ranging from the more empirically pragmatic to the more theoretically rich, each bringing their own strengths and vulnerabilities. The more empirically pragmatic models of cognition have the advantage of workability, communicability, and thus utility with practitioners. The potential cost is that they can miss valued aspects of history education. To get a sense of both commonalities and differences, we can consider models of cognition from the two ends of this array.

Devised specifically to meet pragmatically the demands for an "ongoing, nationally representative survey of student achievement," recent reforms in the National Assessment of Educational Progress (NAEP) U.S. History Test divide the field of history into "content" and "skills," acknowledging their interrelation (Lazer, this volume). "Content" specifies themes, chronological periods, and regions, and is also called "historical knowledge and perspective." This category includes knowing and understanding people, events, concepts, themes, movements, contexts, and historical sources; sequencing events; recognizing multiple perspectives and seeing an era or movement through the eyes of different groups; and developing a general conceptualization of U.S. history.

The skills, "historical analysis and interpretation," consist of explaining issues, identifying historical patterns, establishing cause-and-effect relationships, finding value statements, establishing significance, applying historical knowledge, weighing evidence to draw sound conclusions, making defensible generalizations, and rendering insightful accounts of the past. (NAGB, 2013, p. 32, cited in Lazer, this volume.)

"Content" and "skills" as two large framing categories are almost common sense to American educators. On the other hand, in the European chapters in this volume, they play a much-reduced role, with "skills" rarely even mentioned except to refer to reading, writing, or "generic" skills.

In the European chapters, the models of cognition bear the inheritance of a long, rich, theoretical tradition, based not in education but in philosophy of history. The challenge for the current generation of researchers, those included in this volume, has been to ground theory in an empirically testable model of cognition, ultimately useful in shaping history education (Kölbl & Konrad, this volume; Körber & Meyer-Hamme, this volume; Waldis, Hodel, Thünemann, Zülsdorf-Kersting, & Ziegler, this volume).

Kölbl and Konrad introduce "historical consciousness" as perhaps the "key concept" in history education in Germany (this volume, p. 17). Their chapter provides evidence of the energies that German history educators have devoted to its elaboration, while noting the problems in operationalizing it, "resulting in rather vague proposals which could not actually orient teaching" (this volume, p. 24). Körber and Meyer-Hamme further explore what operationalization might look like, in the "FUER" model of historical thinking. In contrast to NAEP's "content and skills," the cognition model is built around broad "competencies," defined along four dimensions: competence in questioning, methodological competence, orientation competence (ability to relate history to one's own life), and subject area competence, which refers to facility with *all* of the conceptual terms used in discussing the subject of history, both substantive (like "revolution") and procedural (like "periodization").

A further expression of the difference between the more empirically pragmatic and more theoretically rich models of cognition in history is the treatment of one of the core issues in the philosophy of history: the relationship between present and past (Seixas, 2012). Models of cognition influenced by the German writing on historical consciousness (e.g., Rüsen, 2004) make the relationship between past and present explicit and teachable. In addition to "orientation competence" in Kölbl and Konrad and Körber and Meyer-Hamme, we can see it in Duquette's definition of historical consciousness, in Waldis et al.'s definition of "historical questions," in van Boxtel et al.'s heritage education (van Boxtel, Grever, & Klein, this volume), and in the Swedish national assessment, where the curriculum specifies students' ability "to reflect upon their own and others' use of history" in the present as one of three curricular pillars. Yet, as an explicit dimension of students' historical thinking, the relationship between past and present is largely absent from the American contributions.

Other clear differences in the cognition models can be seen in respect to "narrative competence" in historical thinking, ranging from centrality (Körber & Meyer-Hamme, Waldis et al., this volume) to total absence (Charap, this volume; Lazer, this volume). Students' reading of documents or sources (again, with some variation in terms) is present in every chapter, and forms a centerpiece of the cognition model in some (e.g., Reisman, this volume; Smith & Breakstone, this volume). Yet, exactly what cognitive moves are expected in the reading of documents varies across cognition models.

By juxtaposing these sometimes overlapping, sometimes contradictory, more and less theoretical, more or less operationalizable models of historical cognition in a single volume, we can, perhaps for the first time, start to minimize cross-purposes, noting strengths and weaknesses not only in conceptions of desirable educational goals, but also in the translation of these goals into efficient and meaningful, empirically based assessment strategies. Some key issues that assessment scholars and practitioners have encountered in that translation comprise the next section.

Issues in Designing Assessments of Historical Thinking

Several issues arise in designing tasks for assessing historical thinking. Some are common across multiple subject areas; others are specific to history. Among the former is that of developing tasks that truly engage students in complex thinking. Research on assessments of complex constructs has demonstrated the difficulty of designing tasks that actually capture complex thinking (Baxter & Glaser, 1998; Ferrara & Chen, 2011). For example, empirical investigations conducted by Ferrara et al. (2003, 2004) found significant mismatches between cognitive processes targeted by the tasks and actual cognitive processes students engaged in.

Three key issues arise in designing tasks to assess the target constructs in history assessments: (1) the relationship of the assessment tasks to the targeted constructs of historical thinking; (2) the relationship of factual, or "content" knowledge to historical thinking; and (3) the problems of basic reading and writing literacy and their centrality to most historical thinking tasks. The chapters in this book discuss and demonstrate different ways of addressing these issues.

Issue 1: The Relationship of the Assessment Task to the Targeted Constructs of Historical Thinking

Two examples demonstrate different solutions to the problem of aligning assessment tasks and targeted constructs.

In addressing the challenge of engaging students in historical thinking, Seixas et al. (this volume) describe a multistep process. The first step is the translation of the conceptual definition of the construct into "student understandings" (see Seixas et al., Appendix 1). The second step involves a description of "observable behaviors" that would constitute evidence of the expected cognitive processes. Based on these observable behaviors, they defined "tasks that could generate those observable behaviors." The same expected student understandings used for designing tasks are also used for interpreting student responses to tasks. Thus, both tasks and interpretation of student responses are connected with the construct definition.

VanSledright (this volume) describes multiple-choice items that are intended not only to capture historical thinking but also to provide information about students' standing in a progression of historical thinking. He describes designing weighted multiple-choice items that have a tiered weighting structure for item choices as interpretive solutions that define most-to-least defensible responses to the prompt. Unlike typical multiple-choice items where only one choice is correct and defensible, options are weighted from acceptable, but least defensible given the evidence available, to most defensible, based on expected levels of the targeted construct. The structure of the tiered weighting is intended to align with levels of progression in historical thinking.

Issue 2: How to Deal with "Content" Knowledge

All of the chapters deal in one way or another with the relationship of "content" to historical thinking. "Content" is variously referred to, in this volume, as knowledge, context, factual knowledge, content knowledge, contextual knowledge, or prior knowledge. That there is so little agreement on terms suggests that, despite the ubiquity and facility with which it is deployed, "content" actually contains a variety of categories deserving of further exploration. For our purposes, we use the term "content" to identify what is actually a multifaceted issue in the context of the assessment of historical thinking.

Readers will find at least three different approaches to dealing with content in the chapters that follow. In one approach, assessment tasks are designed in an attempt to minimize the need for previous knowledge. Here the factual and contextual information that students need for completing the tasks is provided either in the primary source documents that they will analyze (e.g., Smith & Breakstone, this volume), or in summary information sections or in both (Seixas et al., this volume).

In a second approach, tasks are designed to assess knowledge and thinking jointly. This approach is seen in assessments of cognition and learning models that do not separate out content and skills, such as in the Swedish national assessments described by Eliasson and his colleagues (Eliasson, Alvén, Yngvéus, & Rosenlund, this volume).

In a third approach, content or factual knowledge is one component of the cognition model, and therefore an important piece, in its own right, of history assessment (Charap, this volume; Lazer, this volume; and Kaliski, Smith, & Huff, this volume). In the Advanced Placement (AP) reforms, knowledge of most particular details is not to be tested, but understanding of broad developments within large themes is (Charap, this volume).

The appropriateness of various approaches depends not only on whether content is a targeted construct, but also on the assessment context. In the history classroom, teachers are generally less interested in isolating historical thinking from content knowledge.

In some external assessments such as the AP, the assessment of content knowledge is based on a common curriculum. These assessments test students' historical knowledge and thinking using tasks that integrate the two requirements. Unlike the classroom situation, but consistent with the historical thinking cognition model used in these assessments, separate scores for history content knowledge and historical thinking are developed and reported.

Issue 3: How to Deal with Reading and Writing Requirements

The third issue arises, again, from the integral relationship of reading and writing literacy with historical thinking, and the question of when and where it makes sense to try to disentangle them. When history assessments ask students to read historical documents and write substantial paragraphs, questions arise as to what extent the assessment is measuring historical thinking and to what extent it is actually measuring basic literacy skills. Reading and writing literacy are often highlighted as two of the most fundamental educational goals: Competence in reading and writing is a prerequisite for success across the curricular subject areas. Again, there is variation in how this issue is dealt with across different chapters in the book. In the Smith and Breakstone chapter (this volume), reading literacy is presented as an integral part of assessing historical thinking. In the FUER assessment described by Körber and Meyer-Hamme (this volume), tasks are designed to assess subject-specific reading abilities as well as a respondent's ability to use the information as evidence for historical conclusions. The authors argue that subject-specific reading ability is an important aspect of the ability to compose historical accounts. Seixas et al. (this volume) describe efforts to minimize the burden of reading by shortening the documents presented to students, designing tasks that require students to engage in historical thinking, and eliminating items that could be answered by simply understanding what is presented in the source documents.

If we are interested in making claims about students' historical thinking independent of their reading and writing literacy, then efforts should be made to minimize the burden of reading and writing in the assessment and not penalize students for their literacy skills in an assessment of historical thinking. This becomes a critical issue when the assessment is administered to students with limited proficiency in the language of the assessment. A separate but related issue is the limitation in the claims we can make about students' historical thinking, if the assessment is not designed to distinguish historical thinking from literacy. In some contexts, there is a need to assess distinct subject matter learning and reasoning, such as historical thinking. This can happen in classroom contexts where history teachers are interested in assessing learning specific to history and not literacy skills developed elsewhere. This need is heightened in accountability contexts where assessment of learning is separated by subject areas. In both of these contexts, assessing historical thinking independent of literacy skills is necessary for making meaningful inferences.

Validity of Score Interpretations

The assessment design issues described above highlight the importance of validity evidence for making meaningful score interpretations. Unlike assessments of factual recall, where simple evidence that the assessment covers all relevant topics based on judgments by curricular experts may be adequate, such evidence is not sufficient for assessments of complex thinking. Validation of score meaning requires making intended inferences explicit at the outset. This makes it possible to conduct evaluations of the adequacy of the evidence required to support the intended inferences (Kane, 2013). Determining whether scores from the assessment are accurate indicators of students' history knowledge and thinking involves the examination of: (1) the relationship between the target construct(s) and the tasks; (2) the connection between the tasks and interpretation of performances on the tasks; and (3) the degree to which interpretation of performances in relation to the target constructs are supported by evidence.

The alignment of tasks with constructs and the degree of construct representation is central to the validity of inferences about score meaning. Therefore, clear definitions of cognition and learning models with expected progressions of student development based on empirical research are the starting place for quality assessment design and meaningful score interpretations. Although validation of score meaning requires gathering evidence after the test is developed and scores are generated, it is equally important to gather evidence for the validity argument in the early phases of assessment design before scores are generated—and while there may still be an opportunity to modify the tasks or even the overall design. Therefore, steps used in designing tasks and aligning them with the cognition and learning models, such as the ones described in Seixas et al., VanSledright, and Körber and Meyer-Hamme (all this volume), are important aspects of the validity argument.

Another source of validity evidence is based on the interactions of students with tasks, in particular the cognitive processes in which they engage. In educational research, the most commonly used methods for gathering data about students' cognitive processes are different types of think-aloud protocols (TAPs). TAPs require participants to verbalize their thoughts while they are engaged in an educational activity (Ericsson & Simon, 1993). They can be used to gather evidence of students' cognitive processes; their understanding of test questions; whether specific words, phrases, and sentence structures create confusion or difficulty; and how their understanding of test items affects their formulation of solutions and responses (Ercikan et al., 2010).

It is important to clarify that validity of score meaning cannot be based solely on student response processes. Other psychometric evidence such as that based on dimensionality of test data structure, item and task psychometric properties, including item difficulty and discrimination indicators, as well as indicators of measurement accuracy also need to be considered. However, the focus on response processes as a source of validity evidence by all four chapters in the validity section of this book highlights the criticality of such evidence in assessments of historical thinking.

Structure of the Book

In Part I, contributors describe and discuss different articulations of history education goals—models of cognition and learning—and their implications for assessment. A dominant strain of history education scholarship, worldwide, has its roots in the British Schools Council History Project (SCHP) of the 1970s and 1980s. SCHP provided the notion of "second-order historical thinking concepts" or "procedural concepts" that provided a means to reshape history curriculum and pedagogy along the lines of disciplinary criteria. Though we do not have a chapter on the British model, its legacy can be seen throughout. Competing conceptions of history education developed concurrently in Germany and much of continental Europe, where the idea of "historical consciousness" played a leading role. In the first chapter Carlos Kölbl and Lisa Konrad provide a thorough explanation of the genealogy of the term over the past two decades, through functional, structural, and psychological iterations. Most recently, they explain, a "world turned global" has introduced categories of race, class, and gender and made more complex the models of cognition of historical consciousness developed earlier.

In the United States, public concern, curricular support, and government funding for improving literacy have mobilized research on reading and writing in the disciplines, including history, a trend exemplified by the work of Abby Reisman. Her chapter begins, "Historical thinking depends on the ability to reason about written text. . . ." The apparent contrast with the starting point of Kölbl and Konrad's "historical consciousness" could not be starker. And yet, as readers will see in this chapter and subsequent ones, even very different starting points lead to many overlapping assessment concerns, two of which Reisman highlights: the way that students' background knowledge and their basic reading comprehension confound efforts to assess their historical thinking.

In the work of the research team of Carla von Boxtel, Maria Grever, and Stephan Klein, we can see further evidence of the overlaps among apparently divergent goals of history education and their associated models of cognition. Taking their cue from a new element in Dutch history curriculum, "the changing significance of the past for different groups of people," they propose "heritage education," according a central place for critique of present uses of the past. Quite remarkably, the Dutch curricular moves towards a variant of historical thinking began, like the British and German, in the 1970s and 1980s. The coincidence of temporal origins is striking, no matter how different their models of cognition. Moreover, in the Dutch team's approach, we begin to see the intersection of a "second order concept," (i.e., historical significance) as a curriculum goal, with present and future orientation (central to historical consciousness) as a component of history education.

In the final chapter of Part I, Catherine Duquette explicitly weaves together at least two of the divergent models of historical thinking: the six second-order concepts of the Canadian Historical Thinking Project, and European "historical consciousness" (Duquette, this volume). She does so through both a theoretical analysis and an empirically based assessment project. Her chapter suggests the larger questions that we might apply not only to the four chapters in this section, but to the entire volume: how do the various models of historical cognition differ; to what extent are they compatible; and how can we begin to identify their various strengths and weaknesses in relation to assessment?

In Part II, contributors present research on assessment design and provide models of assessments aimed at measuring various aspects of historical thinking. As in Part I, the variety of cognition models will be striking to readers of these chapters. But the focus shifts in this section to how various history education and assessment scholars deal with issues in designing assessments that capture students' complex thinking.

Bruce VanSledright lays out his own cognition model in an original configuration. He considers assessment at the classroom level, with an approach to task design that, he argues, will be usable and useful for teachers in "assessing for learning." He explores it by providing specific examples, and then drawing out the design principles they embody. Central to his contribution is the "weighted multiple-choice" item, which, he argues, provides information to teachers about students' ways of thinking more efficiently than either the multiple-choice or the constructed response items.

In the chapter by Andreas Körber and Johannes Meyer-Hamme, we see the next steps in translating "historical consciousness" explored by Kölbl and Konrad in Part I, into a model of assessable competencies and tasks suitable for large-scale assessments. They acknowledge the importance of students' ability to both analyze and synthesize in historical studies, and focus on an original approach to tasks aiming to assess students' abilities to construct narratively coherent accounts. Like VanSledright, they draw further general principles from their example.

Peter Seixas, Lindsay Gibson, and Kadriye Ercikan base their chapter on yet another model of historical cognition, one widespread in Canada, structured around second-order concepts that occupy only a small corner of the Körber/Meyer-Hamme model. They provide not individual tasks but a one-hour test, key features of which they suggest as practical solutions to assessment design challenges: multiple short document excerpts, all related to a particular topic, each with a small number of questions, but building towards a summative constructed response paragraph. They locate a key moment in the design process, working with the excerpts, the cognition model, and draft test items, in a series of "mutually determined adjustments and revisions" achieved through piloting, analysis of student responses, and validity research. The last of those is discussed more thoroughly in their chapter in Part IV.

In the final chapter of Part II, Monika Waldis and her colleagues start from a variation on the cognition model of Körber and Meyer-Hamme, and, like them, focus on narrative competence. Like Seixas et al., they provide multiple documents for students to work with. However, after some smaller questions, the central task for students was to construct a narrative for one of three scenarios: a panel discussion, blog, or student newspaper. The students were provided with one of two tests, one on a familiar topic covered in the curriculum, or another unfamiliar topic. These elements of design enable them to make a series of comparisons valuable for history assessment designers. However, most importantly for those interested in their cognition model, they examine the relationship between multiple "quality features" scored through low-inference coding and high-inference, qualitative assessment of the narratives by history education experts.

In Part III, contributors describe three large-scale assessments of historical thinking, two based in the United States and one from Sweden. The differences between the two American and the Swedish assessments are striking. As in Parts I and II, there are clear distinctions between the cognition models in these assessments that reflect the North American and German traditions described earlier on. In this part of the book, we can see how these distinctions are operationalized in real large-scale assessment contexts. The Lazer and Charap chapters provide clear demonstrations of efforts to design large-scale assessments that are expected to hold against strict psychometric criteria in order to provide accurate trend data, in the case of National Assessment of Educational Progress (NAEP), and inform high-stakes decisions, in the case of Advanced Placement (AP) history exams. As a result, there are detailed specifications and descriptions of cognition and learning models and discussions of trade-offs of different assessment design choices. On the other hand, in the Swedish assessment the primary goal of the national test is to influence history instruction and learning in the classroom.

Part III of the book opens with a chapter by Stephen Lazer on NAEP history assessments and the challenges and trade-offs in designing historical thinking assessments for tens of thousands of students. He presents sample tasks for grades 4, 8, and 12 that illustrate different levels of complexity assessed at different grades. The discussion of the future of the NAEP history assessments is inspiring. These include using technology in assessments that may facilitate working with reference materials, such as textbooks, atlases, and archives, and eliminate challenges created by assessing simultaneously historical thinking and content knowledge. Lazer also sees a role for simulations and games in history assessments that may include collaborations among multiple students. These futuristic visions for history assessments can open doors for conceptualizing historical thinking in different ways that may include a group level construct, collaboration, and dynamic exchange of perspectives, among others.

The second chapter in Part III by Lawrence Charap describes motivations for and the assessment design issues in the new AP history assessment. One of the motivations for redesign of the AP history assessments stemmed from criticisms of the exam's use of multiple-choice items. Charap discusses limitations of multiple-choice items in assessing historical thinking and trade-offs between multiple-choice and other item types. The outcome of the redesign has been elimination of disconnected recall-based multiple-choice questions in favor of multiple-choice and writing questions intended to engage students in historical thinking.

The third chapter in this part of the book, by Per Eliasson and his colleagues, describes a Grade 9 national history test in Sweden (Eliasson et al., this volume). The differences in assessment contexts in Sweden versus North America are evident in their respective assessment designs. First, the Swedish assessments focus on historical consciousness with associated broader competencies compared to, for example, the AP assessments with tasks targeted to assess historical causation, patterns of continuity and change over time, periodization, comparison, contextualization, historical argumentation, appropriate use of historical evidence, interpretation, and synthesis. Second, the Swedish national assessment involves teachers in both the administration and the scoring of the assessment as part of their strategy to influence teaching and learning. These broader learning goals and focus on classroom teaching and learning distinguish the Swedish national test from the two American ones.

Four chapters in Part IV describe and discuss validity research in assessments of historical thinking. The primary focus of all four chapters is the extent to which assessments engage students in historical thinking. The first chapter by Pamela Kaliski and her colleagues discusses two approaches for gathering such validity evidence, dimensionality and cognitive validity evidence. In the Kaliski et al. chapter, dimensionality evidence is defined as evidence that supports the claim that items and components of the assessment are related to each other in ways that are consistent with the definition of the construct. Cognitive validity evidence is defined as evidence that the examinees are engaging in intended cognitive processes. The chapter provides clear guidelines for conducting validity research to gather dimensionality and cognitive validity evidence.

The latter three chapters describe validity research on specific assessments and provide insights about task design and limitations of multiple-choice item types. The chapter by Kadriye Ercikan and her colleagues is a natural follow up to the Kaliski et al. chapter in its demonstration of how cognitive validity evidence may be obtained and discussion of the value and limitations of such evidence. The authors describe a three-step process for identifying cognitive validity evidence from student think-aloud protocols. The first step involves determining what types of historical evidence each task elucidates. The second step examines which tasks require historical thinking from students more consistently. The third step examines the relationship between evidence of historical thinking in student verbalizations and historical thinking scores. The authors argue for the importance of these steps in using student verbalization for validity evidence.

The importance of cognitive validity evidence is emphasized in the third chapter, by Gabriel Reich. He convincingly demonstrates limitations of multiple-choice questions in assessing historical thinking. This chapter demonstrates the importance of careful assessment design in order for the assessment to measure competencies beyond general literacy and test-wiseness.

The theme of item type continues in the Mark Smith and Joel Breakstone chapter. These researchers argue for tasks that are not as limiting as multiple-choice items but not as open-ended as document based questions (DBQs). These research-ers argue for tasks targeted to specific historical thinking skills that may be used by teachers in classroom contexts. Using think-aloud protocols, they obtain evi-dence that the tasks are indeed capturing historical thinking among the students who were strategically selected to have had advanced history education and lit-eracy skills.

Commentaries at the end of each part of the book summarize, discuss, and critique chapters included in that part. These commentaries play an important role in synthesizing similarities and differences among the chapters and high-lighting how each contributes to the discussion and practice of assessment of historical thinking.

As this volume goes into publication, educational assessment is top news worldwide. In the United States, the discussion concerns the decline in scores on state-wide assessments (e.g., Kentucky and Maryland) after the states moved to the Common Core Curricula (Common Core State Standards Initiative, 2012). In Canada, hypotheses about the drop in Canada's mathematics scores on the latest Programme for International Student Assessment (PISA) revolve around a greater emphasis on problem solving rather than basic mathematics. Worldwide, there is concern about 15-year-olds' financial literacy levels revealed by the latest PISA. These all reflect high expectations of educational assessments to provide information about outcomes of education processes and preparation of children and youth for the challenges of contemporary society. The book is intended to highlight the importance of historical thinking as a key learning outcome and to promote and provide guidance for good quality assessments of historical think-ing. We hope that academics, practitioners, and policy makers will find rich insights to build upon and move the field forward.

References

Baxter, G., & Glaser, R. (1998). Investigating the cognitive complexity of science assess-ments. *Educational Measurement: Issues and Practices, 17*, 37–45.

Common Core State Standards Initiative. (2012). Common core state standards for English language arts & literacy in history/social studies, science, and technical subjects: Common Core Standards Initiative. Retrieved from www.corestandards.org

Ercikan, K., Arim, R., Law, D., Domene, J., Gagnon, F., & Lacroix, S. (2010). Application of think aloud protocols for examining and confirming sources of differential item functioning identified by expert reviews. *Educational Measurement: Issues and Practice, 29*(2), 24–35.

Ericsson, K., & Simon, H. (1993). *Protocol Analysis: Verbal Reports as Data* (Rev. ed.). Cam-bridge, MA: MIT Press.

Ferrara, S., & Chen, J. (2011). *Evidence for the accuracy of item response demand coding cat-egories in think aloud verbal transcripts.* Paper presented at the annual meeting of the American Educational Research Association, New Orleans, LA.

Ferrara, S., Duncan, T., Freed, R., Velez-Paschke, A., McGivern, J., Mushlin, S., Mat-tessich, A., Rogers, A., & Westphalen, K. (2004, April). *Examining test score validity by examining item construct validity: Preliminary analysis of evidence of the alignment of targeted and observed content, skills, and cognitive processes in a middle school science assessment.* Paper presented at the annual meeting of the American Educational Research Association, San Diego, CA.

Ferrara, S., Duncan, T., Perie, M., Freed, R., McGivern, J., & Chilukuri, R. (2003, April). *Item construct validity: Early results from a study of the relationship between intended and actual cognitive demands in a middle school science assessment.* Paper presented at the annual meeting of the American Educational Research Association, Chicago, IL.

Kane, M. (2013). Validating the interpretations and uses of test scores. *Journal of Educational Measurement, 50,* 1–73.

National Assessment Governing Board (NAGB). (2013). *U.S. History Framework for the 2014 National Assessment of Educational Progress.* Washington, DC: National Assessment Governing Board.

National Research Council. (2001). *Knowing What Students Know: The Science and Design of Educational Assessment.* Washington, DC: National Academy Press.

Rüsen, J. (2004). Historical consciousness: Narrative structure, moral function, and ontogenetic development. In P. Seixas (Ed.), *Theorizing Historical Consciousness* (pp. 63–85). Toronto: University of Toronto Press.

Seixas, P. (2012). Progress, presence and historical consciousness: Confronting past, present and future in postmodern time. *Paedagogica Historica, 48*(6), 859–872.

PART I

Goals of History Education

Models of Historical Cognition and Learning

1

HISTORICAL CONSCIOUSNESS IN GERMANY

Concept, Implementation, Assessment

Carlos Kölbl and Lisa Konrad

Historical consciousness ("Geschichtsbewusstsein") is one of the major concepts in history education in Germany, perhaps even its key concept. It is widely discussed in academia but has also left deep footprints in educational practice. In the wake of what has become known as "PISA-shock" in 2001—compared to pupils in other countries German students scored below the international average—the concept of historical consciousness is being transformed into an assessable competence. The assessment of historical thinking in Germany is inextricably linked with the concept of historical consciousness; thus, an understanding of this concept is an indispensable requirement for understanding German school curricula and models of assessment. Accordingly, we mainly focus on such conceptual explications in this contribution.

The chapter is organized into three sections. The first section defines historical consciousness and its core components as reflected in different conceptualizations. The second section describes the extent to which historical consciousness has been implemented in school curricula. The third section discusses how and to what extent historical consciousness is being transformed into an assessable competence in Germany.

What is Historical Consciousness?

History education cannot claim a monopoly on the term historical consciousness for it is a term also used in other related disciplines, such as psychology (e.g. Kölbl & Straub, 2001; Straub, 2005a), sociology (e.g. Leitner, 1994), or ethnology (e.g. Schott, 1968). Moreover, it is not a recent invention. Rather it dates at least back to empirical explorations in the era of Weimar (Sonntag, 1932). The term began to receive its greatest prominence, though, just when it was declared a core concept in matters of history education from the 1970s onwards. Rolf Schörken's

(1972) and Karl-Ernst Jeismann's (1977) terminological explications and programmatic arguments can be viewed as pioneering in this respect. In subsequent years, different functional, structural, and developmental approaches were proposed (Schönemann, 2012, pp. 102–109).[1] We will first focus on two of the most prominent of these, Jörn Rüsen's (1993) highly influential functional approach revolving around the act of narrating history, and Hans-Jürgen Pandel's (1987) broadly received structural approach, which divides historical consciousness into seven different categories. Then we present an approach stressing the psychological and developmental basis of the concept of historical consciousness. Recently, theoretical efforts inspired by diversity studies have been undertaken to more or less fundamentally rethink historical consciousness. The main focus of these studies is to analyze social categories like race, class, and gender, their complex intersections, and the ways in which they contribute to social inequalities. Martin Lücke's approach, drawing on diversity studies will be discussed at the end of this section. The discussion will point to possible relations between Lücke's and other models of historical consciousness. Also, links between theory and empirical phenomena will be addressed.

Types of Narrative Construction of History

In Jörn Rüsen's conceptualization of historical consciousness (see Rüsen, 1993 and Rüsen, Fröhlich, Horstkötter, & Schmidt, 1991), narrating history and understanding historical narratives play essential roles, as do narrative abbreviations such as "Auschwitz." Rüsen proposes a multifaceted understanding of historical consciousness and does so by offering several conceptual distinctions: (a) different degrees of consciousness and awareness; (b) different dimensions (political, cognitive, rhetorical, and aesthetic); (c) different modes of articulation ranging from ordinary to highly complex; (d) different topoi, e.g. the prominent topos of "historia magistra vitae"; and (e) four types of narrative construction of history. This last differentiation constitutes the most prominent part of Rüsen's concept and consists of what he calls traditional, exemplary, critical, and genetic types.

In the traditional type, the past is regarded as an ensemble of events and interpretations that have immediate meaning for the present. No differences are seen in principle between present and past. Maxims of action of the past can be transferred without attention to historical perspective.

In the exemplary type, past events and phenomena are distilled into laws that possess trans-historical (that is, without change over time) validity. To learn from history means in this case to identify exemplary historical phenomena, to examine them as to their suitability for the formulation of universal laws, and to apply them in the present.

The critical type operates in opposition to the first two types. Here, counter-evidence and counter-narratives contest the immediate meanings that might be drawn from past phenomena for the present.

In the genetic type, the inevitability of historical change, even radical change, is acknowledged. Change is not only a threat, but also brings possibilities with it.

Rüsen's typology originates from a reconstruction of modes of professional historiographical thinking including such diverse thinkers as Leopold von Ranke, Johann Gustav Droysen, Hayden White, or Frank Ankersmit. An investigation on modes of historical thinking of students in the Ruhr area showed the potential of this typology for empirical study (Rüsen et al., 1991; see also Seixas, 2005). Rüsen postulates a progressive logic for his typology, with development moving from the first (lowest) to the last (highest), but never fully abandoning the lower levels. Convincing empirical evidence for this, however, is still lacking.

Dimensions of Historical Consciousness

Hans-Jürgen Pandel (1987) advocates a concept of historical consciousness that takes society seriously. In his structural approach, historical consciousness is a mental structure consisting of seven intertwined forms of consciousness. These forms of consciousness can be divided into three basic (time, reality, historicity) and four social (identity, politics, economy-society, morality) categories (ibid., p. 132). The three basic categories constitute the domain of history. Each category is characterized via central descriptors: "yesterday," "today," and "tomorrow" (time), "real" and "fictitious" (reality), "static" and "changeable" (historicity), "we" and "you" (identity), "above" and "below" (politics), "poor" and "rich" (economy-society), "right" and "wrong" (morality). More detail follows (see also Sauer, 2009, p. 15).

Consciousness of time is important in order to discern between past, present, and future, and in order to put events into temporal order. Moreover, the distinction between physical and historical time is decisive: October 13, 1812 has twenty-four hours just the same as its "sibling" October 13, 2013. Nevertheless, the first date is meaningful for Canadian history as the date of the battle of Queenston Heights, whereas the latter—at least from today's perspective—does not claim historical meaning for Canadian history.

Consciousness of reality is needed in order to identify "real" historical phenomena in contrast to fictitious phenomena, a difficult task. This is true in particular for children but of course not only for them. Procedures of historical validation are often extremely complex operations. Leopold von Ranke's dictum that historians should tell "how it really was" ("wie es eigentlich gewesen") is an easy postulate only on the surface level.

Consciousness of historicity means awareness of change. Groups of persons, segments of societies, societies as a whole, and the interplay among nations and supranational associations and organizations are subject to more or less radical and visible changes. Those changes can take place abruptly or with little notice by contemporaries, sometimes identified only in retrospect. Consciousness of identity points to people's membership in social groups and their feelings of belonging to the group. Consciousness of identity as a competence includes the ability to realize and to reflect historically grounded feelings of belonging—both others' and one's own. Consciousness of politics refers to the idea that societies are structured by relations of power and the ability to identify and analyze such structures. Consciousness of economy-society relates to the ability to analyze social inequalities. Consciousness of morality is the competence to evaluate historical phenomena adequately. This is difficult insofar as today's moral horizon may not be congruent with yesterday's norms and values. A consciousness of morality implies a detailed reconstruction of yesterday's norms and values without totally suspending today's moral convictions, which would result in a dubious moral relativism.

Pandel's concept has also been used as theoretical scaffold in empirical studies (e.g. El Darwich, 1991). Proposals to transform Pandel's concept to better meet the challenges of a globalizing, power-differentiated world will be discussed after the presentation of a developmental approach below.

Historical Consciousness as a Psychological Concept

Developmental approaches to historical consciousness in Germany go as far back as 1932, the year in which Kurt Sonntag's influential theoretical and empirical study into the development of historical consciousness was published (Sonntag, 1932). Our own much more recent efforts (Kölbl, 2009; Kölbl & Straub, 2001; Straub, 2005b) conceptualize the development of historical consciousness drawing on selected theoretical means originating from the tradition of genetic structuralism (Piaget, Kohlberg, Gilligan), sociohistorical psychology (Vygotsky, Luria, Leontiev), narrative psychology (Bruner, Sarbin), and theory of historiography and history education (Rüsen, Koselleck, Danto). Historical consciousness here is not conceptualized only by purely theoretical means but is also—partly—grounded in empirical analyses focusing on children and adolescents. This leads to a psychologically grounded concept of historical consciousness: Historical consciousness is understood as a mental structure or competence that underlies our dealing with collectively important aspects of past, present, and future. This competence articulates itself via narrative acts, i.e. telling and understanding historical narrations. The narrative mode of thinking can be regarded as specific for the domain of history differentiating it from other domains. Thus, a developmental psychology of historical consciousness may be regarded as one particular domain-specific cognitive developmental path (Carey, 1985). Historical consciousness here is, however, not reserved to historical thinking alone. Rather two forms of historical consciousness are differentiated, one scientific and the other existential, i.e. with historically mediated identities and interests.

If historical thinking is taken seriously then one also has to take into account the historicity of historical consciousness itself not only with regard to its contents but also to its very structure and functions. At least in "Western" societies historical consciousness often takes a specific *modern* form. What are the constituents of such a modern historical consciousness? An answer to this question includes the following: an awareness of contingency, otherness, and difference, a critical attitude towards a straightforward acceptance of the idea that history can teach us something ("historia magistra vitae"), a secularization of historical narratives, and, last but not least, a scientifically mediated dealing with history. The causes of modern historical consciousness can be seen in various interrelated processes, including the expansion of the means of telecommunication, increased migration, mass tourism, and repeated experiences of the unpredictability of events and radical social shifts. Modern historical consciousness is in part an answer to the challenges of a world turned global, insofar as it provides a historical consciousness suitable for intercultural communication. Modern historical consciousness is not a privilege of professional historians. Our empirical analyses have found it—in rudimentary forms—in youth and, to a lesser degree, in very young pupils (elementary school level). These analyses revolve around differentiations of the concept of time and history, categories on the structuring of history, concepts of historical development, forms, and foundations for the validation of historical statements, and types of historical understanding and explanation.

A World Turned Global, a World Full of Inequalities: Challenges for Historical Consciousness

A world turned global requires a modern historical consciousness, most importantly in respect to increased awareness of difference and otherness. Such an awareness may be both urgent and insufficient in a world where differences are used to exercise power and justify social, political, and economic inequalities. This is the forceful argument recently made in German history education by advocates of a revised concept of historical consciousness heavily informed by diversity studies (Crenshaw, 1989; McCall, 2005). In 2009, Barricelli and Sauer wrote:

> An estimated third of all students in Germany today bear an intercultural background (with a growing tendency). All didactical [i.e. educational, C. K. & L. K.] research should duly take care of this undeniable *diversity* among pupils when conceiving empirical studies. Perspectives need to be broadened even more: What could history mean to highly heterogeneous student communities of different *race, class* and *gender,* what advantage could individuals and collectives of varying ethnic heritage, social origin or sexual orientation take of considering their own, their family's, the others' past? These issues are not even discussed in a convincing way yet, and they are far less accounted for in empirical studies.
>
> (p. 70)

The research field has changed considerably in a short period. In any case, there is a promising beginning of an important theoretical discussion. Martin Lücke's (2012) approach, relying on Rüsen and Pandel and transforming the latter, is such a contribution to the emergent discourse on the challenges of diversity studies in German history education. Lücke is very much interested in history lessons that enable students to inquire competently about the historical origins of social inequalities and to narrate complex histories of race, class, and gender. A particular focus lies on the complex intersections of these categories, or as critical race theorist Kimberlé W. Crenshaw put it "classically":

> The point is that Black women can experience discrimination in any number of ways and that the contradiction arises from our assumptions that their claims of exclusion must be unidirectional. Consider an analogy to traffic in an intersection, coming and going in all four directions. Discrimination, like traffic through an intersection, may flow in one direction, and it may flow in another. If an accident happens in an intersection, it can be caused by cars traveling from any number of directions and, sometimes, from all of them. Similarly, if a Black woman is harmed because she is in the intersection, her injury could result from sex discrimination or race discrimination.
> (Crenshaw, 1989, p. 149)

Where is the place for race, class, and gender in models of historical consciousness? Lücke (2012, p. 143ff.) answers this question by drawing on Pandel's structural model. He argues for keeping the three basic categories (consciousness of time, reality, historicity) since they form the backbone of the domain of history. However, for the four social/societal categories, he proposes two dimensional fields, including consciousness of categories and consciousness of levels.

Consciousness of categories addresses the pedagogical task of improving students' ability to identify the concepts of difference that led to social inequalities. Race, class, and gender are important candidates, but one might add religion, health, or sexual orientation. Such a consciousness of categories asks for the substantial "what" of social inequality.

Consciousness of levels addresses the pedagogical task of improving students' ability to identify where social inequalities were established in history. These levels are structural relations of power, symbolic forms of representation, and constructions of identity. Such a form of consciousness of levels asks for the "where" of social inequality, i.e. for places and levels of power at which inequalities emerge.

Lücke's transformation of Pandel's model helps to end fruitless questions as to why there are four and not more social/societal categories, e.g. a consciousness of gender (Sauer, 2009, p. 17). Pandel's model may not be the only one, however, which helps to place race, class, and gender into the concept of historical consciousness. Rüsen's critical type of the narrative construction of history may also provide a place for histories of diversity. The concept of a specifically *modern* form of historical consciousness with its emphasis on the importance of awareness for otherness and difference may offer a gateway for such histories, too, particularly if it is directed explicitly towards questions of power and oppression. A serious problem, however, is the almost complete absence of empirical studies that take the challenges of diversity seriously. The demand to fully consider intersections of various social categories poses difficult methodological problems, which may best be addressed by using qualitative methods sensitive to ambiguities, connotations, and ambivalences. For a start, approaching intersectionality pragmatically could imply empirical analyses highlighting mainly one social category (for such an analysis in respect to [un]doing gender in history lessons, see Konrad, 2014).

Historical Consciousness in the Curriculum

Debates concerning historical consciousness have not remained limited to scientific discourse but have also affected the construction of curricula, a prerequisite for the promotion and assessment of historical consciousness in educational contexts. Due to the federal structure of the educational system in Germany, it is not easy to formulate overall statements concerning the implementation of conceptual reflections into the curricula. Analyses of a representative sample of the curricula of all sixteen German states ("Bundesländer") are still missing. But even a quick reading of curricula shows that the term historical consciousness is present in most of them, from Berlin over Lower-Saxony and North-Rhine-Westphalia to Thüringen, to name but just a few.[2] Without going into details, we would like to point in summary to some aspects of special interest for the purpose of this volume:

1   Curricula in Germany contain more or less consensually shared core constituents of the concept of historical consciousness, e.g. historical consciousness as a mental structure operating with the collectively important past, present, and future; historical consciousness as a fundamentally narrative competence; historical consciousness not so much as a reservoir of factual knowledge but rather as a (cognitive) apparatus to analyze history in a methodologically reflective way.

2   Overarching educational goals of history in school as reflected in curricula include the promotion of a (self-)reflexive historical consciousness and the preparation of students to participate competently in a pluralistic and democratic society in general and in the historical culture ("Geschichtskultur") of society in particular.

3   More specific educational goals include the acquisition of domain-specific factual knowledge and of domain-specific methods to construct such knowledge.

4   Jörn Rüsen and Hans-Jürgen Pandel's conceptualizations are implicitly and partly present in curricula. Pandel's basic categories—consciousness of time,

of reality, and of historicity—appear as relevant abilities to be promoted in history lessons.

5 Models of historical competence are used more and more to formulate specific educational goals for specific sub-competences of historical thinking/ historical consciousness in specific school years. We will turn to them below.

6 Intercultural aspects and language concerning intersectionality and diversity are not completely omitted from curricula. Again and again, one finds that other cultures, with the history of men and women or with structures of power, should be an important aspect of history lessons. Yet, as formulations such as "other cultures" or the "history of men and women" suggest, a full appreciation of advanced discourses on culture, diversity, and intersectionality may not yet have found its way into curricula.

Transforming Historical Consciousness into an Assessable Competence

Attempts to operationalize historical consciousness for curricular purposes were criticized as resulting only in rather vague proposals which could not actually orient teaching (see Barricelli, Gautschi, & Körber, 2012; Schönemann, 2012). Such criticism was strongly nourished in the course of debates concerning the "PISA-shock" of 2001. In that year, the results of this international, large-scale assessment study testing reading, mathematical, and scientific literacy showed that German students scored below average. What was sometimes dramatized as a "declaration of bankruptcy" of the German educational system led to demands to focus more on domain-specific competences and not so much on content. Although the domain of history was not directly concerned since it had not been a subject tested in PISA or other large-scale assessment studies, history educators began to intensify work on models of competence, too. This work has not yet been finished nor is there an overall consensus of one specific model of competence. Rather there are several different, sometimes competing, models (for an overview see e.g. Barricelli, Gautschi, & Körber, 2012). We limit our discussion to two particularly influential models.

Historical Thinking

The model "Historical thinking" worked out by Bodo von Borries, Andreas Körber, Waltraud Schreiber, and others (Barricelli, Gautschi, & Körber, 2012; Körber, Schreiber, & Schöner, 2007; Schreiber, 2008) is the most extensively described and discussed model of competence in German discourse. Its close connection to theoretical elaborations on historical consciousness is obvious; the authors come back again and again to Rüsen's approach, to mention only one. The model consists of four fields of partially overlapping competences:

Competences to ask historical questions: Heuristic competences are needed here in order to formulate questions which help to address puzzles in regard to historical phenomena originating in everyday practice. Such questions may first be formulated rather vaguely but should successively be elaborated in terms belonging to the domain of history. The ability to use specific media to gather relevant information is also important in this context. Competences in this field include the ability to identify such questions of other persons. To formulate a historical question is a basic operation in this field.

Methodological competences: These include the ability to analyze historical sources or to analyze historical statements or narratives in respect to their assumptions, their factual base, and their conclusions. On a more advanced level, methodological competences extend to a critical reflection on the suitability of specific techniques, their scope, and their limitations. To re- and deconstruct narratives is a basic operation in this field.

Orientation competences: Historical insights gathered in the course of working on historical questions have to be related to one's own time and life-world, one's own group, and one's own identity. This implies the ability and the willingness to revise understandings of what belongs to oneself and of one's perspective on others in light of new knowledge. If necessary, terms and concepts also have to be adapted to new insights. To reflect one's own historically mediated identity is a basic operation in this field.

Subject matter competences: This field is relevant for all of the competences described above. The knowledge of specific results of historical thinking is not relevant here. Rather it is imperative to use and reflect historical and related terms, even to reflect the very premises of historical thinking itself.

Below the level of core competences, "individual competences" such as "intercultural competence" are postulated. Such single competences do not always have to be categorized below one single core competence.

A unique feature of this model is its detailed definition of different levels of complexity for each field ranging from a-conventional to conventional and transconventional. Another unique feature is the attempt to make it fruitful for the construction of an instrument to assess historical thinking. This instrument is being developed in the HITCH Project (Historical Thinking Competencies in History), similar to instruments used in the PISA-study and other large-scale assessment studies (see Körber & Meyer-Hamme, this volume).

National Educational Standards for History

The drafts for national educational standards for history ("Bildungsstandards Geschichte") from the association of German history teachers ("Verband der Geschichtslehrer Deutschlands"; VGD, 2006, 2010) do not provide a model of competences, like "historical thinking" described above, but rather, proposals to define binding standards which themselves necessarily rely on more or less clear-cut ideas about historical consciousness and historical competence. As far as the latter are concerned, the drafts resort to Sauer's (2006) "pragmatic" model of competence. In the first draft (VGD, 2006), three basic components of historical thinking are identified (Barricelli, Gautschi, & Körber, 2012, p. 226ff.): subject matter competences, interpretative and reflexive competences, and a combined field of media-methodical competences. Although the terms used here are similar to those in the model of "Historical thinking" (above), they are not equivalent. Concrete historical contents play a much more central role in these competences. Accordingly, the insights gained from a constructivist theory of history, which are integrated into the field of interpretative and reflexive competences, remain disconnected to the dominant field of subject matter competences, which centers around concrete historical knowledge (ibid., p. 227ff.). Lücke (2012, p. 145), who reads these drafts against the background of diversity studies, also notes their uncritical adherence to a national master narrative.

What is gained and what is possibly lost with models of historical competence? The answer to this question depends on the specific model in question. Advantages of elaborated and comprehensive models like "Historical thinking" can be seen as interesting, thought-provoking, detailed specifications of competences and sub-competences of historical thinking. They can also provide the basis for rich empirical data gathered with standardized diagnostic instruments. Consequently, such models help to clarify what is meant by the term historical consciousness, and they help in assessing historical consciousness in a more transparent and a more methodologically consistent way. What has been said in respect to historical consciousness in the curriculum, however, may also hold true here: Questions of culture, diversity, and intersectionality in an ambitious sense of the word are in danger of not getting full appreciation when historical consciousness is transformed into an assessable competence, at least as far as the present models are concerned. Moreover, despite of all their well-known advantages, standardized instruments are not always sensitive to the ambiguities, ambivalences, and contradictions inherent in concrete forms of historical consciousness. In the end, models of historical competence can present a danger of becoming rigid guidelines that limit creativity (see also Schönemann, 2012, p. 110). It is, however, an open question whether they will do so, or, alternatively, offer themselves as helpful regulative ideals. Of course, further scientific discourse will be relevant here but educational policy will certainly be far more important in shaping these outcomes.

Notes

1 These categories serve accentuating purposes for conceptualizations of historical consciousness—at least the ones considered here can certainly not completely be subsumed to just one of the three categories.

2 The curricula we touch upon exemplarily can all be found at: http://www.berlin.de/
imperia/md/content/sen-bildung/schulorganisation/lehrplaene/sek1_geschichte.pdf?
start&ts=1150101699&file=sek1_geschichte.pdf; http://www.berlin.de/imperia/md/
content/sen-bildung/unterricht/lehrplaene/sek2_geschichte.pdf?start&ts=1283429419
&file=sek2_geschichte.pdf; http://db2.nibis.de/1db/cuvo/datei/kc_gym_gesch_08_
nib.pdf; http://www.standardsicherung.schulministerium.nrw.de/lehrplaene/upload/
klp_SI/RS/GE/RS_Geschichte_Endfassung.pdf; http://www.standardsicherung.schul
ministerium.nrw.de/lehrplaene/upload/lehrplaene_download/gymnasium_g8/
gym8_geschichte.pdf; http://www.schulportal-thueringen.de/web/guest/media/
detail?tspi=2847

References

Barricelli, M., Gautschi, P., & Körber, A. (2012). Historische Kompetenzen und Kompe-
tenzmodelle. In M. Barricelli & M. Lücke (Eds.), *Handbuch Praxis des Geschichtsunterrichts, Bd. 1* (pp. 207–235). Schwalbach/Ts., Germany: Wochenschau-Verlag.

Barricelli, M., & Sauer, M. (2009). Current Issues in German Research on Historical
Understanding. In M. Martens, U. Hartmann, M. Sauer, & M. Hasselhorn (Eds.),
Interpersonal Understanding in Historical Context (pp. 61–79). Rotterdam, Netherlands:
Sense Publishers.

Carey, S. (1985). *Conceptual Change in Childhood*. Cambridge, MA: MIT Press.

Crenshaw, K. W. (1989). Demarginalizing the intersection of race and sex: A black feminist critique of antidiscrimination doctrine, feminist theory and antiracist politics.
The University of Chicago Legal Forum, 140, 139–167.

El Darwich, R. (1991). Zur Genese von Kategorien des Geschichtsbewußtseins bei
Kindern im Alter von 5–14 Jahren. In B. von Borries, H.-J. Pandel, & J. Rüsen (Eds.),
Geschichtsbewußtsein empirisch (pp. 24–52). Pfaffenweiler, Germany: Centaurus.

Jeismann, K.-E. (1977). Didaktik der Geschichte. Die Wissenschaft von Zustand, Funktion und Veränderung geschichtlicher Vorstellungen im Selbstverständnis der Gegenwart. In E. Kosthorst (Ed.), *Geschichtswissenschaft. Didaktik—Forschung—Theorie* (pp. 9–33).
Göttingen, Germany: Vandenhoeck & Ruprecht.

Kölbl, C. (2009). What Can a Developmental Psychology of Historical Consciousness
Look Like? In M. Martens, U. Hartmann, M. Sauer, & M. Hasselhorn (Eds.), *Inter-
personal Understanding in Historical Context* (pp. 81–96). Rotterdam, Netherlands: Sense
Publishers.

Kölbl, C., & Straub, J. (2001). Historical consciousness in youth. Theoretical and exemplary
empirical analyses [paragraph 103]. *Forum Qualitative Sozialforschung / Forum: Qualitative Social Research, 2*(3), Art. 9, http://nbn-resolving.de/urn:nbn:de:0114-fqs010397.

Konrad, L. (2014). (Un)Doing Gender im Geschichtsunterricht. In A. Bothe & C. Brüning
(Eds.), *Geschlecht und Erinnerung im digitalen Zeitalter—neue Perspektiven auf ZeitzeugIn-
nenarchive*. Münster, Germany: LIT.

Körber, A., Schreiber, W., & Schöner, A. (Eds.) (2007). *Kompetenzen historischen Denkens.
Ein Strukturmodell als Beitrag zur Kompetenzorientierung in der Geschichtsdidaktik*. Neuried, Germany: Ars una.

Leitner, H. (1994). *Gegenwart und Geschichte. Zur Logik des historischen Bewußtseins*. University of Trier, Germany: Habilitation.

Lücke, M. (2012). Diversität und Intersektionalität als Konzepte der Geschichtsdidaktik.
In M. Barricelli & M. Lücke (Eds.), *Handbuch Praxis des Geschichtsunterrichts, Bd. 1*
(pp. 136–146). Schwalbach/Ts., Germany: Wochenschau-Verlag.

McCall, L. (2005). The complexity of intersectionality. *Signs, 30*(3), 1771–1800.

Pandel, H.-J. (1987). Dimensionen des Geschichtsbewußtseins. Ein Sersuch, seine Struktur für Empirie und Pragmatik diskutierbar zu machen. *Geschichtsdidaktik, 12,* 130–142.

Rüsen, J. (1993). *Studies in Metahistory.* Pretoria, South Africa: Human Sciences Research Council.

Rüsen, J., Fröhlich, K., Horstkötter, H., & Schmidt, H.-G. (1991). Untersuchungen zum Geschichtsbewußtsein von Abiturienten im Ruhrgebiet. In B. v. Borries, H.-J. Pandel, & J. Rüsen (Eds.), *Geschichtsbewußtsein empirisch* (pp. 221–344). Pfaffenweiler, Germany: Centaurus.

Sauer, M. (2006). Kompetenzen für den Geschichtsunterricht—ein pragmatisches Modell als Basis für die Bildungsstandards des Verbandes der Geschichtslehrer. *Informationen für den Geschichts- und Gemeinschaftskundelehrer, 74,* 7–20.

Sauer, M. (2009). *Geschichte unterrichten. Eine Einführung in die Didaktik und Methodik.* Kallmeyer, Germany: Seelze.

Schönemann, B. (2012). Geschichtsbewusstsein—Theorie. In M. Barricelli & M. Lücke (Eds.), *Handbuch Praxis des Geschichtsunterrichts, Bd. 1* (pp. 98–111). Schwalbach/Ts., Germany: Wochenschau-Verlag.

Schörken, R. (1972). Geschichtsdidaktik und Geschichtsbewußtsein. *Geschichte in Wissenschaft und Unterricht, 23,* 81–89.

Schott, R. (1968). Das Geschichtsbewußtsein schriftloser Völker. *Archiv für Begriffsgeschichte, 12,* 166–205.

Schreiber, W. (2008). Ein Kompetenz-Strukturmodell historischen Denkens. *Zeitschrift für Pädagogik, 54*(2), 198–212.

Seixas, P. (2005). Historical Consciousness: A Scheme of Progress in Knowledge for a Post-Progressive Age. In J. Straub (Ed.), *Narration, Identity, and Historical Consciousness: The Psychological Construction of Time and History* (pp. 44–98). New York: Berghan.

Sonntag, K. (1932). *Das geschichtliche Bewusstsein des Schülers. Ein Beitrag zur Bildungspsychologie.* Erfurt, Germany: Stenger.

Straub, J. (Ed.). (2005a). *Narration, Identity, and Historical Consciousness.* New York: Berghan.

Straub, J. (2005b). Telling Stories, Making History: Toward a Narrative Psychology of the Historical Construction of Meaning. In J. Straub (Ed.), *Narration, Identity, and Historical Consciousness* (pp. 44–98). New York: Berghan.

Verband der Geschichtslehrer Deutschlands (VGD) (Eds.). (2006). *Bildungsstandards Geschichte. Rahmenmodell Gymnasium 5.-10. Jahrgang.* Schwalbach/Ts., Germany: Wochenschau-Verlag.

Verband der Geschichtslehrer Deutschlands (VGD) (Eds.). (2010). *Bildungsstandards Geschichte (Sekundarstufe I).* http://www.geschichtslehrerforum.de/Standards/index.html.

2

THE DIFFICULTY OF ASSESSING DISCIPLINARY HISTORICAL READING

Abby Reisman

Historical thinking depends on the ability to reason about written text. Writing in 1899, American historian Frederick Jackson Turner encouraged history educators to replace "the old ideal of history as pleasant literature" with "the ideal of history as a discipline of the mind, valuable particularly as a training of judgment in the criticism of material like that which is placed before the citizen in current political and industrial questions" (p. 301). Nearly a century later, the Bradley Commission on History in Schools—a body that advocated a renewed emphasis on historical study in K-12 social studies instruction—recommended "training in critical judgment based on evidence, including original sources" (Bradley Commission, 1989, p. 23).

It seems somewhat perplexing to consider, then, that history assessments have not mirrored this consistent emphasis on the value of reasoning across sources. By 2011, twenty-six of the United States required testing in history/social studies, with half of these using multiple-choice-only measures and the other half using a combination of constructed-response and multiple-choice (Martin, Maldonado, Schneider, & Smith, 2011). Fogo's (in press) account of California's 1987 *History-Social Science Framework* shows how broad curricular recommendations became discrete content standards that were ultimately assessed with decontextualized multiple-choice items on the (now defunct) Standardized Testing and Reporting (STaR) exams. And Reich (2009) discovered a striking misalignment between the reasoning of students who achieved correct answers on the 10th grade New York Regents exam in global history and the historical analysis standard that the test claimed to measure. When we look to explain this persistent misalignment between the stated goals of history instruction and the tests designed to assess them, we find that test-makers have been more concerned with efficiency and psychometric reliability than with disciplinary validity (Wineburg, 2004). But I would like to make the case that a more nagging problem underlies the longevity of multiple-choice tests as historical assessments: the difficulty of disentangling disciplinary historical reading—or, the ability to evaluate the reliability of sources in order to construct an intertextual account of the past—from students' incoming background knowledge, on the one hand, and general reading comprehension, on the other.

Historical Reading and the Common Core Standards

As has been well documented (cf. Lee, 2005), historical thinking depends upon, but extends beyond historical reading. In the United States, the few efforts to design assessments that move beyond factual recall to measure historical thinking have primarily focused on historical reading, students' ability to construct an account of the past from written sources. Wineburg (1991a, 1991b) characterized disciplinary historical reading as an epistemological orientation towards texts that allows the historian to view the texts as human constructions whose probity can and should be interrogated. Wineburg further distilled three discrete heuristics that historians applied while reading historical texts: sourcing (considering the document's source and purpose), contextualization (placing the document in a temporal and spatial context), and corroboration (comparing the accounts of multiple sources against each other).

While neither Wineburg's work nor the subsequent research on disciplinary historical reading was initially framed within a broader reading research agenda, the work dovetailed well with other developments in American education. In 2002, the Rand Corporation, an American non-profit policy think tank, published a report on reading comprehension that highlighted the dearth of research on reading comprehension in middle and high school, even as demands for advanced literacy continued to grow (Snow, 2002). Soon after, the Carnegie Corporation published *Reading Next* in 2004, which charted "an immediate route to improving adolescent literacy" (Biancarosa & Snow, 2006). The report was followed by the formation of the Carnegie Council for Advancing Adolescent Literacy and the subsequent publication of several additional reports, culminating with *Time to Act* in 2010, which "pinpoints adolescent literacy as a cornerstone of the current education reform movement."

By emphasizing domain-specific literacy and the particular demands of content area texts, the reports provided a national platform for work on historical reading. Two findings, in particular, related directly to history instruction: the first was that students need exposure to a range of textual genres in order to be prepared for college; the second was that how one reads differs by content area (Biancarosa & Snow, 2006; Carnegie Council on Advancing Adolescent Literacy, 2010; Heller & Greenleaf, 2007; National Institute for Literacy, 2007). In other words, historians read and ask different questions of texts than do scientists or poets; primary sources, presumably, afford students the opportunity to practice these domain-specific reading practices. These two findings have most recently found their way into the Common Core State Standards for English Language Arts and Literacy in History/Social Studies, Science, and Technical Subjects (2010), literacy standards that have been adopted by all but seven states. The first appears as a "key design consideration," with the authors citing "extensive research establishing the need for college and career ready students to be proficient in reading complex informational text independently in a variety of content areas" (p. 4). The second appears later in the document: in the introduction to reading in the remaining subjects—history, science, and technical subjects—the authors state that "college and career ready reading in these fields requires an appreciation of the norms and conventions of each discipline" (p. 60).

The energy and momentum accompanying the Common Core Initiative has been, on the one hand, exhilarating. The initiative promises a national platform for assessments on *historical reading*, a reality few would have considered possible a mere decade ago. On the other hand, the fact that the standards emerged from the work on adolescent literacy, with only cursory engagement with the literature on historical thinking and reading, has direct implications for the sorts of assessments that will likely emerge. A close look at the Reading Standards for History/Social Studies (p. 61) finds that they are almost indistinguishable from the Reading Standard for Informational Texts (pp. 39–40), aside from the inclusion of inter-textual reading as a core feature of the history/social studies standards. Conspicuously absent from Reading Standards for History/Social Studies, however, is any reference to history or historical knowledge. This stands in contrast to the consensus that has emerged in the research on historical thinking: that meaningful historical thinking requires familiarity and facility with disciplinary ways of interpreting historical texts, an appreciation of the interpretive nature of historical knowledge, *and the application of conceptual, narrative, and discrete factual knowledge.* If test developers infer from these standards that historical reading assessments can be designed without considering students' background knowledge, they will fall into an old trap.

Role of Background Knowledge in Historical Reading

"Disciplinary literacy" has become something of a buzzword in educational circles in the United States, thanks in large part to the Common Core State Standards. In the name of promoting "disciplinary literacy," educators have focused on identifying reading "strategies" employed by expert historians, or pinpointing the particular linguistic demands of history textbooks. The intention—to focus attention on *reasoning* and *interpretation* rather than on memorization and retention—should be applauded. However, it is also important to recognize the essential role that background knowledge plays in allowing experts to employ these various disciplinary reading strategies. A baseline level of knowledge is evident even in the research that has been marshaled most frequently to make the case for teaching disciplinary historical reading. Wineburg (1991b, 1998) finds repeatedly that deep expert knowledge is not essential for historians to navigate a particular problem in history—in his studies, Medievalists and Sinologists expertly read and contextualize texts about the Battle of Lexington and Abraham Lincoln. However, if we consider the context of typical classrooms, we still must ask: what baseline level of knowledge did these non-experts possess? Certainly, they were familiar with the basic narrative of the American Revolution. Certainly they possessed knowledge of Abraham Lincoln's signature achievement—the Emancipation Proclamation.

In a more recent but comparable study, Baron (2012) examined how expert historians "read" a historical space, namely, the Old North Church in Boston, Massachusetts. Arguing that Wineburg's heuristics for reading documentary texts did not account for how experts reason about space, Baron identified five new heuristics from the historians' think-aloud protocols and argues that familiarity with these heuristics might allow novices to begin to ask "What are the multiple time periods evident in this building, and what do they tell me about its history?" (p. 844). Yet, Baron's historians heavily depend on their historical knowledge and experience. Their "heuristics" represent different ways that they used their knowledge to make inferences about the building; indeed, three of the five heuristics—origination (considering the building's origin), stratification (identifying the multiple strata of time evident in the building), and empathetic insight (considering the affective response of people who occupied the space at particular historical moments)—were largely unavailable to those historians with little background knowledge.

Van Boxtel and Van Drie (2012) asked a different question related to historical texts. What allows students to successfully contextualize historical images and documents: historical knowledge or strategy use? The authors found that providing students with knowledge of key substantive historical concepts, and helping them construct an associative network around those concepts, was most predictive of student success on contextualization tasks. This study underscores the importance of historical knowledge in leveraging student reasoning with and about historical texts.

The entwined nature of historical knowledge and historical reading poses formidable challenges to large-scale history assessment developers. Below I discuss two examples of history assessments where the effort to capture historical reading was caught between the confounding factors of background knowledge and reading comprehension.

Example 1: Learning-Based Assessments of Historical Understanding

In a 1994 special issue of *Educational Psychologist*, Eva Baker describes a six-year effort to design performance-based assessments of historical understanding (Baker, 1994). The project, a collaboration between UCLA's National Center for Research on Evaluation, Standards, and Student Testing (CRESST) and Los Angeles Unified

School District, was an effort to create large-scale assessments that would capture broad patterns in student achievement or educational reform, and simultaneously provide classroom teachers important formative information about their students' learning and content understanding. An important distinction must be drawn between "historical thinking"—or disciplinary ways of thinking about the past—and "historical understanding." Baker's project did not purport to measure "historical thinking"—a term that had yet to be popularized; indeed, Baker's conception of "historical understanding" can best be understood as the *result* of historical thinking—namely, a textured understanding of what happened, say, during the Lincoln-Douglas debates (see Figure 2.1). Yet, in attempting to design an assessment of historical understanding that required students to reason across multiple documents, Baker's efforts shed light on the potential pitfalls of measuring historical reading.

In designing the assessment, the researchers faced three constraints. First, they had to avoid designing assessments that captured stable traits or general talents that would not be affected by historical study. In other words, the assessment needed to measure historical understanding as something that was distinct from fluid writing, for example. Second, to ensure content validity, the assessments needed to invite student interpretation. Yet, they needed to simultaneously remain "relatively insensitive to varying content emphasis and epistemological differences among history experts and teachers" (p. 99). This constraint raised a natural dilemma: if students' thinking processes are given greater weight than the specific substance of their answers (so as not to penalize unpopular interpretations), at what point does the assessment cease to measure historical understanding? The third constraint was more universal: any large-scale assessment is limited by practical scoring considerations and feasibility.

Writing Assignment

Imagine that it is 1858 and you are an educated citizen living in Illinois. Because you are interested in politics and always keep yourself well informed, you make a special trip to hear Abraham Lincoln and Stephen Douglas debating during their campaigns for the Senate seat representing Illinois. After the debates you return home, where your cousin asks you about some of the problems that are facing the nation at this time.

Write an essay in which you explain the most important ideas and issues your cousin should understand. Your essay should be based on two major sources: (1) the general concepts and specific facts you know about American History, and especially what you know about the history of the Civil War; (2) what you have learned from the readings yesterday. Be sure to show the relationships among your ideas and facts.

FIGURE 2.1 CRESST performance assessment in history writing prompt (Baker et al., 1992, p. 11)

The assessments ultimately took the form of explanation tasks whereby students read two primary sources that offered competing positions on a historical topic, and explained to a friend or colleague what was happening and why it was important (see Figure 2.1). Developers decided to incorporate primary sources not only for reasons of disciplinary validity—historians, of course, read primary sources—but also to "level the field" for students who may have received varying exposure to the historical topic. The assessment was designed to align with extant processing models that viewed text-comprehension, integration, and application as the core features of "deep content understanding" (Glaser, 1992). The assumption was that students would draw both on their background knowledge and understanding of the historical topic as well as on the information in the provided texts to write the essay.

Six years of field-testing yielded mixed results that informed subsequent design decisions. To begin, researchers quickly discovered that students rarely, if ever, incorporated outside knowledge—even those students whose teachers claimed to have taught the content. Moreover, students generally did not evaluate or assess historical significance, but rather "tried to cover all information with an equally light hand" and they made numerous factual and conceptual errors (p. 101). This finding stood in sharp contrast to the essays written by experts in their subsequent expert-novice study, who incorporated extensive prior knowledge and organized their essays around broad principles, using the provided texts to illustrate key points. In subsequent iterations, developers incorporated a 20-item, short-answer prior knowledge measure that preceded the main task. The goal of this measure was both to activate student prior knowledge and to assess the relationship between such knowledge and student performance on the written component of the assessment. The researchers also added a 14–15-item multiple-choice literal comprehension test to determine if students could make literal sense of the historical texts that were provided. Although Baker did not report on the relationship between these measurement components, their inclusion speaks to the difficulty of disentangling historical reading from background knowledge and literal reading comprehension.

Baker and her colleagues also found disappointing patterns among raters. Initially four expert teachers identified essential criteria for historical understanding (e.g., evidence of historical analysis, detail, etc.), yet factor analyses conducted on these criteria yielded a single factor; in other words, "rating only one element (e.g., logical structure) or using a single overall rating would provide the same amount of information as scoring multiple elements" (p. 100). Ultimately a scoring rubric was designed that included the following dimensions: (1) Overall content quality; (2) Prior knowledge; (3) Principles/themes; (4) Text detail; (5) Misconceptions; and (6) Argumentation. Later, when factor analyses were conducted on these dimensions, researchers found a consistent two-factor solution, in which Prior Knowledge, Principles, and Overall Content Quality loaded on one factor, while Text Detail and Misconceptions formed another. The factor structure matched differences between expert and novice essays. Subsequent exploratory analysis found an interaction between raters' content knowledge and their scores: "Raters with less knowledge tended to overvalue text material in students' writing, and consequently the relation between their ratings of text detail and rater judgment of general content quality increased" (p. 103). Raters' content knowledge also had implications for what was considered a "misconception."

CRESST has engaged in several assessment development projects since the 1990s—most recently in response to the content literacy demands of the Common Core State Standards. However, this earlier effort stands out for both its duration and its attempt to substantively engage with the demands of historical subject matter. For those same reasons, it demonstrates the inherent challenges in designing assessments of historical understanding based on primary sources, assessments that demand that students bring a degree of background knowledge and basic reading comprehension. One could argue that the assessment that was ultimately developed—an explanation task based on two documents—does not constitute authentic engagement with primary sources. Because the assessment ultimately equated historical knowledge with the ability to summarize the views expressed in primary sources, with no opportunity for argumentation or interpretation, one could argue that it demanded little more from students than general reading comprehension. In the example below, I demonstrate how the effort to design an argumentation task around multiple sources encountered similar challenges.

Example 2: Advanced Placement Document-Based Question

The Advanced Placement program was developed in the 1950s in an effort to give "able school boys and girls" an opportunity to challenge themselves with advanced coursework (Schneider, 2009). Run by the College Board since 1955, college credit for the course is determined by one's score on a summative exam. The signature feature of the history exams is the Document-Based Question (DBQ), first created in the 1970s in an effort to prompt students to do more than simply recite memorized factual information—their typical response to the non-document essay prompt. The DBQ, by contrast, assessed students' ability to assess and synthesize multiple primary sources. To many, the AP's DBQ represents the gold standard in authentic historical assessment, a model for assessing disciplinary literacy. Others have criticized the DBQ for being too broad and unfocused to provide classroom teachers with formative information about their students' learning (Breakstone, Smith, & Wineburg, 2013). A peek into the development of the current DBQ sheds some light on its shortcomings as an assessment of historical reading.

Writing in the American Historical Association's publication *Perspectives* in 1983, Stephen Klein, an Educational Testing Services (ETS) consultant to the College Board Development Committee for Advanced Placement American History, discussed the committee's reasoning for shortening the DBQ on the

American History examination from 15–20 documents to a mere half dozen. The committee had discovered two persistent problems in student responses to the longer DBQ: (1) the extensive, self-contained document set provided students with sufficient information about the given topic that they did not need—and, indeed, rarely bothered—to incorporate prior background knowledge into their written responses; and (2) because the prompts emphasized the *analysis* and *synthesis* of documents, it was less apparent how students were to demonstrate their ability to assess relevance and reliability, skills that arguably constitute the heart of historical reading. Klein shows how both skills were gradually deemphasized in the essay prompt: by 1975, both requirements—to incorporate background information not included in the documents and to assess the reliability of the evidence—became optional.

Although the decision to shorten the DBQ initially emerged from practical considerations, not least of which was the time required to assemble longer document sets, the hope was that it would address the two concerns discussed above. The committee reasoned that a shorter document set would force students to incorporate outside knowledge, though it might inadvertently result in the inverse problem: that students would use the documents as mere launching points for a recitation of memorized factual information. The problem of assessing reliability was even more elusive. As Klein (1983) explained,

> Relevance and reliability are determined either by a pat formula having nothing to do with historical knowledge, or by a depth of historical knowledge unlikely to be possessed by a survey course student. An example of the former would be: "A witness to an event is more reliable than someone who hears about it second-hand." An example of the latter would be: "Calhoun was a less reliable judge of Jackson's political motives after their falling out in 1830 than before." The nice thing about the latter example is that one could argue just the opposite . . . but the main point is that whichever side one argues for, substantial historical knowledge would be necessary.
>
> (p. 23)

The committee concluded that in order to keep students focused on the actual documents, the prompt would have to ask about historical significance. As Klein explained, "The committee assumed that, ultimately, questions about historical significance would probably reduce themselves to 'To what extent do the documents support and/or contradict what you already know about historical topic X?'" (p. 24). Furthermore, as Baker and her colleagues concluded, the topic would have to be a mainstream topic that most students could be expected to have encountered in their course.

In Fall 2014, the College Board released a new curricular framework for the AP United States History Exam (College Board, 2014). The DBQ remains a key feature of the free-response section, though the number of documents included in the prompt has been reduced to 7 after several decades of including 9 or 10 documents. The rubric reflects more significant changes, stipulating that document analysis should address "intended audience, purpose, historical context, and/or point of view" and that students should support their arguments with "analysis of historical examples outside the documents." It remains unclear whether and how students will respond to these changes. Klein found in the administration of the first "shorter" DBQ in 1982 that few students incorporated outside knowledge. If the document sets do contain sufficient information, and students are not required to evaluate the reliability or relevance of the evidence, to what extent is the exam assessing general reading comprehension rather than disciplinary reading and historical understanding?

Conclusion

The recent focus on disciplinary historical reading in the United States brings with it the promise of long-awaited assessment reform, a shift away from multiple-choice questions about decontextualized facts towards assessments that ask students to interpret and reason across multiple historical texts. However, as is evident both in the research literature and from previous efforts to design large-scale assessments of historical reading, reasoning about texts requires a degree of background knowledge. Furthermore, any large-scale assessment of historical reading must address the varying degrees of familiarity with a given topic that students will bring to the task. If the assessment includes background knowledge (to "level the field"), and does not explicitly require students to assess reliability and relevance, at what point does it become a reading test that simply asks students to summarize or explain the substance of the historical documents? Assessment developers will need to think carefully about what knowledge students are expected to bring to the task, how students will be asked to use this knowledge when engaging with texts, and whether or not any background knowledge will be provided. Without attending to the relationship between background knowledge and historical reading, new, innovative assessments that attempt to address the historical reading standards of the Common Core run the risk of foundering on the same challenges that have limited previous assessment initiatives.

Lest I be accused of ending on a dire note, I should add the silver lining: the above conundrum concerns large-scale assessment-designers, not individual classroom teachers. Whereas the large-scale designer cannot know what background knowledge students bring to the test, the classroom teacher can know whether students have sufficient background knowledge to interpret certain texts. A teacher who is interested in assessing historical reading might think of the process as three-fold: (1) assessing students' background knowledge; (2) assessing students' ability to evaluate the reliability and relevance of textual evidence; and (3) assessing students' ability to synthesize multiple documents into an account. These three assessments need not be administered together. The assessment of

(2), students' ability to evaluate a source's reliability and relevance, for example, could be comprised of intermittent short assessments, such as the ones designed by the Stanford History Education group (beyondthebubble.stanford.edu). By contrast, an assessment of (3), students' ability to synthesize documents, might be designed as a short DBQ about a topic/event with which students are unfamiliar but that occurred in a context and time period that they have studied extensively. The goal is for teachers to disentangle the various threads that comprise historical thinking in order to better target instruction and assessment.

References

Baker, E. (1994). Learning based assessments of historical understanding. *Educational Psychologist, 29*(2), 97–106.

Baker, E., Aschbacher, P., Niemi, D., & Sato, E. (1992). *CRESST performance assessment models: Assessing content area explanations.* Los Angeles, CA: University of California, National Center for Research on Evaluation, Standards, and Student Testing.

Baron, C. (2012). Understanding historical thinking at historic sites. *Journal of Educational Psychology, 104*(3), 833–847.

Biancarosa, C., & Snow, C. (2006). *Reading next—A vision for action and research in middle and high school literacy: A report to Carnegie Corporation of New York* (2nd ed.). Washington, DC: Alliance for Excellent Education.

Bradley Commission on History in Schools. (1989). Building a history curriculum: Guidelines for teaching history in schools. In P. Gagnon (Ed.), *Historical literacy: The case for history in American education* (pp. 16–47). Boston, MA: Houghton Mifflin.

Breakstone, J., Smith, M., & Wineburg, S. (2013). Beyond the bubble in history/social studies assessments. *Phi Delta Kappan, 94*(5), 53–57.

Carnegie Council on Advancing Adolescent Literacy. (2010). *Time to act: An agenda for advancing adolescent literacy for college and career success.* New York, NY: Carnegie Corporation of New York.

College Board. (2014). The AP United States History Exam. Retrieved from http://apcentral.collegeboard.com/apc/members/exam/exam_information/2089.html

Common Core State Standards for English Language Arts & Literacy in History/Social Studies, Science, and Technical Subjects. National Governors Association Center for Best Practices, Council of Chief State School Officers, Washington D.C. Retrieved from http://www.corestandards.org/wp-content/uploads/ELA_Standards.pdf

Fogo, B. (in press). The making of California's history standards: Enduring decisions and unresolved issues. *The History Teacher.*

Glaser, R. (1992). Leaning, cognition, and education: Then and now. In H. L. Pick, Jr., P. van den Broek, & D. C. Knill (Eds.), *Cognition: conceptual and methodological issues* (pp. 239–265). Washington, DC: American Psychological Association.

Heller, R., & Greenleaf, C. (2007). *Literacy instruction in the content areas: Getting to the core of middle and high school improvement.* Washington, DC: Alliance for Excellent Education.

Klein, S. (1983). The genesis of shorter document-based questions in the advanced placement American history examination. *American Historical Association Perspectives* (May/June): 22–24.

Lee, P. (2005). Putting principles into practice: Understanding history. In M. S. Donovan and J. D. Bransford (Eds.), *How students learn: history in the classroom* (pp. 31–74). Washington, DC: National Academies Press.

Martin, D., Maldonado, S., Schneider, J., & Smith, M. (2011). A report on the state of history education: state policies and national programs. *National History Education Clearinghouse.* Retrieved from http://teachinghistory.org/system/files/teachinghistory_special_report_2011.pdf

National Institute for Literacy. (2007). *What content-area teachers should know about adolescent literacy.* Washington, DC: Author.

Reich, G. (2009). Testing historical knowledge: standards, multiple-choice questions and student reasoning. *Theory and Research in Social Education, 37*(3), 325–360.

Schneider, J. (2009). Privilege, equity, and the advanced placement program: tug of war. *Journal of Curriculum Studies, 41*(6), 813–831.

Snow, C. (2002). *Reading for understanding: toward a research and development program in reading comprehension.* Santa Monica, CA: RAND.

Turner, F. J. (1899, October). *Educational Review, 18,* 301–304.

Van Boxtel, C., & Van Drie, J. (2012). "That's in the time of the Romans!" Knowledge and strategies students use to contextualize historical images and documents. *Cognition and Instruction, 30*(2), 113–145.

Wineburg, S. (1991a). Historical problem solving: A study of the cognitive processes used in the evaluation of documentary and pictorial evidence. *Journal of Educational Psychology, 83*(1), 73–87.

Wineburg, S. (1991b). On the reading of historical texts: Notes on the breach between school and academy. *American Educational Research Journal, 28*(3), 495–519.

Wineburg, S. (1998). Reading Abraham Lincoln: An expert/expert study in the interpretation of historical texts. *Cognitive Science, 22*(3), 319–346.

Wineburg, S. (2004). Crazy for history. *Journal of American History, 90*(4), 1401–1414.

3

HERITAGE AS A RESOURCE FOR ENHANCING AND ASSESSING HISTORICAL THINKING

Reflections from the Netherlands

Carla van Boxtel, Maria Grever, and Stephan Klein

Introduction

In every country, there are historical issues that are vital in collective memory and repeatedly give rise to public debates. In the Netherlands, the transatlantic slave trade and its associated traces of the past aptly illustrate the sensitivity of such issues. It is only very recently and hesitantly that the Dutch government has acknowledged the historical role of the Dutch. For instance, in 2002 a national slavery monument was unveiled in Amsterdam and the annual commemoration of the Dutch abolition of slavery on July 1 implemented. It is only in the last ten to fifteen years that the topic has been integrated in both academic historiography and school history curricula, although specialists are still very critical. With respect to school history, they argue that the slave trade is often represented as a side story and that the emphasis is mainly on the abolition by the Dutch, ignoring the agency of enslaved people themselves (Van Stipriaan, 2007).

Whereas the Dutch involvement in slavery has been acknowledged at the national level, for many descendants it remains an emotionally charged issue. Part of the Afro-Caribbean Dutch community has demanded substantial "reparations" for what they call the "Black Holocaust". The recent controversy in the Netherlands about the phenomenon "Black Pete", which attracted international attention, can also be connected to the legacy of Dutch slavery. Every year in November, Dutch children eagerly look forward to the arrival of St. Nicholas and his Black Petes (Zwarte Pieten), coming from Spain on a steamboat with lots of presents. However, particularly since the 1980s with the arrival of migrants from the Dutch former colonies Suriname and the Antilles, some people began to protest against the performances of Black Petes: white men who paint their faces black and wear wigs with black curly hair. But the Dutch cherish their traditions and heritage. Moreover, it is argued that the character of Black Pete has changed over time from a single servant who disciplines children to a variety of male and female Petes with various responsibilities and emotions. However, the outward appearance is still close to the (re)invented nineteenth century character, and evokes associations with a black slave.

What do students in high school learn about the ways people attribute significance to the past in everyday life and in the communities in which they participate? In this particular case, do they understand the sensitive nature of slavery history? Do they understand how their own identity and that of others affect the questions asked and the interpretations and evaluations given in the debates about the slavery monument and Black Pete? Are they aware that the attribution of significance changes over time? These questions all relate to an important key concept for the learning of history: historical significance. Recently, the upper level key-targets of the Dutch history curriculum that are assessed in a combination of school examinations and one central written examination, have been extended with two new elements under the header "significance nowadays". The first target concerns understanding of the changing significance of the past for different groups of people in the past and in current society. The second target concerns the recognition of various present motives, values, and expectations when people make moral judgments about the past. In this chapter, we will focus on the first target, in particular on the changing significance of the past for different groups of people in *current society*.

The first target is particularly related to what has been called *present significance* (e.g. Cercadillo, 2006; Phillips, 2002; Seixas & Morton, 2013) or *memory-significance* (Lévesque, 2005; 2008). The "significance nowadays" targets of the Dutch history examination program actually focus attention on heritage practices in current society. Much has already been written about differences between disciplinary history and heritage or memory history (e.g. Bodnar, 1992; Lowenthal, 1999) and about the relationships between those practices (e.g. Lee, 2004; Rüsen, 2007). With "heritage", we mean the selection and preservation of remains within a community—objects, monuments, trails, traditions, and memories—that people consider valuable for the present and the future. The construction and justification of identities play an important part in this process (Ashworth, Graham, & Tunbridge, 2007; Savenije, Van Boxtel, & Grever, 2014; Smith, 2006). When heritage—whether material or immaterial—becomes a resource for the learning and teaching of history, two questions arise. First, to what extent does school history itself reflect either a disciplinary or a heritage approach to the past? When school history is more like collective memorialization, not history (VanSledright, 2008), teaching present significance may result in enforcing students to appropriate particular meanings and to adapt to certain identities. Second, how can we use heritage as a resource for enhancing and assessing students' understanding of present significance?

To address these questions, we start by describing the extent to which history education in Dutch upper secondary school (students aged 16 to 18) reflects a disciplinary historical approach to the past. Next, on a more general level, and illustrated with examples about the Dutch slave trade and slavery, we shall argue that in the context of a disciplinary school history both material and immaterial heritage may provide interesting entrances to assess and further enhance students' understanding of present significance.

Dutch History Education: Continuation of a Disciplinary Approach

In the Netherlands, debates about the teaching and assessment of historical thinking skills are no recent phenomenon. In the 1970s and 1980s teacher educator Leo Dalhuisen developed a history textbook with many assignments containing historical sources and higher level questions to enhance historical thinking and reasoning. In 1993, a new history examination program was implemented. For the first time, second order concepts (e.g. fact and objectivity, causes and consequences, continuity and change) were introduced to assess students' ability to think about history. The idea of present significance was rather implicit. Students should recognize that every time period "carries the past within her" and they should acknowledge that every individual, including the students themselves, is "bound by place and time". The central written examinations focused on in-depth knowledge of two alternating themes, while school examinations would assess other themes; each type of examination counting for 50%. After the implementation of the new history examination programs in the late 1990s (Van Boxtel & Grever, 2011), all Dutch history textbooks included a variety of historical sources and assignments to develop historical thinking skills. The implicit "present significance" targets, however, were not defined in more detail.

Not all history teachers were equally content with the increased emphasis on skills. Opponents argued that history education was not meant to create "little historians", and doubted whether these higher-order skills could be a realistic attainment target for all types of education. Furthermore, they argued that the emphasis on skills reduced the time to provide a historical overview. In the new millennium, two independently operating commissions suggested a historical overview that was subsequently implemented in the history curriculum (Van Boxtel & Grever, 2011; Wilschut, 2010). The first commission designed a chronological framework of ten eras including European and national developments. The framework consists of ten eras with round numbers, based on the pedagogical idea that this kind of periodizing is easier to memorize rather than historiographical standards. Each era carries three to six so-called key features, consisting of historical developments or structures, such as Romanization, Industrial Revolution, or decolonization. The assumption was that teachers and history textbook authors could choose dates, events, and persons themselves to explain the key features, preventing the imposition of a master narrative. Furthermore, the designers of the framework emphasized a conceptualization of historical overview knowledge as "orientation knowledge": knowledge that can be used to situate historical and present events, persons, and developments in time (Van Boxtel & Van Drie, 2012; Van Drie, Logtenberg, Van der Meijden, & Van Riessen, 2009). In 2015, the national central examination will assess this historical overview knowledge of ten eras for the first time. This shift is accompanied by a reformulated section in the curriculum on the assessment of historical thinking and reasoning skills. These are now organized in three clusters: Time, Interpretation, and Significance Nowadays. Chronological overview knowledge has to be assessed in combination with these historical thinking and reasoning skills. Hence, the disciplinary skills of history are still a substantial component of the subject of history in upper secondary school.

While the implementation of the chronological frame of reference was still disputed, under political pressure from the Dutch Parliament, the government required the development of a "genuine canon" of Dutch history and installed a second commission. This was the result of a call for a strengthening of national identity and cohesion through history, a development similar to other European countries (Grever & Stuurman, 2007). Despite the protests of historians and negative advice from the Council of State, in 2008 a canon of Dutch history and culture was implemented: *entoen.nu De canon van Nederland* (for an English translation see Van Oostrom, 2008). It received a semi-official status in primary education and the first three years of secondary education. Schools have to use fifty "windows" (specific items) from the canon to illustrate key features of the framework of ten eras. Museums, memorial centers, and heritage organizations increasingly provide schools with opportunities to use local and national heritage as a resource for teaching the windows of the canon (Grever, De Bruijn, & Van Boxtel, 2012). In contrast with the ten-era framework, the canon did not become part of the attainment targets in upper secondary education.

In sum, despite the pressure to assess chronological overview knowledge and a canon of national history, since the 1990s considerable attention to the development of historical thinking and reasoning skills has characterized the history curriculum in the upper level of Dutch secondary school. Interestingly enough, the implementation of the canon of national history and particularly the extension of the attainment targets for history in upper secondary education with skills related to present significance both contribute to a growing attention to heritage practices. When using (material and immaterial) heritage in an educational context that is characterized by a disciplinary approach to the past, as is the case in Dutch upper secondary school history, we cross the supposed boundaries between heritage and history and bring together different practices. Such boundary crossing may result in difficulties, but it also represents a potential to open up space for negotiation of meanings (see Akkerman & Bakker, 2011). The difficulties arise from the unpredictability of students' reactions and from the demands of the knowledge base of teachers and their skills of guiding the process of nego-tiation in a particular context. Hawkey and Prior (2011) for example showed that the influence of students' ethnic identity on their positioning towards a national narrative is often diverse and ambiguous (Grever, Pelzer, & Haydn, 2011). Klein (2010) showed how teachers' knowledge, values, and skills impact their ability to deal with multiple and ambiguous perspectives in the classroom. These difficul-ties taken into account, we now turn to the potential of the boundary crossing, i.e. the question of how we can use heritage as a resource for enhancing and assessing students' understanding of present significance.

Using Heritage to Enhance and Assess Understanding of Present Significance

In the Netherlands, material and immaterial heritage is mainly used to enrich students' image of historical events and periods and to engage them in histori-cal inquiry activities. The framework of the Dutch curriculum and in particu-lar the "significance nowadays" targets do, however, provide room for several approaches to learning and assessing present significance through heritage. We will elaborate on two of these approaches, using examples from a recently devel-oped historical website on the Dutch slave trade and slavery in the Atlantic world (Klein, 2013).

Multiple Perspectives: Fort Elmina and Slavery Monuments

The "significance nowadays" targets require that students come to understand different reasons why people in the present care about certain events, develop-ments, or issues in history. Although in conceptualizations of historical think-ing relevance for the present is often mentioned as one of the reasons to attribute significance (e.g. Lévesque, 2008; Phillips, 2002; Seixas, 2008), few scholars further elaborate this relevance for the present category. Lévesque (2008) uses the term "memory significance" when describing criteria that are less used in the community of historians: intimate interest, symbolic significance, and contemporary lessons. People can attribute significance because of a perceived connection to their ancestry, religion, culture, or nation. Something can gain symbolic significance when used for present-day national or patriotic justifica-tion. The past can also be used to draw analogies to guide present-day actions, usually away from "errors" of the past. Next to understanding why people attribute present significance, students also need to understand that what is considered significant varies from group to group. The website on slave trade and slavery in the Atlantic world contains two activities in which students can explore how people from a variety of backgrounds attribute significance to traces from the past.

The first activity is about Fort Elmina. This fort on the coast of Ghana is one of the most important locations connected with the transatlantic slave trade. Thousands of enslaved people from African kingdoms were transported from this place over the Atlantic. Today, it is visited by millions of tourists from various cultural backgrounds. It is a *lieu de mémoire* for many, but not with a fixed meaning. The learning assignment in the website takes this as a point of departure. First, students are introduced to four types of people who represent larger collectives. They are, first, tourists from Creole Suriname backgrounds who feel a close connection to the age of the transatlantic slave trade, being descendants of those who were transported. Students see an excerpt of a documentary by a Surinamese film director. The tourists perform a remembrance ritual by lighting some candles in a dark space within Fort Elmina. Second, students view a photo of the village near Fort Elmina, whose inhabitants profit from mass tourism by offering services such as transport in fishing boats. They are not descendants of slaves who were transported. Third, the website includes a photo of President Obama and his wife Michelle (and their children). Students learn that Obama does not descend from slaves in the Atlantic region, but that his wife does. Finally, students see the former Crown Prince Willem-Alexander (today: King) and Princess Maxima (today: Queen) of the Netherlands as official visitors in 2002. They represent a country that has been deeply involved in the slave trade; in fact, the Dutch owned Fort Elmina and coordinated the transportation across the Atlantic from this place. From the 1990s, there has been an active community in the Netherlands of people from Suriname and the former Dutch Antilles, who ask for recognition of this past. After this introduction, students are to read four citations pertaining to these persons. These show multiple perspectives. Students are then asked to link the citations to the persons. The target here is for pupils to learn how one and the same physical place elicits different views and emotions in the present (or very recent past), depending at least in some way on the personal backgrounds of the visitors (cultural, political, economic).

The second activity on the website anticipates a variety of student perspectives. A study of students' views on the significance of slavery heritage (Savenije, 2011; Savenije, Van Boxtel, & Grever, 2014) shows the various perspectives on present significance they bring into the classroom. Although the study researched the age group 13 to 14, students' responses provide a good picture of how various interpretations were related to their diverse backgrounds. Students mentioned, for example, that they could understand that descendants of enslaved people would consider it important to preserve historical remains of slave trade and slavery for the future. Some students of Surinamese and Antillean background made a connection to their own families. Other students considered slavery heritage important as an historical example of inequality.

The website assignment about slavery monuments works in two steps. First, students encounter photos of five slavery monuments without any information regarding what these represent or where they are located. Students are asked to drag and drop these monuments in one of three boxes offering the following choices: (a) I like this as a monument to remember slavery; (b) I don't like it as a monument to remember slavery; or (c) I do not understand the monument. The rationale of this first step is to let students decide first on the aesthetic appearance of the monuments. Some are specific (slaves resisting or breaking chains) while others are more symbolic. For the next step, students are offered new photos of the monuments, now as objects where memory rituals are performed. They see flowers placed at some of them and ceremonies performed. They also learn what exactly the monuments are supposed to represent, where they are located, and when they were erected. The second step is the question: "To which monument do you relate the most? Explain your answer". The rationale here is that when they possess knowledge of the monuments' intended meanings, students may change their opinion. This provides possibilities for teachers to organize discussion about the engagement of students with the topic and its present significance for them, linked to their own social and cultural backgrounds. Students in upper secondary education are able to reflect on their own identity and the ways in which it affects their ideas (Savenije, 2014, pp. 126–127). However, organizing a discussion requires teachers to be knowledgeable of student diversity and skilled in guiding learning processes that are "negotiations of meaning" rather than the learning of facts.

An old African Statue: Biography and Changed Meanings

Heritage can also be used as a resource to enhance students' understanding that the significance that people attribute to phenomena, persons, events, or objects from the past may change over time. One assignment on the website works with a museum object: a very rare statue of a woman with an oracle scale on her head. Today, it occupies a high profile place in the Rijksmuseum Volkenkunde in Leiden. It has done so, however, only since 1992 when its age was discovered. The object apparently was mentioned and illustrated in a book, published in the year 1700. The author explained it as the product of an unrefined hand, which resembled—so he thought—the ancient Egyptian goddess of Isis. He saw it on the chimney shelf of the Dutch West Indian Company (WIC) in the city of Groningen. This evidence shows how the object travelled through time and space, starting in the seventeenth century. It must have been bought from the Owo-people in the environs of the old city of Benin and then transported on a slave ship to the Dutch Republic. When the Dutch WIC was dissolved at the end of the eighteenth century, the statue ended up with a baker in Groningen, from whom it was bought by a former director of the museum in 1903. It was placed in the depot until its real history was discovered. The assignment asks students to reconstruct the whereabouts of this statue in four steps and invites them to reflect on its changed meanings, when changing from owner to owner. It represents a biographical approach, suited to also foster learning about continuity and change.

Not only objects, but also monuments have their own biographies that interconnect with larger historical developments. Students do not always understand memorials as a reflection of the times and values in which they were built (Nemko, 2009; Seixas & Clark, 2004). Therefore, students must also learn to consider monuments as reflecting a certain stance and as a product of their time. A study by Nemko (2009) shows that although pupils practiced a critical approach to historical sources such as documents and pictures in the history classroom, they had difficulties with considering monuments as reflecting a particular stance. Understanding of present significance also includes the ability to critically assess the narratives that are constructed around objects, sites, buildings, paintings, archival documents, or other remains of the past that are selected as heritage. Enhancing historical inquiry and reasoning activities related to heritage can make students aware of possible simplifications, presentism, and inaccuracies.

The activities provided by the website are meant to enhance students' understanding of the variety and changing perspectives on the significance of a particular history. The aim of the website activities is not to assess this type of understanding. In particular, students' reflection on the way they personally relate to a particular heritage is difficult to assess. However, assessment of students' understanding of *present* significance should be preceded by activities such as those provided by the website or a visit to a museum, monument, or site of remembrance. When students have explored different (including their own) and changing perspectives on the significance of particular remains of the past, they can be asked, for example, to construct an oral presentation or write a reflection that displays their understanding. In that case, one needs to elaborate a rubric specifying levels of understanding present significance. A paper-and-pencil assessment task could present two or three different perspectives in the debate about the erection of the national slavery monument or about Black Pete. Students could be asked to identify and explain different or changing perspectives within the historical context (also using their chronological overview knowledge). Or, when no background information is provided about the authors, students could be asked to identify the kind of extra information needed in order to better understand the debate. It might even be possible to develop multiple-choice questions in which a heritage practice becomes a resource; for example, in what VanSledright (2014) describes as upside-down weighted multiple-choice items in which several answers are possible but the most compelling option receives most points.

Conclusions and Discussion

Heritage is often associated with essentialist narratives focused on self-confirmation, patrimonial pride, and a lack of historical distance. From this perspective heritage does not seem to be an attractive "partner" for history education that aims at historical thinking and reasoning abilities. However, students regularly come across heritage in everyday life outside school and become participants in heritage practices themselves. In many school subjects the question is raised as to how to connect learning in school to the contexts in which knowledge and skills taught need to be applied. We consider heritage as such as a context for history education. When we want to achieve transfer of students' historical thinking and reasoning ability to situations external to the school setting, we need to think about heritage as a potential resource for history learning. In this chapter, we explored how heritage might be a resource to enhance and assess students' understanding of present significance. It is self-evident that to enhance this understanding, school history itself needs to adopt a disciplinary approach allowing for a dynamic notion of heritage (Ashworth, Graham, & Tunbridge, 2007; Smith, 2006). Heritage must be viewed as a continuous process of selection and meaning making related to our (changing) orientations towards the future. In this chapter, we first discussed the extent to which history education in Dutch upper secondary school reflects a disciplinary approach. We concluded that, despite the pressure to teach a chronological overview and a canon of national history, the official attainment targets, history textbooks, and national examinations positively contribute to a practice in which relatively much attention is paid to historical thinking and reasoning skills. In this context, Dutch historians who work as history teachers or educators in museums, archives, or heritage organizations have an important role. They can be considered mediators who must manage and combine multiple, divergent discourses and practices in order to further promote students' historical thinking and understanding.

Our examples showed how material and immaterial heritage can be used as instructional resources. Students can explore how the past is used in the present by different people in different ways. They also learn how perspectives on significance are shaped by identity and change over time. When they are stimulated to think about how they themselves attribute significance, they can learn something about how their own identity can play a role. When teaching about such issues, we need to be careful. People's identities may play a role in how they attribute significance, but they do not necessarily result in particular perspectives. Negotiating between different perspectives on the past is a difficult task. It requires teachers with deep content knowledge and the skills to organize a genuine dialogue by asking questions, listening to answers, and prompting students to make sense of differences of opinions by taking into account the underlying knowledge, experiences, and values of people in the past and in the present.

Heritage can also be used as a resource for assessing students' understanding of what is called "present significance". The most obvious way is a visit to a museum, monument, or heritage site, or a research project in which students have the opportunity to explore how people today or in the past attributed significance. This can be done by a written reflection or an oral presentation. However, a well-designed case about a particular heritage practice might also be included in test items. Further research is needed to describe in more detail what it means to understand present significance and what subtypes can be discerned. In order to examine students' progression, we also need to discern levels of understanding. Finally, more research is needed to further explore the potential of heritage as a resource to teach historical thinking. We believe that crossing the supposed boundaries between heritage and history and bringing together different practices will open up new possibilities for enhancing historical thinking and reasoning.

References

Akkerman, S., & Bakker, A. (2011). Boundary crossing and boundary objects. *Review of Educational Research, 81,* 132–169.

Ashworth, G., Graham, B., & Tunbridge, J. (2007). *Pluralising pasts: Heritage, identity and place in multicultural societies.* London: Pluto Press.

Bodnar, J. (1992). *Remaking America: Public memory, commemoration, and patriotism in the Twentieth Century.* Princeton: Princeton University Press.

Cercadillo, L. (2006). 'Maybe they haven't decided yet what is right:' English and Spanish perspectives on teaching historical significance. *Teaching History, 125,* 6–9.

Grever, M., De Bruijn, P., & Van Boxtel, C. (2012). Negotiating historical distance. Or, how to deal with the past as a foreign country in heritage education. *Paedagogica Historica, 48*(6), 873–887.

Grever, M., Pelzer, B., & Haydn, T. (2011). High school students' views on history. *Journal of Curriculum Studies 43,* 207–229.

Grever, M., & Stuurman, S. (Eds.). (2007). *Beyond the canon. History for the twenty-first century.* New York: Palgrave MacMillan.

Hawkey, K., & Prior, J. (2011). History, memory cultures and meaning in the classroom. *Journal of Curriculum Studies, 43*(2), 231–247.

Klein, S. (2010). Teaching history in the Netherlands: Teachers' experiences of a plurality of perspectives. *Curriculum Inquiry, 40,* 614–634.

Klein, S. (Ed.). (2013). Slave trade in the Atlantic world. Center for Historical Culture, Erasmus University Rotterdam. www.atlanticslavetrade.eu

Lee, P. (2004). "Walking backwards into tomorrow": Historical consciousness and understanding history. *International Journal of Historical Learning, Teaching, and Research, 4*(1). http://centres.exeter.ac.uk/historyresource/journal7/7contents.htm

Lévesque, S. (2005). Teaching second-order concepts in Canadian history: The importance of "historical significance". *Canadian Social Studies, 39*(2). www.quasar.ualberta.ca/css/Css_39_2/ARLevesque_second-order_concepts.htm

Lévesque, S. (2008). *Thinking historically. Educating students for the twenty-first century.* Toronto, ON: Toronto Press.

Lowenthal, D. (1999). *The past is a foreign country.* Cambridge, England: Cambridge University Press.

Nemko, B. (2009). Are we creating a generation of 'historical tourists'? Visual assessment as a means of measuring pupils' progress in historical interpretation. *Teaching History, 137,* 32–39.

Phillips, R. (2002). Historical significance—The forgotten 'key element'? *Teaching History 106,* 14–19.

Rüsen, J. (2007). How to make sense of the past—salient issues of Metahistory. *The Journal of Transdisciplinary Research in Southern Africa, 3*(1), 169–221.

Savenije, G. (2011). Discussion in chains. Pupils' ideas about slavery heritage. In C. van Boxtel, S. Klein, & E. Snoep (Eds.), *Heritage education. Challenges in dealing with the past* (pp. 32–39). Amsterdam, Netherlands: Erfgoed Nederland.

Savenije, G. (2014). *Sensitive history under negotiation. Pupils' historical imagination and their attribution of significance during heritage projects.* PhD thesis, Erasmus University Rotterdam.

Savenije, G., Van Boxtel C., & Grever, M. (2014). Sensitive 'heritage' of slavery in a multicultural classroom: pupils' ideas about significance. *British Journal of Educational Studies. 62*(2), 127–148.

Seixas, P. (2008). *"Scaling Up" the benchmarks of historical thinking. The Vancouver meetings,* February 14–15, 2008. Vancouver, BC: Centre for the Study of Historical Consciousness.

Seixas, P., & Clark, P. (2004). Murals as monuments: Pupils' ideas about depictions of civilization in British Columbia. *American Journal of Education, 110,* 146–171.

Seixas, P., & Morton, T. (2013). *The big six historical thinking concepts.* Toronto, ON: Nelson Education.

Smith, L. (2006). *Uses of heritage.* London, England: Routledge.

Van Boxtel, C., & Grever, M. (2011). Between disenchantment and high expectations. History education in the Netherlands, 1968–2008. In E. Erdmann & W. Hasberg (Eds.), *Facing, mapping, bridging diversity. Foundation of a European discourse on history education* (vol. 2; pp. 83–116). Schwalbach/Ts., Germany: Wochenschau-Verlag.

Van Boxtel, C., & Van Drie, J. (2012). "That's in the time of the Romans!" Knowledge and strategies pupils use to contextualize historical images and documents. *Cognition and Instruction, 30*(2), 113–145.

Van Drie, J., Logtenberg, A., Van der Meijden, B., & Van Riessen, M. (2009). "When was that date?" Building and assessing a frame of reference in the Netherlands. *Teaching History, 137,* 14–21.

Van Oostrom, F. (2008). *The Netherlands in a nutshell. Highlights from Dutch history and culture.* Amsterdam, Netherlands: Amsterdam University Press.

VanSledright, B. (2008). Narratives of nation-state, historical knowledge and school history education. *Review of Research Education, 32,* 109–146.

VanSledright, B. (2014). *Assessing historical thinking and understanding. Innovative designs for new standards.* New York: Routledge.

Van Stipriaan, A. (2007). Disrupting the canon: The case of slavery. In M. Grever & S. Stuurman, (Eds.), *Beyond the canon. History for the twenty-first century* (pp. 205–219). New York: Palgrave MacMillan.

Wilschut, A. (2010). History at the mercy of politicians and ideologies: Germany, England, and the Netherlands in the 19th and 20th centuries. *Journal of Curriculum Studies, 42*(5), 693–723.

4

RELATING HISTORICAL CONSCIOUSNESS TO HISTORICAL THINKING THROUGH ASSESSMENT

Catherine Duquette

In 2003, the Ministry of Education, Leisure, and Sport (MELS) of the province of Quebec, Canada, published its new history and citizenship education curriculum which specified that the learning of history should not be limited to memorizing a set of dates, names, and events but should promote the development of a form of historical thinking (MELS, 2003). Quebec's choice to emphasize historical thinking is not unique, as other Canadian provinces, such as Ontario and Alberta, have also developed similar history curricula over the years. However, research has shown that the teaching and learning of historical thinking are far from simple. As Lee and Ashby (2000), Barton (1997), and VanSledright (2002) note, students find it arduous to move away from an understanding of history as a true, never-changing story to narratives based on the interpretation of the past that may differ from one person to another. Teachers, on their part, seem to struggle with the assessment of historical thinking, finding it time-consuming and difficult to observe in students' work. An abundance of research promoting numerous concepts such as historical thinking, historical consciousness, or historical understanding does not help the teachers confront this challenge, as the connection between the concepts is rarely adequately explained in the available literature. Moreover, teachers are not always provided with models or categories on which they might base their assessments, leaving them with the difficult task of identifying and assessing these concepts in the works of their students. An example of this can be found in Quebec's History and Citizenship Education curriculum, which demands that students develop their ability to identify the causes and consequences of a specific historical event from grade 7 on. Yet, the curriculum does not provide teachers with a clear progression of students' expected cognitive development, which causes confusion on what can be expected of a grade 7 student compared to one in grade 11. In order to find answers to this problem, we feel that a better understanding of the precise nature of the relationship between historical consciousness and historical thinking might prove beneficial for teachers faced with the task of assessing their students' ability to interpret the past. The research question addressed in this chapter is: what is the relationship between the concept of historical consciousness and historical thinking, and how can a clearer understanding of this relationship enhance the assessment of historical thinking? In order to answer this question, we will present the results of an empirical study conducted with 148 French-speaking students in their final year of high school in the province of Quebec, Canada. Before discussing the results of this study, a brief explanation of its theoretical framework and methodology is presented.

Theoretical Framework

One of the first problems that confronts history teachers is the ambiguity of the vocabulary used in both official and academic publications. The meaning behind terms such as historical thinking, historical consciousness, and historical understanding is rarely defined. For example, Christian Laville (2004) tends to associate historical consciousness with a form of collective memory while the members of the *Pasts Collective* view it as a form of interplay between memory, identity, and a critical understanding of the past (Conrad et al., 2013). Similar confusion is found when comparing the definitions associated with historical thinking and with historical understanding (Duquette, 2014). For the purpose of our study, a clear definition of what is understood by historical thinking and historical consciousness is necessary if we wish to define their relationship.

Historical Thinking

In this chapter, historical thinking is understood as a series of specific cognitive operations needed to carefully interpret the past. It consists of two main elements: a historical perspective and a historical method (Laville, 2004). In particular, a historical perspective is understood as the framework guiding the interpretation of past events. Seixas's (2010) model of historical thinking provides us with our inspiration for five elements found under the term historical perspective; these are historical significance, continuity and change, causes and consequences, historical empathy,[1] and taking into account the complexity of the past. The historical method, in turn, refers to a deductive approach that requires students to question the past, propose a hypothesis, check the available sources, and analyze sources with respect to their reliability in order to offer a response to the initial question (Martineau, 1999). It is the historical method, together with the historical perspective, that enables students to interpret and develop their own understanding of the past (see Table 4.1 for an illustration of this model).

TABLE 4.1 Elements of historical thinking

Historical Thinking	
Historical Perspective	*Historical Method*
Establish historical significance	Question social phenomena of the past
Identify elements of continuity and change	Propose hypotheses
Analyze causes and consequences	Check available sources
Develop historical empathy	Analyze sources with respect to their reliability
Take into account the complexity of the past	Answer initial query

Historical Consciousness

Historical consciousness is best defined as the understanding an individual has of temporality. That is to say, historical consciousness is the interpretation of the past that allows the understanding of the present and the consideration of the future (Charland, 2003; Rüsen, 2004; Seixas, 2006). Historical consciousness can be observed through the narratives used by an individual to make sense of the complex ties between past events and today's ever-changing world:

> The linguistic form within which historical consciousness realizes its function of orientation is that of the narrative. In this view, the operations by which the human mind realizes the historical synthesis of the dimensions of time simultaneous with those of value and experience lie in narration: the telling of a story.
>
> (Rüsen, 2004, pp. 69)

Thus, historical consciousness is not in itself a form of critical thinking (Laville, 2004), but it may become so if the individual is made aware of his own subjectivity vis-à-vis his understanding of the past. Therefore, it may be useful to think of historical consciousness as divided into two levels: first a non-reflective level and second a reflective level. To be reflective, historical consciousness must base its understanding of the past on the interpretations emanating from the process of historical thinking.

Hence, historical consciousness and historical thinking provide two different frames for making sense of the past. However, what influence historical consciousness has on historical thinking and vice versa is still unknown. This question is the focus of the empirical research described in this chapter.

Research Method

In order to define the relationship between historical thinking and historical consciousness, a qualitative study was carried out with 148 French-speaking Quebec students in their final year of secondary school.[2] If others before us have conducted empirical studies concerned with similar concepts, it was impossible to use their research protocols for our purposes. Indeed, studies led by Charland (2003), von Borries (1997), and Létourneau (2014) are designed to "define the basic elements of students' historical consciousness and to determine its structure (our translation)" (Charland, 2003, p. 23) rather than to establish its relationship with historical thinking. The same applies to studies interested in historical thinking, where the implication of historical consciousness in the development of the latter is rarely taken into account. Thus, a research design specifically targeted to address the purposes of this empirical study was employed.

Our research was designed using the model of problem solving advocated by Dalongeville (2000). The objective of the research was to place students in a learning process, which allowed the researcher to observe how students' ability to think historically might affect their historical consciousness. This led to the development of a four-step research design:

Step one: each participant responds to an open-ended question in which they need to solve a contemporary problem to which the past is relevant (of three possible—on the reasons for disparities between wealthy and poor countries, the consequences of immigration on Quebecois culture, or voluntary enlistment in armed services).[3] Step one promotes the emergence of the narratives employed by their historical consciousness (Rüsen, 2004).

Step two: the same participants complete an interview that starts with the researcher creating a cognitive conflict to bring students to question their initial understanding of the problem.

Step three: participants analyze historical documents relevant to the problem, supplied by the researcher, using a think-aloud method, a process that involves their ability to think historically.

Step four: in light of the information found in the historical documents, participants are asked to answer the initial problem once more, allowing the researcher to observe the relationship between students' ability to think historically and the narratives expressing their historical consciousness.

The Development of Historical Consciousness

Before the relationship between historical thinking and historical consciousness could be observed, it was necessary to categorize how students' historical consciousness evolved through the experiment. In an attempt to do this, a classification was carried out using the stages proposed in the Rüsen taxonomy, which are: traditional, exemplary, critical, and genetic (Rüsen, 2004). However, our data did not reflect the characteristics of Rüsen's four stages of historical consciousness. In his categories, Rüsen considers that the individual constantly refers to the past when confronted with a contemporary problem in which history is relevant. This does not seem to be the case with our participants as a number of them did not take into account the past in their responses to the contemporary problem posed in the questionnaire. For example, many students associated third-world poverty with bad climate and did not see the influences of past imperialism or decolonization on the situation. Because of this, we abandoned Rüsen's taxonomy and, after a careful reading of student responses, developed our own empirically based categorization based on whether the participants included references to the past in their answers. This process led us to conceive a four-tier developmental model.

Primary Level of Historical Consciousness

Students at the primary level of historical consciousness are not able to provide a precise answer to the contemporary problem found in the questionnaire. Students often denounce the third-world poverty problem as an example of social injustice without much explanation. In response to the question of the consequences of immigration on Quebecois culture, students at that level will be either strongly in favor of immigration or opposed to it, without being able to explain why they hold such convictions. At this level, participants never refer to past events in their answers. For these students poverty, culture, and voluntary enlistment in armed services are unchangeable situations that cannot be explained because they are just too complex.

Intermediate Level of Historical Consciousness

At this level, students answer the historical problem by mentioning causes taken from their everyday lives. For example, participants attempt to explain poverty by comparing the economic situation in the province of Quebec with the one they expect to find in third-world countries. Thus by using Quebec as a model, they determine the criteria that ensure prosperity. Again, at this level students never mention past events in their answers.

Composite Level of Historical Consciousness

Students at the composite level mention both causes from the past and the present in their answers but without necessarily linking them. For these students, the events that have occurred in the past have no influence on the events of the present. Therefore, past causes, such as colonization, explain poverty in the past, while the abuse of the rich countries of today gives rise to the current situation.

Narrative Level of Historical Consciousness

At this final level, students are able to explain how past events have influenced the situations found today. In other words, they are able to build a narrative that explains the evolution of the different concepts found in our questionnaires. Indeed, unlike students at the composite level, they do not just enumerate a long series of causes, they tell a story. That is to say, they combine different events in the past to construct a narrative explaining the evolution of a historical phenomenon from past to present. Participants at the narrative level are the ones who come closest to displaying a form of reflective historical consciousness.

Our four-level developmental model was used to evaluate the variation in the level of historical consciousness in participants. The level of historical consciousness at step 1 was compared to the level at step 4. The results of this operation are found in Figures 4.1 and 4.2.

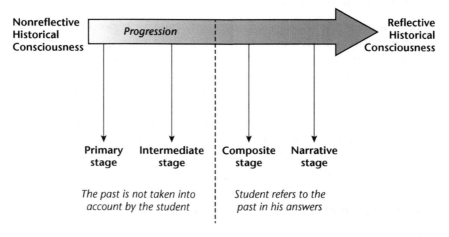

FIGURE 4.1 Levels of the development of historical consciousness

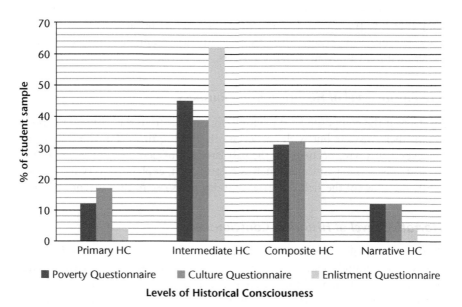

FIGURE 4.2 Levels of historical consciousness at step 1

The progress of historical consciousness between step 1 (Figure 4.3) and step 4 (Figure 4.4) is evident by comparing the two figures. As we move from step 1 to step 4, the percentages of participants having primary and intermediate levels of historical consciousness decrease while those at the composite and narrative levels increase. Specifically, after students are asked to think historically (in step 3)

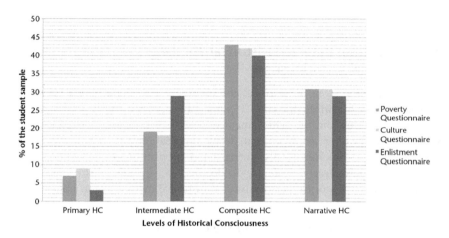

FIGURE 4.3 Levels of historical consciousness at step 4

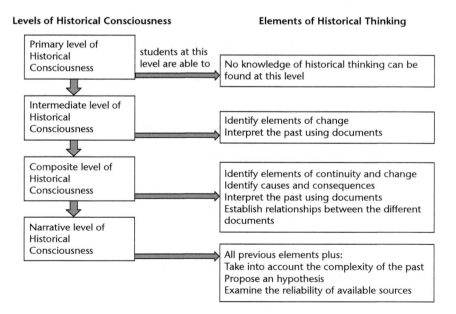

FIGURE 4.4 Assessment model

the number of students at the intermediate level *decreases* by an average of 27% at step 4 while, in contrast, the narrative level *increases* by an average of 21%. Obviously, something is happening between step 1 and step 4 of the research. Is the change in students' demonstrations of historical consciousness related to their ability to think historically? In order to answer this question, we proceeded with a detailed analysis of students' historical thinking at each level of historical consciousness.

The Correlation Between Historical Thinking and Historical Consciousness

By comparing the levels of historical consciousness with the different elements associated with historical thinking, a connection between the development of historical thinking and the achievement of a level of reflective historical consciousness can be observed. In order to define this relationship, we compared students' ability to think historically during step 3 of our protocol with their levels of historical consciousness at step 4. To do this, both components of historical thinking, namely historical perspective and historical method, were analyzed.

Historical Thinking of Students in the Category of Primary Historical Consciousness

Students at the primary level seem to struggle when asked to solve a problem in which history is relevant. The elements associated with a historical perspective are rarely found in their answers. Indeed, no statement could be classified as "continuity and change" and all attempts at historical empathy were based on common sense rather than on information found in the given documents. Similar conclusions can be drawn when analyzing students' abilities to use the historical method. Again, students at the primary level do not seem to question the documents provided, they do not see the links between events, they do not have any nuance in their interpretations of the documents, and they do not cite any other sources in their answers. These results suggest that the boundaries between past and present are still unclear for these participants. In fact, they seem to understand the past through the filters of today's morals and values. Essentially, their discourse is rooted in the present with little to no connection to the past. These students do not seem to have developed any of the intellectual skills related to historical thinking.

Historical Thinking of Students in the Category of Intermediate Historical Consciousness

Students at the intermediate level, like those at the primary level, struggle when asked to perform a task based on historical thinking. For example, 78% of our sample uses elements from their everyday lives rather than their knowledge of the past (15% of the sample) when interpreting the documents provided. This impairs their ability to use the elements of historical perspective and historical method. Historical empathy, for example, is more often based on common sense rather than on the interpretation of the given documents. However, what distinguishes participants at the intermediate level seems to be their understanding of the past as having no connection with the present. Indeed 47% of our sample emphasizes elements of change between past and present rather than elements of continuity (15% of the sample). In doing this, participants underline how today's society is morally better than past societies. Moreover, students at the intermediate level are those who mention most frequently their history course and the movies they have watched as the best sources of information. Films appear to be just as reliable and accurate as the information provided by their history teacher. These results lead us to believe that participants at the intermediate level are just beginning to learn how to think historically. The links between the present and the past are still unclear and although students are sometimes able to identify important information from a historical source, the elements of perspective are not integrated enough to allow a proper interpretation. In sum, for these participants, the questions raised in our questionnaires are not perceived as being linked to history but to morals.

Historical Thinking of Students in the Category of Composite Historical Consciousness

Students at the composite level of historical consciousness seem to have developed a form of historical thinking. Indeed, 50% of our sample provides answers to the historical problem based on the interpretation of the documents provided. In contrast to students at the intermediate level, these participants are able to identify elements of continuity and change and of causes and consequences. Yet, they still lack some understanding of history as an interpretation of the past. In other words, the majority of them (56%) are still looking for the "right" answer. Nevertheless, the data show an increase in students' ability to use elements of historical thinking. This leads us to suggest that the composite level is a moment of transition where students are in the midst of learning how to think historically. A further analysis of students' ability enables us to identify the elements of historical thinking that have been mastered in large part and the ones still needing to be learned. According to the data, the elements that have more to do with a form of critical thinking are the ones still in development. For example, few students at the composite level question the reliability of the historical documents proposed by the researcher. They also have difficulty showing caution when providing an interpretation. In other words, students at this level are quite certain of providing the single right answer to the historical problem, while other interpretations are considered "wrong" and thus discarded. Finally, the lack of critical thinking also leads participants at this level to consider representations of the past proposed by movies or TV shows to be as reliable as information found in historical documents. All things considered, students at the composite level have yet to understand history as plural interpretations of the past. It is this that seems to hinder their ability to master the elements of historical thinking that have more to do with a form of critical thinking.

Historical Thinking of Students in the Category of Narrative Historical Consciousness

Students at the narrative level distinguish themselves from other levels of historical consciousness by their greater capability of thinking historically. For example, instead of using their common sense to solve a problem, they tend to refer to the information found in the documents provided. In their discourse, elements associated with historical empathy, continuity and change, and causes and consequences can be found. Yet what distinguishes the majority of these students, in our view, is their ability to take into account the complexity of the past. That is to say that these participants are aware of the subjectivity of historical sources and they accept that a single event might bring forward different interpretations. However, 32% of our sample at this level still interpret the past using a set of values supported by their society. This number is nevertheless a significant drop when compared to other levels of historical consciousness (74% for the intermediate level and 56% for the composite level). Taking into account the complexity of the past thus appears to be one of the most difficult elements of historical thinking for students to master. Another characteristic of the participants at the narrative level is the fact that they are the most likely to include links between past and present when answering our questionnaire (88% for the narrative level compared to 48% for the intermediate level and 50% for the composite level). In addition, students at the narrative stage are the only ones that question the reliability of the documents provided in the course of the interview. Participants at the narrative level are also the ones who are most likely to question their own interpretations. This also seems to be a difficult element of historical thinking to master, for even at the narrative level only 18% of our sample seems to systematically do this. The following example shows a student (Colb, 126–131) questioning his own interpretation:

> Well the more international actions are taken the more other countries are going to go to [Afghanistan] to help. But again, this is perhaps another form of propaganda . . .

In this example, the participant questions his answer using a concept that he has developed during the interview: the concept of propaganda. Therefore, it is plausible to say that this student has managed to transfer his knowledge from one situation to another. Thus, if we trust our results, the transfer of knowledge and skills in history cannot be done until students have a certain mastery of historical thinking. In sum, it is when students become aware of the complexity of the past and are able to take into account their own subjectivity when interpreting available sources that the narrative level of historical consciousness is reached. That is to say that students who attain a narrative level of historical consciousness are the ones who can think historically.

Historical Consciousness as a Means to Assess the Development of Historical Thinking

The results of this research tend to underline a strong relationship between the development of a reflective historical consciousness and the ability to think historically. Students' level of historical consciousness can be understood as an indicator of their ability to think historically. Moreover, it seems that to move from one level of historical consciousness to another, students must have previously developed specific elements of historical thinking. For example, to move from an intermediate level to a composite level, students must have developed their ability to identify causes and consequences as well as the elements of continuity and change. An assessment model can thus be drawn from the available data as shown in Figure 4.4.

The assessment model can be considered an effective means to assess students' historical thinking: It simplifies the process of evaluation since teachers do not need to evaluate every single element of historical thinking individually but can instead assess their students' general level of historical consciousness. Indeed, since the four levels of historical consciousness are part of a move towards a mastery of historical thinking, once the level of historical consciousness is known to the teachers, they can in turn infer which elements of historical thinking still need to be developed. For example, if students are mostly at the intermediate level, the teacher will know that they need to work on the concepts of continuity and change so that students come to understand the links between past and present. Furthermore, this assessment model allows teachers to discern how their students understand the discipline of history, thus enabling them to focus on the specific misconceptions they might hold.

Illustration of a Practical Usage of the Assessment Model in the History Classroom

To be of use to teachers, the assessment model must be associated with a teaching of history based on problem solving. Lessons must be constructed around a large question that will act as the central theme. Following the steps associated with the historical method, students provide an initial answer to the problem at the beginning of the lesson. It is at this moment that their teacher can evaluate their initial level of historical consciousness using our four-tier model. The rest of the lesson must be aimed at answering the large question. Teachers can at that moment decide to focus on the different elements of historical thinking, knowing, thanks to their assessment of their students' initial historical consciousness levels, which elements of historical thinking are mastered and which are still in development. At the end of the lesson, the teacher can assess once more their students' levels of historical consciousness and compare them with their initial levels in order to verify if and how students have progressed in their learning of historical thinking. However, teachers must be aware that historical thinking is not an ability that is quickly mastered. It would not be surprising that their students stagnated at a level of historical consciousness for some time before moving on because they have not sufficiently mastered the required elements of historical thinking. Despite this, our four-tier model of historical consciousness combined with our assessment model have the potential of becoming a tool for teachers to quickly assess the progression of their students regarding their ability to think historically.

Conclusion

In its 2003 program, the MELS of the province of Quebec asked its teachers to assess their students' historical thinking rather than their factual knowledge of history. Compared to longstanding assessment practices that focus on the memorization of factual knowledge, this new type of assessment demanded that teachers significantly change their assessment habits. To date, assessing historical thinking remains one of the sensitive issues associated with the Quebec history and citizenship education curriculum. Although we are conscious that replication studies are necessary to test and confirm our findings, we believe that our assessment model proposes a possible answer to teachers' difficulties. Indeed, the data seem to point out that our four-tier model of the development of historical consciousness can act as an effective indicator to monitor the development of historical thinking, thus rendering the process of assessment easier and less time consuming for busy teachers.

Notes

1 This is called historical perspective in Seixas's text. However, we feel that historical perspective is a larger concept. Thus, we prefer, as Ashby and Lee (1987), to use the term historical empathy when referring to the act of trying to understand the underlying reasons of an individual's actions in the past.
2 The sample of 148 students consisted of 65 boys and 83 girls. Their average age was 16.2 years.
3 Different questions were used to see whether the topic studied might affect the relationship between historical thinking and historical consciousness (Rüsen, 2004). As we will see, the topic of the question had very little influence on the results.

References

Ashby, R., & Lee, P. (1987). Children's Concepts of Empathy and Understanding in History. In Portal, C. (Ed.), *The History Curriculum for Teachers* (pp. 62–88). New York: Falmer Press.

Barton, K. C. (1997). History—It can be Elementary. An Overview of Elementary Students' Understanding of History. *Social Education, 61*(1), 13–16.

Charland, J.-P. (2003). *Les Elèves, l'Histoire et la Citoyenneté: Enquête auprès d'Élèves des Régions de Montréal et de Toronto.* Québec: PUL.

Conrad, M., Ercikan, K., Friesen, G., Létourneau, J., Muise, D., Northrup, D., & Seixas, P. (2013). *Canadians and Their Pasts.* Toronto: University of Toronto Press.

Dalongeville, A. (2000). *Situations-Problèmes pour Enseigner l'Histoire au Cycle 3.* Paris: Hachette Éducation.

Duquette, C. (2014). Through the Looking Glass: An Overview of the Theoretical Foundations of Quebec's History Curriculum. In Sandwell, R. & von Heyking, A. (Eds.), *Becoming a History Teacher* (pp. 139–157). Toronto: University of Toronto Press.

Laville, C. (2004). Historical Consciousness and Historical Education: What to Expect from the First for the Second. In Seixas, P. (Ed.), *Theorizing Historical Consciousness* (pp. 165–182). Toronto: University of Toronto Press.

Lee, P., & Ashby, R. (2000). Progression in Historical Understanding among Students Ages 7–14. In Stearns, P., Seixas, P., & S. Wineburg (Eds.), *Knowing, Teaching and Learning History* (pp. 199–222). New York: New York University Press.

Létourneau, J. (2014). *Je me Souviens? Le Passé du Québec dans la Conscience de sa Jeunesse.* Montréal: Fides.

Martineau, R. (1999). *L'Histoire à l'École, Matière à Penser.* Montréal: L'Harmattan.

Québec, Ministère de l'Éducation, du Sport et des Loisirs du Québec (MELS). (2003). *L'École, Tout un Programme, Programme de Formation au Premier Cycle du Secondaire* (pp. 337–368).

Rüsen, J. (2004). Historical Consciousness: Narrative Structure, Moral Function, and Ontogenetic Development. In Seixas, P. (Ed.), *Theorizing Historical Consciousness* (pp. 63–85). Toronto: University of Toronto Press.

Seixas, P. (2006). What Is Historical Consciousness. In Sandwell, R. (Ed.), *To the Past: History Education, Public Memory and Citizenship in Canada* (pp. 11–22). Toronto: University of Toronto Press.

Seixas, P. (2010). A Modest Proposal for Change in Canadian History Education. *International Review of History Education, 6*, 11–26.

VanSledright, B. (2002). *In Search of America's Past: Learning to Read History in Elementary School.* New York: Teachers College Press.

von Borries, B. (1997). Linking Time Levels in Historical Consciousness. Interpretations of the Past, Perceptions of the Present and Expectations of the Future by East and West German Youth. In Létourneau, J. (Ed.), *Le Lieu Identitaire de la Jeunesse d'Aujourd'Hui, Étude de Cas* (pp. 139–174). Montréal: L'Harmattan.

COMMENTARY

Into the Swampy Lowlands of Important Problems

Robert B. Bain

The chapters in this first section make one thing very clear: it was much easier for teachers and policy makers when they only cared about how much factual information history students retained rather than developing students' historical consciousness or enhancing their capacity for historical thinking. Few complications existed when the learning goal was simply memorizing the "stuff" of history. However, the authors of these chapters implicitly question whether such simplicity was ever the goal of history instruction, at least over the past century in the West.

For example, Carlos Kölbl and Lisa Konrad point out that in Germany discussions about historical consciousness stretched back to the 1930s, and since the 1970s, it has become a "core concept" in German history education. Neither are discussions about teaching historical thinking new in the Netherlands, as Carla van Boxtel, Maria Grever, and Stephen Klein explain, offering as one example a 1970s textbook replete with primary sources and historical reasoning questions. Though focusing on contemporary issues of disciplinary literacy in the United States, Abby Reisman traces the interest on domain-specific historical reasoning back over 100 years while centering her analysis on 40-year-old attempts to assess historical reasoning. It seems that trying to extend students' thinking beyond mastery of historical facts has been the once and future goal for educational reformers and, possibly, for state systems of public education.

Seeing this as a goal with a longer historical trail sharpens our understanding of the *enduring* difficulties educators confront in trying to develop and assess students' historical thinking, consciousness, understanding, habits of mind, and practices. The great value in these chapters resides in how they illuminate the challenges—some hidden—and in a few cases, how they offer plausible ways to manage the issues.

Of course, a central challenge is political. Many people fear that such history instruction will encourage students to reject the received or "official" versions of a nation's past and thus they put up fierce opposition. Discussions of these politics all too often fill the air, something these chapters, to their credit, largely avoid. Indeed, one of their strengths rests in how they rarely mention political firestorms created by opponents. Rather, they target conceptual confusion, poorly constructed assessments, and a dearth of evidence and effective models created by supporters of this more ambitious form of history instruction. Collectively, they suggest that the failure to provide conceptual clarity and usable models of assessment, possibly even more than political tension, has hindered and continues to hinder reform. As Catherine Duquette points out in this volume, "[a]n abundance of research promoting numerous concepts such as historical thinking, historical consciousness, or historical understanding does not help the teachers confront this challenge, as the connection between the concepts is rarely adequately explained in the available literature." Furthermore, Duquette continues, researchers have not offered teachers "models or categories on which they might base their assessments," thus forcing practitioners to construct these while teaching.

In speaking to and about the supporters of disciplinary teaching, these chapters provide needed transparency, critical analysis, and a few empirically grounded examples to help teachers identify clear goals for history instruction and to fuel the imaginations of assessors working at both large and small scales.

Such is not easy work. Far easier to stay on the "high hard ground" of "manageable problems," such as designing assessments to measure recognition of historical facts rather than to wade into the "swampy lowlands" where:

> problems are messy and confusing and incapable of technical solution. The irony of this situation is that the problems of the high ground tend to be relatively unimportant to individuals or society at large, however great their technical interest may be, while in the swamp lie the problems of greatest human concern. The practitioner is confronted with a choice. Shall he remain on the high ground where he can solve relatively unimportant problems according to his standards of rigor, or shall he descend to the swamp of important problems where he cannot be rigorous in any way he knows how to describe.
>
> (Schön, 1995, p. 27)

By "deliberately immersing themselves in confusing . . . ill formed, vague and messy" real world problems of history education, these chapters offer ways to get leverage on the conceptual, empirical, and pragmatic problems confronting current reformers, researchers, and practitioners interested in teaching and assessing historical thinking, consciousness, or understanding (Schön, 1995, p. 27).

Part of the problem is the conceptual stew that makes up the goals for history education. With so many nouns and verbs that the adjective "historical" has modified—thinking, consciousness, understanding, and for good measure, the authors in this section add in historical literacy and heritage—how can teachers, assessors, and other actors in history education productively and effectively select and use such ideas to inform practice? What are these varied aims for history education in the West? Do they connect to each other and, if so, how? Are they compatible, incompatible, mutually exclusive, interdependent, or nested within each other? How have researchers or policy makers operationalized each concept for teachers or assessors to enact in practice? How have educators used them to move forward their work with students?

Posing such questions seems to imply that individual concepts—consciousness, thinking, understanding, literacy, or heritage—have an internal coherence awaiting application, an assumption that these chapters, particularly those about historical consciousness in Germany and historical thinking in the United States, challenge.

"Historical consciousness," Kölbl and Konrad argue, "is one of the major concepts in history education in Germany, perhaps even its key concept." It is well-grounded in the theoretical literature, "inextricably linked" to the German assessment of historical thinking, and "an indispensable requirement for understanding German school curricula and models of assessment." Indeed, their reading of all sixteen German states finds the term present in most of them. Thus, there seems to be consensus in Germany around using the term in theory and curriculum. Yet, as Kölbl and Konrad excavate its meaning within the theoretical, curricular, and assessment literatures, they show the great difficulty in translating even elegant theory into usable curricular and assessment practice.

First, it is important to acknowledge the service they provide by constructing a usable categorization scheme—functional, structural, developmental, and intersectional—to frame ways German scholars have conceived of historical consciousness, its components, and interconnections. This reading of the scholarship encourages us to develop a multidimensional and interconnected picture of the various purposes and components of this complex concept. They beautifully move across complicated work by Rüsen, Pandel, Lücke, and others to construct a clear mental model, falling just short of providing an actual diagram to capture the connections between and among the various approaches.

However, as they moved from their discussion of theory into the swampy lowland of curricular design and assessable models, the rich intertextual dialog became a simple identification and listing of places in the German curriculum, standards, or assessment models where certain elements of historical consciousness might be found. Absent the clarity offered in the first section of the chapter, we see a concept-in-pieces listed in seemingly disparate places. Now I am not offering this as a criticism of Kölbl and Konrad, but rather as an observation of the fragmented way curriculum designers and policy makers likely grafted parts of one or the other theory onto existing structures. Ideas offered by Rüsen or Pandel end up being implicit or partly present, often appearing as vague idealistic goals, while Lücke's consciousness of categories or consciousness of diversity are barely seen. Yet, as Kölbl and Konrad describe the situation, the standards or curricula seem to provide far more specificity in declaring the factual knowledge and skills the students should acquire.

Of course, I am making leaps based merely on Kölbl and Konrad's brief sighting of historical consciousness in the instructional landscape, but in other contexts we have seen how policy makers and teachers cobble conceptual fragments onto existing curricular and institutional structures (see, for example, Cohen, 1990; Cuban, 1984). A genetic narrative, as Rüsen might call for, would help us understand how this situation developed, and I would wager such a story would involve key policy makers—absent the conceptual clarity provided in this chapter—appropriating features of various theoretical constructs to offer academic legitimacy and to move their work forward (Kliebard, 2004). These attempts to translate historical consciousness into practice, Kölbl and Konrad argue, fail to provide a full appreciation of or sensitivity to "the ambiguities, ambivalences, and contradictions inherent in concrete forms of historical consciousness." This is all the more worrisome if, as is too often true in the United States, teachers and assessors learn about concepts, such as historical consciousness, through curricular documents and assessment models.

The failure to translate conceptual complexity into practice also shapes Reisman's analysis of U.S. attempts to assess historical reading. Reading historical texts, particularly snippets of primary sources, has become a proxy for historical thinking in the United States. "Historical thinking," Reisman argues, "depends on the ability to reason about written text."[1] Indeed, assessing historical reading has become the key indicator of ambitious history teaching in the United States, though Reisman notes how rarely any state actually assesses such thinking.

Rather than criticizing the national failure to do so, Reisman analyzes extant attempts to assess historical reading. Here again we see a translation problem in moving from a scholarly concept to instructional and assessment practice. In her mini-case studies of two assessment instruments, including Advanced Placement's Document Based-Question (DBQ) that Americans typically view as the gold standard of history assessment, Reisman argues that the assessments ignore how students use background knowledge to comprehend the texts. Such failure negates the disciplinary-specificity of the exams, which thus fail to measure historical thinking.

For at least fifty years, scholars of historical thinking have recognized that to be able to read a text historically demands the reader situate the text in its time and place as well as understanding authorial purpose and audience. To learn from a historical text the reader must *already* possess some understanding of the situation about which the text refers as well as the context that produced the text itself (Bain, 2006). Collingwood captured this learning paradox beautifully in *The Idea of History*.

> The whole perceptible world, then, is potentially and in principle evidence to the historian. It becomes actual evidence in so far as he can use it. And

he cannot use it unless he comes to it with the right kind of historical knowledge. The more historical knowledge we have, the more we can learn from any given piece of evidence; if we had none, we could learn nothing. Evidence is evidence only when someone contemplates it historically. Otherwise, it is merely perceived fact, historically dumb. It follows that historical knowledge can only grow out of historical knowledge.

(Collingwood, 1946, p. 247)

The assessment challenge resides, Reisman explains, in this "entwined nature of historical knowledge and historical reading" and not in some confusion about the concept of historical thinking itself. It is a translation issue, as fidelity to the concept demands an instrument that can not only determine how much and what kind of content knowledge students bring to the assessment task but also capture how they use that knowledge in reasoning about the texts. Failure to do so, Reisman demonstrates, makes these document-based assessments little more than reading comprehension exams, and not tools to assess historical disciplinary literacy.

Grappling with so fluid a concept as historical background knowledge to assess how someone reasons with texts is messy work indeed. It requires, as Reisman argues, "disentangling the measurement of disciplinary historical reading—the ability to evaluate the reliability of sources in order to construct an intertextual account of the past—from students' incoming background knowledge, on the one hand, and general reading comprehension, on the other." It is far simpler to reduce such reading to the use of a set of generic reading strategies or analytical heuristics, the path, as Reisman demonstrates, taken even by respected assessment teams in the United States. While I am less convinced than Reisman that scholars of historical thinking, such as Wineburg, are guilty of such a domain-neutral simplification, I agree with her that reducing historical thinking to a set of reading strategies is evident across a wide-swath of literacy scholarship, curriculum, and "disciplinary" assessments. Thus, Reisman's analysis offers a strong standard to evaluate assessments of historical thinking by highlighting the role content knowledge plays in historical reasoning and demonstrating how difficult it has been for large-scale assessments to meet that standard.

Developing conceptual clarity while alerting us to the dangers, failures, or shortcomings in existing curricular models or assessments is critical and vital work. However, it still leaves the design and enactment of complicated instruction and assessment to practitioners. Such might be as it should be. Reisman tellingly ends her chapter encouraging teachers to take heart since they are best situated to know what historical knowledge their students can and do bring to the work of historical thinking.

The chapter by van Boxtel, Grever, and Klein, and the chapter by Duquette pursue slightly different paths. While also mindful of the importance of conceptual clarity and the problems entailed in translating ideas to practice, both chapters take up the challenge of constructing tasks that required students to engage in historical thinking while making that thinking visible to others. These chapters tackled the design problem by blurring the distinction between learning and assessment. That is, the authors placed students in a problem-saturated learning situation, one that required students to engage in historical reasoning which in turn enabled the researchers to see that reasoning in action. Rather than using the product of students' thinking, such as AP does in evaluating only the students' final DBQ essay, the authors of these two chapters designed the tasks to surface students' thinking along the way. Thus, they made the messiness of thought-in-action a virtue. Further, the tasks did not isolate historical thinking, historical consciousness, or some component of thinking, but were broad enough for researchers to see larger patterns and connections.

The challenge in the Netherlands that van Boxtel, Grever, and Klein discuss is doubly interesting because it involves using heritage within a disciplinary instructional frame. They point out that typically scholars view heritage as "essentialist narratives focused on self-confirmation, patrimonial pride, and a lack of historical distance," which does not make it an "attractive 'partner' for history education that aims at historical thinking and reasoning abilities." While they describe their work as border crossing, I saw them rather as erasing the boundary by making heritage an object of historical inquiry.

The activities they describe concerning Fort Elmina, slavery monuments, and old African statues all required students to think about how people, situated in their own particular time and space, approached particular situations from the past. This historically grounded problem space featured way stations that surfaced students' thinking at key points. While not framed as an assessment, the authors offer productive suggestions for how this learning activity could become an assessment of students' thinking about "significance nowadays," suggestions waiting for others to try.

However, van Boxtel, Grever, and Klein also point out how critical teachers' background knowledge is for using such tasks in the classroom, something that is worth underscoring. Engaging students in empathetic historical inquiry around heritage issues requires far more and different background knowledge on the part of teachers than is needed to reason effectively with historical texts. Of course, teachers need deep knowledge about the historical situation and the historical actors their students will investigate. They must be skillful in reading these historical contexts as well as the historical texts. However, they must also be skillful in reading the instructional contexts and knowledgeable about the background knowledge and perspectives their students bring with them to the task. Such content-knowledge-for-teaching is always important but never more so then when using historical thinking to analyze heritage issues. Ignoring the necessity of such knowledge can have far worse consequences than negating the disciplinarity of a reading assessment.

Caveats aside, van Boxtel, Grever, and Klein's chapter encourages a re-imagining of historical assessments to capture the processes of thinking rather than thinking's products. Duquette's chapter takes the next steps as she constructed a multistage assessment that she administered to 148 fifth-year Canadian students and then analyzed the results. While the results of her study are quite interesting, particularly her claims about a parallel progression for historical consciousness and thinking, I thought her multistep assessment model offered a very valuable way to structure classroom assessments and possibly even large-scale assessment. So, before discussing and tempering some the implications of her results, let me wax enthusiastic about her method.

To answer her research question about the relationship between historical thinking and historical consciousness, Duquette built a four-step assessment program that (1) identified students' initial historical stance toward a problem, (2) generated a bit of cognitive dissonance to destabilize the stance, (3) provided an opportunity to engage in historical analysis to help mediate the dissonance, and (4) presented the initial problem again to identify any change in students' stance toward the problem. While more complicated than a one-time sit-down, paper and pencil exam, the four steps enable the assessor—be it a teacher, external evaluator, or researcher—to identify students' pre-assessment content knowledge as well as making visible the "doing" of historical inquiry before analyzing the impact such inquiry has on initial views. Duquette's procedure captures students' thinking-in-action, an assessment method that enables us to understand what students bring to a study, what they do with historical texts, and what difference their historical capacity makes.

Such a dynamic model helps mitigate the challenges that Reisman describes by finding a way to disentangle students' incoming background knowledge from what follows as well as demonstrating how we might ascertain the impact of historical inquiry on students' consciousness of events. Duquette's assessment in four parts provides a proof of concept that a learning task can become an assessment task—and the reverse. Such an assessment model is worthy of further trials or connections to previous trials both at the classroom level and among far larger populations.

I was also taken with the results of her study, though not yet ready to endorse them, as Duquette seems to do, as a solution to the problems practitioners face in assessing historical thinking. In addition to her clear, near operational statements of historical thinking and historical consciousness, Duquette also reports on both a scheme to describe the growth of historical consciousness, and then on a coordinated growth pattern for historical consciousness *and* historical thinking. For the former, she developed a four-tiered growth model for historical consciousness, different from Rüsen's (2004), to describe how the Canadian high school students she studied progressed. For the latter, she constructed a model that matched the requisite growth in historical thinking students could do at each of four levels in historical consciousness. In short, she argues that growth in thinking and consciousness moved in parallel since the more developed historical thinking an individual could employ the higher was their level of historical consciousness.

There is much to digest here, with its clear definitions of complicated concepts and two concise growth charts that describe progression in consciousness and a linked, parallel graphic of growth in historical thinking and historical consciousness. Given the limits of chapter length, I suspect by necessity Duquette also left out much, such as samples of students' work to illuminate the emergent categories or correlational data to help us see strength of the relationships between the development of historical consciousness and thinking. We need such information to understand more fully her study before we could build on it or use it in a classroom. As a researcher Duquette acknowledges as much, saying her study needs replication to "test and confirm our findings." I would also add we need more research to possibly "disconfirm" the findings or, at least, to understand the context variables of a study conducted with one age cohort of students in one Canadian province.

I mention this only because toward the end of the chapter, Duquette casts off the researcher's caution for a bit of overgeneralization concerning the study's implications. She claims, given her findings and her charts, "teachers do not need to evaluate every single element of historical thinking individually but can instead assess their students' general level of historical consciousness" and then use it to "infer which elements of historical thinking still need to be developed." Thus the process of assessment is simplified since her "model of the development of historical consciousness can act as an effective indicator to monitor the development of historical thinking." While I am enthusiastic about this work, the data presented here does not warrant such a recommendation to teachers, particularly given the study's limited context or other studies that suggest that growth of second-order ideas are "decoupled." Lee and Ashby (2000) reporting on the CHATA study noted that ideas of younger children (7–15 years old) "do not necessarily develop in parallel." In some cases, they often found "changes in skills (e.g., cross referencing a pair of sources) with no accompanying conceptual development" (Lee & Ashby, 2000, pg. 214). Simply, we know far too little about the frames presented in the Duquette chapter to understand under what conditions and instructional contexts one can effectively infer the details of historical thinking from the rubric offered to assess historical consciousness.

Still, my response to a few sentences of implications must not detract from my enthusiasm for the ideas Duquette presents or her desire to help teachers navigate in the swampy lowlands of important problems. Rather, it is because the lowlands are so messy and the problems so important, we must be mindful and cautious in the claims of progress we make as well as the challenges remaining.

In taking on some of the real challenges entailed in assessing historical cognition, these four chapters sharpen our understanding of the theoretical and practical issues we confront while offering a plausible set of categories, procedures, and cautions to help in that endeavor. They should be of considerable value to teachers, other practitioners, and researchers.

Note

1 While I agree with the importance of reasoning with texts, I fear such statements too often encourage and support educators in the United States, particularly those outside the discipline of history, to reduce historical thinking to *only* the thinking that occurs in the presence of historical texts, and *only* primary texts at that. This is not a critique of Reisman, whose work here and elsewhere shows how complicated and nuanced a process is at play, but a caution. Scholars, particularly those in this volume, have demonstrated that embedded within an activity such as historical reasoning with texts are competent practices such as problem framing, empathy, temporal and spatial orientation, significance, and use of situated background knowledge. Thus, those with a disciplinary orientation bring domain-specific nuance, depth, and complexity to phrases such as "historical reasoning with texts." My worry, however, concerns the tendency for those without such disciplinary understanding to see historical reading simply as general comprehension strategies. Challenging this tendency is exactly what Reisman's chapter tackles.

References

Bain, R. B. (2006). Rounding up unusual suspects: Facing the authority hidden in history textbooks and teachers. *Teachers College Record, 108,* 2080–2110.

Cohen, D. K. (1990). A revolution in one classroom: The case of Mrs. Oublier. *Educational Evaluation and Policy Analysis, 12*(3), 311–329.

Collingwood, R. G. (1946). The historical imagination. In *The idea of history* (pp. 232–249). Oxford, UK: Oxford University Press.

Cuban, L. (1984). *How teachers taught: Constancy and change in American classrooms, 1890–1980.* New York, NY: Longman Press.

Kliebard, H. M. (2004). *The struggle for the American curriculum, 1893–1958.* New York, NY: Routledge Falmer.

Lee, P. J., & Ashby, R. (2000). Progression in historical understanding among students 7–14. In P. Stearns, P. Seixas, & S. Wineburg (Eds.), *Knowing, teaching, and learning history: National and international perspectives* (pp. 199–222). New York, NY: New York University Press.

Rüsen, J. (2004) Historical consciousness: Narrative structure, moral function, and ontogenetic development. In P. Seixas (Ed.), *Theorizing historical consciousness* (pp. 63–85). Toronto, ON: University of Toronto Press.

Schön, D. A. (1995). Knowing-in-action: The new scholarship requires a new epistemology. *Change, 27*(6), 26–34.

PART II

Issues in Designing Assessments of Historical Thinking

5

ASSESSING FOR LEARNING IN THE HISTORY CLASSROOM

Bruce VanSledright

Picture this image. A group of students sitting hunched over at their classroom desks, eyes squinted, brows furrowed, #2 pencils clutched tightly between their fingers. They are reading a test booklet. Next to them lies a sheet of paper with numbered columns. Arranged horizontally adjacent to each number are four tiny ovals with the letters A, B, C, and D etched inside their perimeters. Students read a test item, select one from among the options, and color in an oval of choice. This testing practice can last for some time. If the test has high-stakes consequences, the results could mean the difference between graduating from high school or not.

Come spring and at frequent intervals across the school year in similar exercises teachers mandate as preparation, thousands of history students in the United States undertake this ostensible rite of passage. So, what, we might ask, do such history tests attempt to measure? To get some leverage on that question, we can examine items released by states. Figure 5.1 offers an example.

This item is generally representative of the types of items on such released tests. They are what many call content-based items in that they attempt to sample

---

Political and economic ties to which country led to United States involvement in World War I?

  A France

  B Germany

  C Great Britain

  D Austria-Hungary

FIGURE 5.1 An item released from the 2012 Virginia SOL U.S. History Test

students' recall of ostensibly important details and occurrences in U.S. history—knowledge of what happened, where, when, and who was involved. In this case, it concerns political and economic alliances that shaped the combatants in World War I. The item appears to test whether students know that a pivotal U.S. ally in that war was Great Britain.

Occasionally, items utilize photographs, quotes, or charts as initial stimuli followed by a question that asks students to select the correct one from among four options. Despite this somewhat different approach, the items typically test students' recall of particular details and events in history. There are clusters of items that relate to military events, presidents, other national leaders, and cultural developments such as changes in technology and entertainment. Approximately 140 years of the nation's past are boiled down into a handful or two of items—few of which attempt to sample *directly* whether students can do the historical thinking necessary to understand that nation's past.

The Limits of Current Testing Practices

The last clause in the preceding paragraph is important. Research undertaken over the last several decades on the ways students learn history has shown repeatedly that to understand the past requires learning how to think historically (e.g., Barton, 2008; Lee, 2005; Lévesque, 2008; VanSledright & Limon, 2006; Voss, 1998; and Wineburg, 1996). Historical cognition becomes a requirement for historical understanding. Conversely, if students do not learn how to think historically, understanding the past grinds to a halt (Lee, 2005).

Historical cognition of the sort that enables understanding necessitates far more than memorizing details of what occurred in the past and being able to recall who did what when and where. The details and people are important in that they provide substance for thinking and content for claims of understanding. However, if we take seriously the aim of cultivating deeper understandings of that past, then we must educate the mental acts that enable them. Learning to think this way is often counterintuitive and therefore requires considerable effort, for example the fine art of suspending—to the extent possible—our present-day sociocultural assumptions to make sense, say, of Abraham Lincoln, Abigail Adams, or Marcus Aurelius who lived in times not of our making or circumstance (see Lee, 2005; Seixas, 1996; Shemilt, 1984; Wineburg, 2001).

The point here is that our current testing practices in history, at least in many locales in the United States, yield data of largely dubious value if the goal is to make claims about students' historical thinking efforts and the understandings that follow from them. Tests of these sorts, despite their high-stakes consequences, tell us little about how students think through and come to understand the past, and, more importantly, what they can then do with that thinking and knowing process. The data from these tests reveal even less about how history teachers, or students themselves, might approach addressing problems in historical thinking and understanding in order to improve on them. If we can agree on these claims and if we are committed to improving the thinking that deepens understanding, then it follows that a reconceptualization about how we assess for learning in history—and by extension, teaching—is in order. That reconceptualization is the focus of this chapter.

Rethinking Assessment in History

To get some purchase on what assessment—in contrast to testing—in history might look like, it would help to work from research on assessment design. If a key goal involves shifting towards using assessments to identify historical thinking practices and learning difficulties in order to enable teachers and students to systematically address them, then assessment designs need to cohere with that principal goal. One of the better sources for attending to it is entitled *Knowing What Students Know: The Science and Design of Educational Assessment* (Pellegrino, Chudowsky, & Glaser, 2001).

The author team writes, "Needed are classroom and large-scale assessments that help all students learn and succeed in school by making as clear as possible to them, their teachers, and other education stakeholders the nature of their accomplishments and the progress of their learning" (Pellegrino et al., 2001, p. 1). In designing such assessments, the team notes, "Every assessment, regardless of purpose, rests on three pillars. . .": cognition, observation, and interpretation. Attention to cognition comes first because it provides the framework on which the other two pillars depend. The assessment scholars refer to cognition as the "cornerstone of the assessment design process" (p. 3). They observe that a cognitive model should draw from the best research evidence currently available that demonstrates how students learn and develop competence in a subject domain.

My efforts in this chapter involve elucidating classroom-based assessment designs and examples in history education that hinge off these three pillars. My approach is classroom and teacher-learner focused (see Black & Wiliam, 1998). The heart of my reasoning for subscribing to this arguably narrow classroom focus is that I believe that it is history teachers and learners who have the most to gain by reconceptualizing assessment practices (e.g., Nuthall & Alton-Lee, 1995).

Cognition in History Education

The cognitive processes involved in yielding deep understandings in history are complex and multifaceted. I lack the space to trace them out in extensive detail. Their characteristics and elements have been explored and unpacked several times in the work of Peter Lee (2005), Stéphane Lévesque (2008), Peter Seixas (1996), and Sam Wineburg (2001). I also have attempted to make them accessible (VanSledright, 2011, 2014). I draw from this work as I develop illustrations around a staple of historical study referred to as source work, the act of assessing the status of historical accounts in order to draw evidence from them to make claims of understanding.

Accounts and evidence are historical concepts that have procedural dimensions. Putting them into practice involves strategic mental operations, as in *assessing* an account's status to determine if it *provides* evidence on the basis of which we can *make* claims to understanding. Figure 5.2 depicts these relationships and how they flow together. In short, those relationships represent a cognitive model that serves as the basis for the task and interpretive aspects of the assessment designs that follow.

Assessment tasks need to possess ecological validity. That is, a task must be linked to what students have had an opportunity to learn in the history classroom. Therefore, as an example, I focus on Lt. Colonel George Custer's attack on Lakota Sioux and Cheyenne warriors encamped on the Little Bighorn

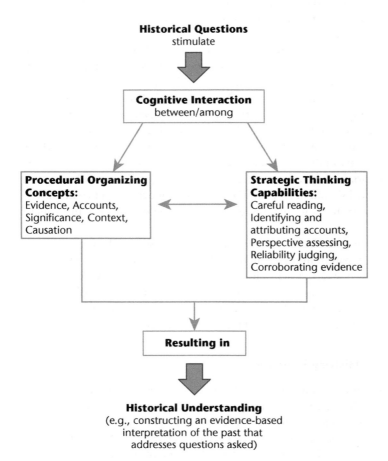

FIGURE 5.2 A model of cognition in history

River in Montana in 1876. This is a commonly taught U.S. history topic on which to establish the workings of the three assessment pillars. The topic allows me to design tasks, describe the forms of cognition that we might look for, and set targets for interpreting the evidence the tasks generate. Pellegrino et al. (2001) proceed along a similar tack by offering readers a number of ecologically valid examples drawn especially from mathematics and science domains. My approach here will be examples-to-design-principles rather than principles-to-examples.

Custer was significantly undermanned and later appeared outmaneuvered by the Lakota and Cheyenne, who in a pitched battle destroyed his attacking cavalry, killed all his troops, and killed Custer himself. This battle of the Little Bighorn came to symbolize a great victory for the Plains Indians and a source of disgrace for Custer and a few surviving commanders who ordered retreat to save their soldiers. The battle and its outcome are well known, but what tends to mystify historians and investigators is what actually happened on June 25, 1876. What accounted for Custer's choice to attack in the face of overwhelming odds and almost certain defeat? Did he think surprise and a flanking maneuver he ordered his two commanders, Frederick Benteen and Marcus Reno, to undertake would give him a battle edge? Or was Custer simply overly ambitious and arrogant, filled with a desire for retribution, or all of the above? Can this incident be understood as another episode in the limits of pursuing Manifest Destiny over peaceful co-existence? What of the Lakota and Cheyenne perspectives?

For students to address these knotty historical questions (top of the cognitive model in Fig. 5.2), they would need to begin by making sense of what happened that day in June and, if possible, what precipitated it. Some historical context would need to be set. Students' minds would need to be transported to the late nineteenth century, to U.S. government-Indian relations, to life on the Plains, to a grasp of a bloody, running confrontation between two different cultures. This way would involve an exploration of accounts (a procedural concept in the upper left box in Fig. 5.2) from the past, especially eyewitness testimony to the extent that that testimony was available (strategic thought in the right box in Fig. 5.2).

A key problem here hinges on the fact that Custer and all his troops died on the battlefield. Surviving commanders Benteen and Reno's view of Custer's skirmish with the Lakota and Cheyenne was obscured by the rolling landscape around Little Bighorn. Benteen and Reno were later interviewed, as were their soldiers. Surviving Indians, who subsequently were captured by the U.S. Army, were also interviewed. However, the accounts are all after the fact, and memory becomes progressively less reliable. The evidence derivable from these accounts could be tendentious, laced as it might certainly be with different and quite possibly conflicting perspectives and protective embellishments in the case of the Indians (requiring careful perspective assessments—right box in Fig. 5.2). There also was a *post hoc* investigation; an effort was made to map the battlefield but it yielded only sketchy evidence.

Given this scenario, we can see that, at a minimum, students would need to engage the accounts available in order to *address the questions* being posed (e.g., what happened here, why, and what was its historical significance?). They would need to *read carefully, identifying* each different account, *attributing* it to an author, and attempting to make sense of who that author was and what her/his *perspective* entailed. Then they would need to *derive evidence* from those accounts as they built a deeper *understanding* of the battle at Little Bighorn. Finally, a process for putting that *understanding on display* with an appropriate evidentiary grounding would need to occur.

In the foregoing, I italicized key concepts and cognitive procedures in play that enable subsequent historical understanding (Fig. 5.2). As I have noted, the assessment tasks would need to address these concepts/procedures and resulting understandings because the former are the *sine qua non* of the latter. Testing only topic understanding (bottom of Fig. 5.2) provides teachers limited diagnostic power, particularly if students' claimed understandings are misguided, naïve, or misconstrued. Breakdowns and impasses in thinking can lead to weak understanding. Identifying cognitive difficulties through assessment becomes crucial if progress is to be made moving students forward.

Observations: Tasks and/or Situations

There are a number of different ways to design tasks that measure historical cognition and an equally broad array of possibilities for getting at resulting understandings of the battle at Little Bighorn (see Donovan & Bransford, 2005; VanSledright, 2014; http://beyondthebubble.stanford.edu; and www.historicalthinking.ca). There is room here to explore only one in detail: weighted multiple-choice items (WMCs).

WMC items can be employed to sample historical thinking as well as topic understanding. Because history is an ill-structured domain in which definitive conclusions are often difficult to obtain and approaches to thinking through the problem and discerning adequate evidence to make claims can allow for various defensible interpretations, a tiered weighting structure for item choices does some justice to the nature of that domain problem. As I will show, they permit more than one possible interpretive solution, but not all are equally defensible. Attempting to gauge students' awareness of this problem and how it operates in history can assist teachers in making the pedagogical adjustments necessary to grow possibilities for understanding.

As one WMC example, consider the sample item in Figure 5.3. What type of thinking and/or understanding does this item sample?

The prompt attends principally to the domain problem I outlined: definitive answers to historical questions (what happened to Custer and his men?) are frequently difficult, if not impossible, to divine with certainty. However, this

Even though we know they all died, it is difficult to figure out exactly how that happened to Custer and his troops at the battle of Little Bighorn because

a. The surviving Indians did not speak English well enough to provide testimony. (0)

b. Colonel Custer and his troops were killed preventing them from recounting the battle. (1)

c. Benteen and Reno heard the battle but could not see it due to the rolling landscape. (2)

d. Reconstructing the battlefield was hampered by the disappearance of evidence. (4)

*weightings in parentheses

FIGURE 5.3 A sample weighted multiple-choice item

problem should not prevent us from using whatever accounts and evidence we can locate to generate conjectures or theories (Kloppenberg, 1989). The response options point toward the idea of relying on accounts and evidence to make this sort of sense. Some theories—given what we know from the accounts and evidence—turn out to be better than others. Evidence can preponderate. Item options pivot off this idea.

The response weights are chosen to represent a theoretical position that defines most-to-least defensible responses to the prompt. The weights need to make sense given the theoretical rationale developed to defend them. In this case, the rationale (all WMC items need a weighting rationale) arises from a first design presupposition that, unlike typical multiple-choice items, we need only one fundamentally erroneous response choice (indefensible). The three other options would be weighted from acceptable, but least defensible given the evidence available, to most defensible. However, because history contains many problems of understanding that are difficult to resolve definitively, all weighting rationales can be debated, as are the ones in the preceding item. Weighting rationales allow teachers, for example, who might use such WMCs, to be intellectually honest about this problem with their students, while also providing some leverage on construct validity (e.g., the types of cognition it takes to discern more from less defensible interpretive choices) and ease of scoring. The rationale for the weights is a form of task-evidence interpretation. I discuss that process below.

This WMC item also samples the cognitive constructs of accounts and evidence and their relationship to fashioning a historical interpretation. Yet, it does so somewhat indirectly. We could construct a WMC item that more directly sampled those two constructs. Accounts and evidence are crucial concepts (constructs) in history. The past makes itself accessible to us in the present via residue in the form of accounts. From them we can glean evidence for constructing interpretations that attempt to explain the past. Learners, therefore, need to have a working understanding of how accounts can (and cannot) be used to draw evidence. The concepts of author perspective and an account's reliability also come

---

An artist's rendering or image of a historical occurrence should be treated as
  a. meaningless for use as evidence. (0)
  b. less reliable than eyewitness testimony. (1)
  c. representative of the artist's viewpoint. (2)
  d. possible corroborating evidence. (4)

All accounts must be read critically because
  a. they may distract historians from presenting the past objectively. (0)
  b. documents can be altered to change how past events are viewed. (1)
  c. events have often been told from the viewpoint of the victors. (2)
  d. they are written from the perspective of a person from the past. (4)

*weightings in parentheses

FIGURE 5.4 Sample WMC items that measure accounts and evidence

into play (Fig. 5.2). With regard to account reliability, the concept of evidence preponderance enters in. See Figure 5.4 for two examples.

Following principles described with regard to the former WMC, both tasks are designed to measure students' understandings of procedural concepts and their strategic applications referenced in the cognitive model. The first WMC explores the idea of what to do with a historical *account* from which *evidence* might be derived. The second attempts to elicit a respondent's sense of why all *accounts* require *careful readings* before *evidence* can be extracted from them. In this way, the task design is driven by the cognitive model (ecological validity is assumed). The tasks attempt to measure conceptual understandings of cognition and the mental efforts that are required to make sense of the past (Lee, 2005; Lee & Shemilt, 2003; Seixas, 1996; VanSledright, 2011).

One method to test whether such items actually measure these types of cognition could be a verbal report protocol in which a small group of students respond to a think-aloud prompt as they read and make sense of the items (see Ercikan et al., 2010; Ericsson & Simon, 1984).[1]

Another test might occur in the classroom itself after the assessment tasks were scored and the assessment was returned. Students could be invited to scrutinize the items, their weighting rationales, and ecological validity. Taken item by item, teachers could query how students understood the prompt, the options, and weighting structures applied. Arguments could be entertained about changes, for example, to weights, shedding light on how items worked and whether the cognitive operations of the items tapped into constructs intended. Students could thereby help modify items to obtain greater validity. Such a process might well cultivate increased self-assessment capabilities.

There are other means by which to sample historical constructs beyond a reliance on WMC items. The document-based question (DBQ) is a good candidate. In such questions, students are invited to put on display what they can do with what they know by reading a series of accounts and drawing evidence from them in order to construct a historical interpretation framed by an initial question prompt that sets parameters and context for the response. Interpretive rubrics can be designed that align with the constructs crucial to thinking and understanding in history (e.g., identifying and attributing the account, extracting evidence, using evidence defensibly, making evidence-based conjectures).

A variation on DBQ design is the single-account-interpretation essay (SAIE) (VanSledright, 2014). In this variation, students can be asked to carefully read an account (e.g., an excerpt from Custer's journal) and then write an essay explaining, for example, (a) how she went about assessing its status as a source (identification, attribution, perspective evaluation); (b) drew evidence from it to generate conjectures about a particular question under study (e.g., was Custer overly ambitious, or was he convinced that his surprise attack would allow him to win the battle?); and (c) speculate on the reliability of the account in making evidence-based claims. A response to such an item could be composed by a student in less time than a DBQ. It could alternatively sample how respondents understood a staple of the cognitive landscape in history, articulated within the learning model sketched earlier—assessing source status (Fig. 5.2).

Interpretations—Scoring Rubrics

To consider ways in which to interpret the data generated by the tasks I have described, I return to the WMC examples to explore their weighting rationales. Rationales for weighting provide a form of rubric in that they provide criteria for scoring. As I noted, making them transparent in the classroom allows students an opportunity to debate them once the assessments are returned. If students understand the idea of weighting structures, the items teach them to think carefully about all the options and therefore think about how they are thinking. These metacognitive acts allow them to become better at those types of tasks as well as better self-assessors.

The four options in the first WMC item hold the following weights:

(a) The surviving Indians did not speak English well enough to provide testimony (0),
(b) Colonel Custer and his troops were killed preventing them from recounting the battle (1),
(c) Benteen and Reno heard the battle but could not see it due to the rolling landscape (2), and
(d) Reconstructing the battlefield was hampered by the disappearance of evidence (4).

Option (a) is weighted as the incorrect choice. The principles for weighting structures emerge from the following argument. While it is the case that many of the Indians who were interviewed about the battle after the fact spoke little English and used sign language and/or required translators, they did indeed provide testimony, albeit of questionable reliability for rather obvious reasons.

On the assumption of ecological validity, students who studied the battle and read accounts of the post-battle investigation would be expected to understand this point.

Option (b) is a weak choice but reasonable on its face. It is weighted at (1) in part because options (c) and (d) are better choices given the prompt. Option (b) plays off a common, everyday idea students sometimes hold that if no witnesses remain to provide firsthand testimony, we cannot know what happened and therefore understanding history stops (e.g., Lee, 2005; Lee & Shemilt, 2003; VanSledright & Kelly, 1998). As such, it functions here to check on whether students still harbor this idea even though they had opportunities to learn about the details of the post-battle investigation via other accounts.

Option (c) is also reasonable given the evidence. Benteen and Reno were at the battlefield at the time, did provide eyewitness testimony when interviewed, but claimed their vision was obscured by hills that blocked their view of what happened to Custer and his 215 troops. Therefore, it functions as a good choice relative to the prompt. However, option (d) is the best choice given that prompt. To convey that point, it receives 4 points in an effort to impress on students that it is the most defensible option given the evidence at hand. In the attempt to reconstruct the battlefield, U.S. military investigators struggled to recreate events even though the Indians had left the scene. Investigators had to study crumpled grass patterns, holes in the earth left by lodge poles, and the layout of bodies. However, these clues yielded only partial answers and surviving Indians were not available to be interviewed until later. As a result, understanding what happened that fateful afternoon is largely incomplete, fueling much continued conjecture about the circumstances of Custer's defeat, his tactics, and his motives.

In many ways, this is the point of an item such as this: Doing history often yields as much mystery as it solves because evidence of whatever kind does not always answer our questions the way we wish. Student investigators must read and analyze carefully. The cognitive model (Fig. 5.2) guiding the task and its rationale structure are rooted in an effort to teach and then assess this pivotal idea in history. Historical investigators may not be able to definitively determine what happened in the past, but with careful, systematic sleuthing, they can come to some defensible conjectures and provisional hypotheses that later can be revised if more evidence is revealed. Put differently, objects from the past tell mixed stories, potentially frustrating knowers' efforts to make sense of them. However, knowers' cognitive capabilities can be cultivated in ways that allow them to produce conditional understandings.

An additional diagnostic benefit of WMCs and how they are scored arises when similar items are employed over time in order to assess the development of ideas in history. If weighting rationales consistently follow the principles I illustrate here, teachers would be able to track potential change and growth, for example, in students' capabilities to move away from the unproductive idea that we cannot know the past if there were no eyewitnesses (option b) and toward the understanding that defensible evidence-based conjectures and interpretations are possible with careful investigative scrutiny (option d).

Likewise, WMC items allow for assessing students' developing under-standings of important procedural concepts of the type noted in the second and third examples, if such items are used several times over the course of a semester's historical study. Those moments present teachers with several data points that suggest change (or the lack thereof) over time with opportunities to learn between them. This allows for evidence-based pedagogical adjust-ments to those opportunities in order to enhance cognition and subsequent understanding.

With four-option WMCs in history, the idea is to generate one option that is categorically inappropriate *given the prompt*. The prompt demarcates the boundaries within which the options must operate. The 1-point mid-weight option may be defensible but is weakly so in the sense that it may tap into a commonly held belief students may hold that is not wrong, but does not assist in them in addressing the question. The 2-point option is more defensible given the evidence available, but it is less defensible than the 4-point option, again given the evidence explored in class. The criterion of defensible histori-cal interpretation/argumentation is crucial to these items as it is to the cogni-tive model (Fig. 5.2).

Checking Task and Rubric Validity

These types of classroom-based, formative assessment tasks must meet at mini-mum four key principles. First, they need to be derived as explicitly as pos-sible from the cognitive model. This in turn means that the model must be domain specific and clearly articulated both conceptually and with respect to how component pieces (constructs) flow and toward what end. Second, the question—does the task measure the constructs it was intended to measure—must be answered through a test such as verbal report protocols or a classroom discussion of the tasks themselves. Tasks/items that fail this test must be modified (e.g., changes to options and/or changes to weighting rationales or rubrics) or discarded. Third, interpretations of the evidence must be carefully aligned to the cognitive model and calibrated to the tasks themselves. And fourth, they must be ecologically valid in the sense that students need clear opportunities to learn what is being assessed.

The Importance of Classroom- and Learning-Based Assessment

If, as I argued at the outset, our current testing practices do little to assist teachers in improving student learning, then teachers will need to find their way toward new approaches. I have tried to sketch some of them here. It is an evidence-based approach (Mislevy, Steinberg, & Almond, 2002; Pellegrino et al., 2001) close to the ground where history teachers work with students to deepen historical understanding and the crucial forms of thinking upon which it depends. Some call this assessment approach formative (e.g., Black & Wiliam, 1998).

History teachers need tools like WMC items, or like those developed by Breakstone, Smith, and Wineburg (2013), Ercikan and Seixas (2011), Monte-Sano (2012), and the Schools Council History Project (Shemilt, 1980). These types of assessments create opportunities for teachers to identify where students are on a trajectory from thinking as novices to becoming more cognitively competent in history. Most large-scale accountability tests used in program evaluation do not.

In a careful study of a four-decade effort to drive changes in schools and among teachers via various authorizations of the Elementary and Secondary Education Act and their embedded reform policies, David Cohen and Susan Moffitt (2009) come to the conclusion that the policies, despite good intentions, largely missed their targets. They argue that no matter the high-stakes or the rigor or rigidity of accountability provisions (e.g., No Child Left Behind; NCLB), we will not be able to test our way to improved practice and learning. That work needs to occur in classrooms, in the interactions between students and their teachers. Teachers need knowledge and tools to facilitate that work.

Research-based models of learning and cognition that are domain specific, tasks that align to those models and generate valid evidence of learning, and sharp rubrics calibrated to those evidences and linked back to the model suggest a promising approach. At a minimum, they provide the people who need it the most—history teachers and their students in this case—with data and evidence that can be used by both to make more robust daily decisions that enhance historical thinking and understanding.

Note

1 We developed and utilized WMCs in our 10 years of Teaching American History grant evaluation work in Maryland. In an effort to validate the WMCs we constructed, such as my examples here, we initially subjected them to a form of peer-review and then pilot tested them among samples of prospective teachers. We followed with a common item-response analysis and discarded ones that did not discriminate adequately. However, we did not have the resources to validate via verbal reports, a more robust process.

References

Barton, K. C. (2008). Research on students' ideas about history. In L. Levstik & C. Tyson (Eds.), *Handbook of research in social studies education* (pp. 239–258). New York, NY: Routledge.

Black, P. J. & Wiliam, D. (1998). Assessment and classroom learning. *Assessment in Education: Principles Policy and Practice, 5*, 7–73.

Breakstone, J., Smith, M., & Wineburg, S. (2013). Beyond the bubble in history/social studies assessments. *Phi Delta Kappan, 94*, 53–57.

Cohen, D. C., & Moffitt, S. L. (2009). *The ordeal of equality: Did federal regulation fix the schools?* Cambridge, MA: Harvard University Press.

Donovan, S., & Bransford, J. (Eds.). (2005). *How students learn: History in the classroom.* Washington, DC: National Academy Press.

Ercikan, K., Arim, R., Law, D., Domene, J., Gagnon, F., & Lacroix, S. (2010). Application of think-aloud protocols for examining and confirming sources of differential item functioning identified by expert reviews. *Educational Measurement: Issues and Practice, 29,* 24–35.

Ercikan, K., & Seixas, P. (2011). Assessment of higher order thinking: The case of historical thinking. In G. Schraw & D. H. Robinson (Eds.), *Assessment of higher order thinking skills: Current perspectives on cognition, learning, and instruction* (pp. 245–261). Charlotte, NC: Information Age.

Ericsson, K., & Simon, H. (1984). *Protocol analysis: Verbal reports as data.* Cambridge, MA: MIT Press.

Kloppenberg, J. (1989). Objectivity and historicism: A century of American historical writing. *American Historical Review, 94,* 1011–1030.

Lee, P. J. (2005). Putting principles into practice: Understanding history. In S. Donovan & J. Bransford (Eds.), *How students learn: History in the classroom* (pp. 31–78). Washington, DC: National Academy Press.

Lee, P. J., & Shemilt, D. (2003). A scaffold, not a cage: Progression and progression models in history. *Teaching History, 113,* 13–23.

Lévesque, S. (2008). *Thinking historically: Educating students for the twenty-first century.* Toronto, ON: University of Toronto Press.

Mislevy, R., Steinberg, L., & Almond, R. (2002). On the structure of educational assessments. *Measurement: Interdisciplinary Research and Perspectives, 1,* 3–63.

Monte-Sano, C. (2012). What makes a good history essay? Assessing historical aspects of argumentative writing. *Social Education, 76,* 294–298.

Nuthall, G., & Alton-Lee, A. (1995). Assessing classroom learning: How students use their knowledge and experience to answer classroom achievement test questions in science and social studies. *American Educational Research Journal, 32,* 185–223.

Pellegrino, J. W., Chudowsky, N., & Glaser, R. (Eds.). (2001). *Knowing what students know: The science and design of educational assessment.* Washington, DC: National Academy Press.

Seixas, P. (1996). Conceptualizing the growth of historical understanding. In D. R. Olson & N. Torrence (Eds.), *The handbook of education and human development: New models of learning, teaching and schooling* (pp. 765–783). Cambridge, UK: Blackwell Publishing.

Shemilt, D. (1980). *History project 13–16: Evaluation study.* Edinburgh, UK: Holmes McDougall.

Shemilt, D. (1984). Beauty and the philosopher: Empathy in history and classroom. In A. Dickinson, P. Lee, & P. Rogers (Eds.), *Leaning history* (pp. 39–84). London, UK: Heinemann.

VanSledright, B. A. (2011). *The challenge of rethinking history education: On practices, theories and policy.* New York, NY: Routledge.

VanSledright, B. A. (2014). *Assessing historical thinking and understanding: Innovative designs for new standards.* New York, NY: Routledge.

VanSledright, B., & Kelly, C. (1998). Reading American history: The influence of using multiple sources on six fifth graders. *The Elementary School Journal, 98,* 239–265.

VanSledright B., & Limon, M. (2006). Learning and teaching in social studies: Cognitive research on history and geography. In P. Alexander & P. Winne (Eds.), *The handbook of educational psychology, 2nd ed.* (pp. 545–570). Mahweh, NJ: Lawrence Erlbaum Associates.

Voss, J. (1998). Issues in the learning of history. *Issues in Education: Contributions from Educational Psychology, 4,* 163–209.

Wineburg, S. (1996). The psychology of learning history. In D. C. Berliner & R. C. Calfee (Eds.), *Handbook of educational psychology* (pp. 423–437). New York, NY: Macmillan.

Wineburg, S. (2001). *Historical thinking and other unnatural acts: Charting the future of teaching the past.* Philadelphia, PA: Temple University Press.

6

HISTORICAL THINKING, COMPETENCIES, AND THEIR MEASUREMENT

Challenges and Approaches

Andreas Körber and Johannes Meyer-Hamme

Introduction

In Europe as well as in the United States and probably around the world, history teaching has been and still is a subject of conceptual debate and change. In Germany and elsewhere, it has also always been political. Across many different approaches, it aimed at providing students with specific interpretations of the past relevant for creating political attitudes and/or orientations—e.g. faith in the Emperor, identification with the people and/or the state, or (allegedly "apolitically") the unchanging human nature behind historical change. Only in the 1970s, after the debate about "emancipatory" history teaching aimed at fostering critical attitudes to the present state by reflecting alleged or actual suppressed perspectives and histories, were more formal definitions of history teaching developed, largely combined under the "central category" (Jeismann, 1980) of "historical consciousness". Methodological skills of historical investigation and judgment (beyond the analysis of given material) were introduced in the 1980s, but largely as optional additions. With the acknowledgment of increased diversity of cultural perspectives in German society since the 1990s, finally, the implicit assumption of the traditional German master narrative as the basis for history teaching, dissolved. Abilities of historical thinking and participation in the social discourse on history became more central.

In recent years, a great part of didactic development has focused on the latter, conceptualizing the innovative understanding of history learning as the development of students' own abilities to think historically, challenging the conventional notion of using history as the introduction of the next generation to an accepted national master narrative. In Germany, this development is mainly connected with the theoretical work of Danto (1968), Rüsen (1983), and others, influencing the concept of "historical consciousness" and the increased acknowledgment of different social, political, and cultural perspectives. Even though this concept is dominant today in the conceptual portions of state curriculum documents, history as it appears in classrooms and textbooks still maintains a strong place for the chronological narrative.

One consequence of this is that assessments of history learning carry the same double focus. Even though the German guidelines of the Federal Education Ministers' Standing Conference (KMK)[1] require upper-secondary exams to combine three different aspects of examination (reproducing, applying, and reflecting as well as problem solving),[2] the bulk of assessments taking place in schools still use conventional written or oral exams or by "handmade", non-standardized multiple-choice tests, referring to specific historical subjects.

As for concepts, techniques, and instruments for assessing students' achievements in this area, two distinctions are fundamental for understanding the testing of students' abilities in historical thinking, as presented in this chapter, each leading to the usage and application of different concepts and techniques:

- One differentiation refers to the *purpose* of assessments, distinguishing between measuring individual learners' achievements, mostly designed for the use of teachers on the one hand, and, on the other, large-scale assessments that offer not individual diagnostics, but rather information on average achievement and its distribution within groups. Qualitative approaches are in large part suitable for the former, quantitative for the latter purpose.
- The other differentiation distinguishes between teaching and learning history focused on a given narrative (usually a country's or society's development), which needs to be learned and "understood", on the one hand, and students' abilities for *thinking historically* in the sense of reflecting on historical problems and needs for orientation, arriving at "new" and possibly varying conclusions and judgments, on the other.

Empirical Research

Empirical research has played a minor role in the developments sketched so far. Starting in the 1930s and again in the 1960s, focusing on the interests of students and—based on a theory of maturation—discerning feasible and problematic subjects (Küppers, 1961; Roth, 1968), there has been some research into the development of historical consciousness (e.g. Noack, 1994) and its internal structures (e.g. von Borries, 1995; in intercultural comparison: Angvik & von Borries, 1997). As a large-scale project applied in countries with very different curricula and perspectives, the latter mainly used a format requiring the participants to assess statements on 5-point Likert scales, designed on the basis of a structural definition of historical consciousness.

These instruments were useful for empirically investigating culture-specific differences of the interpretation of the past, the perception of the present, and the anticipation/expectations of the future (Jeismann, 1977). They do not, however, focus on competencies of individual historical thinking, in the sense that has been developed since PISA 2000. Even where the older research already touched upon aspects of historical thinking, rather than merely assessing knowledge,[3] it needs to be integrated into a concept of testing based on a model of historical thinking—which in our case is given by the FUER model, some aspects of which, focusing on competencies, will be discussed below (Körber, forthcoming; see also Kölbl, this volume). However, the purpose of large-scale assessments (as opposed to individual diagnostics for teachers in their own classes) places additional requirements, which need to be addressed first.

- In federal states with diverse curricula (as in Germany), and under conditions where teachers have at least relative autonomy to organize their classes' learning processes, no guarantee can be given that any specific subjects have been covered. Thus, large-scale testing cannot include substantive/declarative knowledge about specific events, contexts, and/or interpretations of history. In this aspect, they need to be self-contained, meaning that they must offer all the specific context and information needed for fulfilling the tasks. This is no shortcoming in the light of competence theory since the transferability of acquired or developed abilities is fundamental.
- Furthermore, in the light of both practicability and test security, tests for large-scale assessments in their final form need to offer rather large stocks of instruments that are comparable as to their dimensionality and "difficulty". All these requirements place rather strong limits on the thematic context of the individual tasks presented. Tests of this kind, addressing different aspects of competencies in different tasks, cannot be constructed on the basis of one subject (e.g. "Ancient Rome" or "The Weimar Republic"), but must offer the possibility of combining tasks addressing different subjects.

Nonetheless, history cannot be addressed and historical competencies cannot be assessed (any more than taught) without legitimate reference to historical events or contexts. Abstract questions will not suffice, because competencies can only be tested via actual performances in the domain. So, tasks and items need a historical context—in the form of questions and of information and source material.

Large-scale tests using standardized items and focusing on factual as well as conceptual knowledge on a scope of subjects as are common in the U.S. (cf. VanSledright, 2014) were developed in the 1960s and 1970s (Ingenkamp, 1967), and more sophisticated forms of such tests, integrating items requiring more complex operations, have also been suggested (von Borries, 1973) but have never been widely used. In the course of the discussion around how to make the concept of "historical consciousness" comprehensible, methodological skills have been suggested as teaching aims alongside with theoretical insights and concepts. With regard to assessing students' mastery of the former, open strategies of evaluation using qualitative data have been developed, such as portfolios, learning diaries, working reports, posters, exhibitions, etc. (Adamski, 2003). They are suitable for assessing individual students' abilities in a given context and for differential feedback, but not for comparing groups. What is still lacking are instruments applicable for measuring historical thinking in large-scale assessments (e.g. for addressing the question of interrelations of history achievements with reading literacy and with generic skills). In order to be applicable in different settings (e.g. federal states), they need to operate independently of specific historical subjects having been addressed in class. This requirement also fits the theoretical definition of (historical) competencies as the domain specific abilities that enable their holders to reflect on changing historical subjects and problems. Such tests, therefore, need to address contextually non-specific, transferable conceptual and procedural as well as (meta-)theoretical knowledge and abilities. To date, some efforts have been made to develop measures for measuring specific aspects of historical thinking competencies (e.g. Bertram et al., 2013; Hartmann, 2008, 2009; Hartmann & Hasselhorn, 2008). A general measure for historical thinking competencies, however, is still missing.

Towards a Large-Scale test for Historical Thinking Competencies

Challenges

One of the challenges of developing large-scale assessments for historical competencies, therefore, is to exactly define and tailor the amount and depth of context—and to aim the tasks towards the required procedures and the (quality of) performance in them. The latter is then taken as an indicator of the level of the competence that is to be measured.

While conventional, subject-focused tests may prompt the respondents to distinguish correct from incorrect information, contextualization, and/or conclusions (and in doing so require remembering and applying contextual information), they do not necessarily identify whether correct or incorrect answers are due to factual knowledge, understanding of the different concepts used, and/or differences in perspectives and interpretations. Competence testing must address these specific aspects separately. In this approach, some students' responses that yield positive scores may nevertheless represent historically incorrect statements. This feature of some tasks sometimes leads to criticism. We will therefore discuss this feature of assessment tasks using a more concrete example.

The General Approach of the HITCH-Project[4]

Having been skeptical as to the possibility of developing such tests at first—on the grounds that the complex relation between personal/collective positions and perspective(s), complex information on specific subjects and the constructed and judgmental nature of historical statements defies the formulation of standardized items which can be rated as (not) correct (Körber et al., 2008), part of the consortium which developed one of the main theoretical models of historical competencies in German (the so-called "FUER-model"; Körber, Schreiber, & Schöner, 2007) is currently working on such an instrument.

The FUER-Model

The FUER-model[5] defines four dimensions of historical competencies, which—if the development is successful—can be shown to be both empirically discriminable and part of a general factor of historical thinking. These four dimensions have been derived from a procedural understanding of historical thinking developed by Hasberg and Körber (2003) on the basis of Rüsen's (1983) circular model of historical research.

Based on the postulation, taken from Rüsen (1983), that historical thinking is a process of orientation in the temporal dimension originating from a present need for, or uncertainty about, one's own (historical) identity and options, there are four dimensions of historical competence.

- The first dimension (competence in questioning) is the ability to devise operational historical questions (not only questions to be put to an expert, but reflecting one's own possibilities and possible strategies of further thought); and to identify and assess the questions behind historical narratives one comes across.
- The second dimension (methodological competence) is defined as the combination of two aspects, namely the abilities to (synthetically) construct historical statements from information ("re-construction") and to (analytically) assess and reflect given historical statements ("de-construction").
- The third dimension (orientation competence) then defines the ability to relate information and insights about the past, as well as others' conclusions and judgments about the past, to one's own life (including one's society).

These three dimensions of competence are procedural in that they reflect the circular process of historical thinking: from questions arising from the need for orientation in time, through the methods of historical research that might provide that orientation, through the representation of those results, and back to the reflection on one's own newly elaborated identity and orientation. All are interconnected by the following:

- The German title, "Sachkompetenz", of the fourth dimension of historical competencies is controversial. Other models of competencies, as for example the one by Michael Sauer employed by the German History Teachers'

Association (Sauer, 2002; Verband der Geschichtslehrer Deutschlands, 2006), use this term to mark substantive knowledge about past events, individuals, structures, etc. In our model, this is not what is meant by this term, since such knowledge (though important) is not transferable and therefore does not constitute a part of "competencies" proper. In our model, the term refers to another kind of knowledge, which is applicable if not to all then at least to a number of cases, and which constitutes a prerequisite for performing the process of historical thinking in a communicable way. The "subject matter" which is referred to in the title of this dimension is not *the past*, but *history* as a mental construct and *historical thinking*.

Among the areas of knowledge referred to here, are all concepts and categories used for structuring the "historical universe", e.g. patterns of periodization or epochs, but also of sectors (political, economic, cultural, "micro-" vs. "macro history" and so on) and methods. It includes as well concepts used in the process of historical orientation, such as "power", "sovereignty", and "culture." Moreover, epistemological concepts such as "source", "development", and "progress" are also covered. Most "second-order concepts" such as "the big six" historical thinking concepts (Seixas & Morton, 2013) belong here. Lastly, this dimension of competence also includes procedural concepts, such as knowledge (theoretical and/or experience-based) of how to get access to archival sources, how to order information chronologically, and how to analyze and interpret a document.

What all of these concepts and categories have in common is that they are not necessarily taken from the past itself, and if they are, they are to be used in a present form. They constitute part of the fabric of the narratives that are constructed or analyzed. They are not only used in the process of historical thinking proper, but also when thinking or communicating *about* history, historical thinking, its specific epistemology, and its results. When we, for example, discuss the benefits and limits of the concept of "(primary) source"—central in German history school and academic teaching—or "evidence" (more prevalent in Anglo-Saxon theoretical discourse)[6]—we do not perform historical thinking, but rather activate the competencies defined in this area.

In order for this knowledge to be counted as a "competency", it must be not only *declarative,* in that the holder of this competence can name and define these concepts, but also *discursive,* in that she/he can reflect and discuss them, and finally *operational* in that she/he is able to apply them in the operations which the other three dimensions of competence define.

In addition, the model offers a set of levels that apply to all four competencies (cf. Körber 2012):

• aconventional: a basic level at which historical thinking is done in irregular forms without the ability to apply conventional concepts;
• conventional: an intermediate level at which accepted concepts and procedures can be used for formulating and answering individual questions; and

- transconventional: an advanced level at which the conventional concepts and procedures cannot only be used and applied but can also be critically examined as to their scope and limits.

Approaches to Testing

As argued above, the FUER-model upon which our approach is based distinguishes four dimensions of competencies, each of which is further differentiated. In the "methodological competencies" (and elsewhere) a distinction is made between synthetic vs. analytical approaches, each of which is complex. Synthetic "re-construction", for example, consists of a combination of (1) gathering information on past phenomena from primary sources; (2) synthesizing them into a story about the past and—at least implicitly—relating it to the present (and future); and (3) meeting criteria for the plausibility of the story/account thus constructed. Since there is not just one criterion of correctness of a narrative, but at least three different dimensions (empirical, normative, and narrative plausibility; cf. Rüsen 1983/2013) which need to be met independently, tests for students' ability to re-construct must address these aspects *separately*. Tasks for students' ability to construct coherent accounts as to standards of narrativity may therefore use material (information) which need not be historically accurate in itself, if the ability to assess and judge the empirical and normative plausibility are tested in other tasks. This strategy also offers the possibility of constructing tasks on narrating which do not need to anticipate the students' own cultural, social, or other (even individual) perspectives, which would render comparison between students' achievements impossible. The former may therefore refer to supposed perspectives and interests, while tests for abilities of assessing empirical plausibility have to test for mastery of epistemological concepts, largely independent from perspective. An example is given below.

In the following section, three examples of tasks are presented, each of which addresses one aspect of the synthetic aspect of "re-construction". The interrelation of the second and third is of particular importance (Körber, Schreiber, & Schöner, 2007).

Units and Items for Assessing Aspects of Re-constructive Competence

First, let's have a look at some tasks, focusing the competence of composing historical accounts (narrations) on the basis of primary and secondary information (re-construction). Based on the FUER model we can differentiate three aspects of this competence:

The first aspect refers to the ability to extract information from given material. In order to differentiate this from mere (non-history-specific) reading skills, several sources are presented, representing both different perspectives and different types of material (particularly primary and secondary sources). Based on such sets of material, respondents are prompted to conclude whether specific, given statements about the event/subject covered are substantiated or contradicted by the given material or whether the material does not give any clue as to the questions asked. Here, we can directly draw on a format used in earlier research for historical consciousness (e.g. von Borries, 1995 and 466 [items] on the subject of the Crusades).

In this way, the tasks not only require students to find and repeat statements given in the material, but to understand and process the information given with respect to historical accounts. This kind of task builds upon subject-specific reading abilities and also tests for the respondent's ability to use the information as evidence for historical conclusions. However, this is only one important aspect of the ability of "composing historical accounts".

For the second aspect of re-constructive competence, the "narrative synthesis", tasks must confront respondents with the challenge to construct plausible historical narratives, using a set of given components of several historical narratives about the same topic. Since the ability to assess empirical plausibility is tested separately (see above), the test can be constructed as follows.

Respondents are provided with a set of cards containing different portions of stories on a common subject. As shown in Figure 6.1, these portions can be arranged in different ways, yielding coherent and/or incoherent narratives with respect to the interrelated combination of statements about things past and their interconnection (portions A–F) and about their meaning or conclusions (1–4), respectively. Three different stories can thus be constructed, sharing a common beginning portion. The measure for the student's re-constructive ability then is the number of plausible connections they can make within the three stories (see Figure 6.1).

Scores are given not only for complete solutions, but also for partial combinations. Since the resulting accounts (histories) present different sequences, not all

	1	2		3
	A	*C*	< end of story, version 1>	*2*
< beginning of a story about the past >	*E*	*B*	< end of story, version 2 >	*4*
	D	*F*	< end of story, version 3 >	*1*

Statement A	Statement B	Statement C	Statement D	Statement E	Statement F
Conclusion 1		Conclusion 2		Conclusion 3	Conclusion 4

FIGURE 6.1 Task format for re-construction of narration: respondents sort statements A to F into the white and conclusions 1–4 into the light gray cells.

of them will match the "actual" occurrences as presented by the current state of historical research.[7]

For the third aspect of the competence to re-construct, the ability of students to observe criteria of plausibility, specific instruments are needed. Again, in contrast to classical, master-narrative-based tests, the task cannot consist of stating whether the stories are "correct". Instead, the respondents are presented with statements referring to possibilities of judging the plausibility in different dimensions, some of which are fully pertinent, while others are only partially so, and others completely irrelevant. Respondents are asked to judge their appropriateness. The task is to judge the given criteria.

Cautions: Tasks as Multipolar Configuration

In conclusion, our model of assessment of historical learning focuses neither on mastery of given narratives and interpretations nor on second order concepts, but rather on competencies as transferable abilities to perform tasks and operations of historical thinking. It requires a certain amount of context, lest historical thinking itself be reduced to a mechanical operation without any orienting function. These contexts have to be provided by material given in the instruments, which therefore must be somewhat "self-contained", not referring to prior substantive knowledge on the subject. No context presented with tasks and items, however, can be totally free of cultural and social connotations and students necessarily differ in their perspectives and prior knowledge to such contexts (see Beck & McKeown, 1994; Hodel et al., 2013; Meyer-Hamme, 2009). It therefore constitutes a specific challenge for test construction to discern the necessary amount and depth of context as well as its fairness. Furthermore, even assessments, which have been tested and standardized, may be difficult to adapt to other languages and cultures.

Relevance for Teaching

Promoting standardized testing as well as working on the development of the appropriate instruments does always entail the danger of promoting "teaching to the test" and therefore a constriction of teaching aims and outcomes to testable aspects. Therefore, especially in diverse and pluralist countries, standardized testing of historical knowledge and interpretation may be problematic, since differences in perspective may be pushed out of view. On the other hand, constant debate about the past and its representation, as well as its relevance for present societal orientation and identity, is not a weakness, but a democratic strength in such societies. It makes, however, some demands on its members' abilities to participate in such discussions and therefore on their ability to both synthetically and analytically deal with histories of topics not covered in school. In this respect, empirical knowledge about the state of students' abilities in this domain is necessary for developing teaching and training. Large-scale assessments then do not directly yield information for the individual teacher's work, but tests based on standardized instruments may give teachers valuable indicators of strengths and needs for development.

Moreover, some of the test/item formats being developed in such projects may help to focus teaching on the cognitive ("problem solving") aspects of dealing with historical accounts and may even initiate classroom discussions about the thinking operations and the students' own role in "making history". The format of constructing different narratives from given material discussed above, e.g. may in this case not only yield information about students' ability to perform this operation, but also provide tools for discussing their strategies and strengthening their awareness of their active role in historical thinking. In this respect, constructing and using items suitable for large-scale assessments focusing on competencies may be a substantial contribution to the development of what in the German discussion has been coined an innovative "Aufgabenkultur", i.e. a widespread sensitivity to, and discussion about, the relevance and role of assessment tasks in learning processes, as well as a commitment to their refinement.

Notes

1 Ständige Konferenz der Kultusminister der Länder in der Bundesrepublik Deutschland: "Vereinbarung über Einheitliche Prüfungsanforderungen in der Abiturprüfung." (Beschluss der KMK vom 01.06.1979 i.d.F. Vom 24.10.2008).
2 The German terms laid down in the "uniform standards" for final upper secondary exams (Abitur) are "wiedergeben von Sachverhalten . . . (Reproduktion)" being a bit more complex that mere "recall", "selbstständige[s] Erklären, Bearbeiten und Ordnen", as well as "angemessenes Anwenden . . . auf neue Sachverhalte . . . (Reorganisation und Transfer)", and "reflexiver Umgang mit neuen Problemstellungen . . . (Relexion und Problemlösung)" (Ständige Konferenz 2005).
3 Including "strategic" or "procedural" as opposed to "declarative" or "susbstantive" knowledge (cf. VanSledright 2014).
4 The following is based on the ongoing work of the collaborative project "HITCH" (Historical Thinking—Competencies in History), coordinated by Ulrich Trautwein, Waltraud Schreiber, Bodo von Borries, and Andreas Körber with Christiane Bertram, Wolfgang Wagner, Johannes Meyer-Hamme, Michael Werner, and Matthias Hirsch; and associated partners, among them Béatrice Ziegler with Monika Waldis-Weber, Christoph Kühberger, and Nicola Brauch. Cf. Trautwein et al. (2014).
5 For a description in English with graphs see Körber, 2011.
6 "Source" of course is a metaphor and therefore needs reflection as to its connotations. German academe, however, makes a point of reserving this term for primary (documentary and monumentary) material, rather strongly distinguishing it from "account" ("Darstellung")—the term reserved for retrospective narratives. The strictness of this distinction is, of course, problematic. Even though this is known, the metaphorical connotation of the concept "source" reaches deeply into epistemology, when, e.g. Klaus Arnold, in an encyclopedic article, explains: "Sources are the starting points of historical perception ['Erkenntnis']. As is the case with natural watercourses, their mere existence is not enough. They gain their relevance only by human tracking back to their origins"

(Arnold [2002, p. 251]; transl. AK). Horst Walter Blanke commented on Heinrich von Sybel: "The metaphorical term of 'source' already implicated the easiness of its interpretation [Auswertung]: 'Sources' virtually 'pour' mere insight [Erkenntnis]." Accordingly, leading members of German historiography held the view the "historical method" was "nothing more than the application of common sense." (Blanke [1999, p. 4]; transl. AK).
7 For further argumentation about the specifics of the historical aspect in this unit see Meyer-Hamme (forthcoming).

References

Adamski, P. (2003). Portfolio im Geschichtsunterricht: Leistungen dokumentieren—Lernen reflektieren. *Geschichte in Wissenschaft und Unterricht, 54*, 32–50.

Angvik, M., & Borries, B. von (Eds.). (1997). *Youth and History: A Comparative European Survey on Historical Consciousness and Political Attitudes Among Adolescents*. Hamburg, Germany: Körber-Stiftung.

Arnold, K. (2002). Quellen. In S. Jordan (Ed.), *Lexikon Geschichtswissenschaft. Hundert Grundbegriffe* (pp. 251–255). Stuttgart, Germany: Reclam.

Beck, I., & McKeown, M. (1994). Outcomes of History Instruction: Paste-Up Accounts. In M. Carretero & J. F. Voss (Eds.), *Cognitive and Instructional Processes in History and the Social Sciences* (pp. 237–256). Hillsdale, NJ: L. Erlbaum.

Bertram, C., Wagner, W., & Trautwein, U. (2013). Chancen und Risiken von Zeitzeugenbefragungen: Entwicklung eines Messinstruments für eine Interventionsstudie. In J. Hodel, M. Waldis, & B. Ziegler (Eds.), *Forschungswerkstatt Geschichtsdidaktik 12. Beiträge zur Tagung "geschichtsdidaktik empirisch 12"* (pp. 108–119). Bern, Switzerland: hep-Verlag.

Blanke, H. W. (1999). Zur Geschichte und Theorie des Theorie-Gebrauchs und der Theorie-Reflexion in der Geschichtswissenschaft. In A. Jobmann & B. Spindler (Eds.), *Theorien über Theorien über Theorien* (pp. 7–23). Bielefeld, Germany: Universität Bielefeld; Institut für Wissenschafts- und Technologieforschung.

Borries, B. v. (1973). *Lernziele und Testaufgaben für den Geschichtsunterricht, dargestellt an der Behandlung der Römischen Republik in der 7. Klasse* (1st ed.). Stuttgart, Germany: Klett.

Borries, B. v. (1995). *Das Geschichtsbewußtsein Jugendlicher: Erste repräsentative Untersuchung über Vergangenheitsdeutungen, Gegenwartswahrnehmungen und Zukunftserwartungen von Schülerinnen und Schülern in Ost- und Westdeutschland. Jugendforschung*. Weinheim, Germany: Juventa-Verlag.

Danto, A. C. (1968). *Analytical Philosophy of History* (Reprinted). London, UK: Cambridge University Press.

Hartmann, U. (2008). *Perspektivenübernahme als eine Kompetenz historischen Verstehens* (Dissertation). Georg-August-Universität Göttingen, Göttingen, Germany.

Hartmann, U. (2009). Kompetenzprofile historischer Perspektivenübernahme in Klasse 7 und 10. In J. Hodel & B. Ziegler (Eds.), *Forschungswerkstatt Geschichtsdidaktik 07. Beiträge zur Tagung "geschichtsdidaktik empirisch 07"* (1st ed., pp. 79–89). Bern, Switzerland: hep-Verlag.

Hartmann, U., & Hasselhorn, M. (2008). Historical Perspective Taking—A Standardized Measure for an Aspect of Students' Historical Thinking. *Learning and Individual Differences, 28*(2), 264–270.

Hasberg, W., & Körber, A. (2003). Geschichtsbewusstsein dynamisch. In A. Körber (Ed.), *Geschichte—Leben—Lernen. Bodo von Borries zum 60. Geburtstag* (pp. 177–200). Schwalbach/Ts., Germany: Wochenschau-Verlag.

Hodel, J., Waldis, M., Zülsdorf-Kersting, M., & Thünemann, H. (2013). Schülernarrationen als Ausdruck historischer Kompetenz. *Zeitschrift für Didaktik der Gesellschaftswissenschaften, 4*(2), 121–145.

Ingenkamp, K. (1967). *Geschichtstest "Neuzeit"*. Weinheim, Germany: Beltz.

Jeismann, K.-E. (1977). Didaktik der Geschichte. Die Wissenschaft von Zustand, Funktion und Veränderung geschichtlicher Vorstellungen im Selbstverständnis der Gegenwart. In E. Kosthorst & K.-E. Jeismann (Eds.), *Geschichtswissenschaft. Didaktik, Forschung, Theorie* (pp. 9–33). Göttingen, Germany: Vandenhoeck & Ruprecht.

Jeismann, K.-E. (1980). 'Geschichtsbewußtsein': Überlegungen zur zentralen Kategorie eines neuen Ansatzes der Geschichtsdidaktik. In H. Süssmuth (Ed.), *Geschichtsdidaktische Positionen. Bestandsaufnahme und Neuorientierung* (pp. 179–222). Paderborn, Germany: Ferdinand Schöningh.

Körber, A. (2011). German History Didactics: From Historical Consciousness to Historical Competencies—and Beyond? In H. Bjerg, C. Lenz, & E. Thorstensen (Eds.), *Historicizing the Uses of the Past. Scandinavian Perspectives on History Culture, Historical Consciousness and Didactics of History Related to World War II* (pp. 145–164). Bielefeld, Germany: Transcript.

Körber, A. (2012). Graduierung historischer Kompetenzen. In M. Barricelli & M. Lücke (Eds.), *Handbuch Praxis des Geschichtsunterrichts. Historisches Lernen in der Schule* (pp. 236–254). Schwalbach/Ts., Germany: Wochenschau-Verlag.

Körber, A. (forthcoming). Messung historischer Kompetenzen—Herausforderungen für die Erstellung eines LSA-geeigneten Kompetenztests. In M. Waldis & B. Ziegler (Eds.), *Forschungswerkstatt Geschichtsdidaktik 13. Beiträge zur Tagung "Geschichtsdidaktik empirisch 13"* (1st ed.). Bern, Switzerland: hep-Verlag.

Körber, A., Borries, B. von, Pflüger, C., Schreiber, W., & Ziegler, B. (2008). Sind Kompetenzen historischen Denkens messbar? In V. Frederking (Ed.), *Schwer messbare Kompetenzen. Herausforderungen für die empirische Fachdidaktik* (pp. 65–84). Baltmannsweiler, Germany: Schneider Verlag Hohengehren.

Körber, A., Schreiber, W., & Schöner, A. (Eds.). (2007). *Kompetenzen Historischen Denkens: Ein Strukturmodell als Beitrag zur Kompetenzorientierung in der Geschichtsdidaktik.* Neuried, Germany: Verlags-Gesellschaft.

Küppers, W. (1961). *Zur Psychologie des Geschichtsunterrichts: Eine Untersuchung über Geschichtswissen und Geschichtsverständnis bei Schülern.* Bern, Switzerland: Huber.

Meyer-Hamme, J. (2009). *Historische Identitäten und Geschichtsunterricht: Fallstudien zum Verhältnis von kultureller Zugehörigkeit, schulischen Anforderungen und individueller Verarbeitung* (1st ed.). Idstein, Germany: Schulz-Kirchner Verlag.

Meyer-Hamme, J. (forthcoming). Formate geschlossener Aufgaben für thematisch fokussiertes Testen historischer Kompetenzen. In M. Waldis & B. Ziegler (Eds.), *Forschungswerkstatt Geschichtsdidaktik 13. Beiträge zur Tagung "Geschichtsdidaktik empirisch 13"* (1st ed.). Bern, Switzerland: hep-Verlag.

Noack, C. (1994). Stufen der Ich-Entwicklung und Geschichtsbewußtsein. In H.-J. Pandel (Ed.), *Zur Genese historischer Denkformen. Qualitative und quantitative empirische Zugänge* (pp. 6–46). Pfaffenweiler, Germany: Centaurus-Verlagsgesellschaft.

Roth, H. (1968). *Kind und Geschichte: Psychologische Voraussetzungen des Geschichtsunterrichts in der Volksschule* (5th ed.). *Psychologie der Unterrichtsfächer der Volksschule.* München, Germany: Kösel.

Rüsen, J. (1983). *Historische Vernunft: Grundzüge einer Historik I: Die Grundlagen der Geschichtswissenschaft.* Göttingen, Germany: Vandenhoeck & Ruprecht.

Rüsen, J. (2013). *Historik: Theorie der Geschichtswissenschaft.* Köln, Germany: Böhlau.

Sauer, M. (2002). Methodenkompetenz als Schlüsselqualifikation. Eine neue Grundlegung des Geschichtsunterrichts? *Geschichte, Politik und ihre Didaktik, 30*(3/4), 183–192.

Seixas, P. C., & Morton, T. (2013). *The Big Six Historical Thinking Concepts.* Toronto, ON: Nelson Education.

Ständige Konferenz der Kultusminister der Länder in der Bundesrepublik Deutschland (1979/2005): *Einheitliche Prüfungsanforderungen in der Abiturprüfung. Geschichte.* Retrieved from http://www.kmk.org /fileadmin/veroeffentlichungen_beschluesse/ 1989/1989_12_01-EPA-Geschichte.pdf

Ständige Konferenz der Kultusminister der Länder in der Bundesrepublik Deutschland. (1979/2008). *Vereinbarung über Einheitliche Prüfungsanforderungen in der Abiturprüfung.* Retrieved from http://www.kmk.org/fileadmin/veroeffentlichungen_beschluesse/ 2008/2008_10_24-VB-EPA.pdf

Trautwein, U., Bertram, C., Borries, B. v. Körber, A., Meyer-Hamme, J., Schreiber, W., Zuckowski, A., et al. (2015, forthcoming). *Kompetenzen historischen Denkens erfassen: Konzeption, Operationalisierung und erste Befunde des Projekts, "Historical Thinking— Competencies in History" (HiTCH).* Stuttgart, Germany: Kohlhammer.

VanSledright, B. A. (2014). *Assessing Historical Thinking and Understanding: Innovative Designs for New Standards.* New York, NY: Routledge.

Verband der Geschichtslehrer Deutschlands. (2006). *Bildungsstandards Geschichte: Rahmenmodell Gymnasium, 5.- 10. Jahrgangsstufe. Studien des Verbandes der Geschichtslehrer Deutschlands.* Schwalbach/Ts, Germany: Wochenschau-Verlag.

7

A DESIGN PROCESS FOR ASSESSING HISTORICAL THINKING

The Case of a One-Hour Test

Peter Seixas, Lindsay Gibson, and Kadriye Ercikan

Introduction: Context and Rationale

In recent years, history curricula and standards have increasingly incorporated goals of historical thinking, consistently outpacing corresponding changes in assessments (see Introduction). One reason for the persistence of assessment of history as memorization of facts is relative ease and efficiency. By comparison, the assessment of historical thinking poses a daunting challenge. On top of conceptual issues, history assessment developers face challenges related to reliability, scoring efficiency, and limits of test-taking time, among others. This chapter examines the design of a single one-hour test with features that we believe can be used, developed further, and adjusted to a variety of assessment contexts. The objective of the chapter is to highlight those features in order to define principles, challenges, and potential solutions for teachers and other test developers with similar aims. However, it stops short of issues of validity, as those will be discussed in Chapter 13 (this volume).

The design process discussed in this chapter builds on the research on historical thinking conducted as part of Canada's Historical Thinking Project (hereafter, the HT Project, originally "Benchmarks of Historical Thinking"). The HT Project ran from 2006 to 2014, with the aim of making historical thinking central to history education (Peck & Seixas, 2008; Seixas, 2010). It proposed a definition of historical thinking based on six concepts that have been highly influential in recent Canadian provincial curriculum revisions:

- establish *historical significance* (why we care, today, about certain events, trends, and issues in history. Why are the Plains of Abraham significant for Canadian history?)

- use primary source *evidence* (how to find, select, contextualize, and interpret sources for a historical argument. What can a newspaper article from Berlin, Ontario in 1916 tell us about attitudes towards German-Canadians in wartime?)
- identify *continuity and change* (what has changed and what has remained the same over time. What has changed and what has remained the same about the lives of teenaged girls, between the 1950s and today?)
- analyze *cause and consequence* (how and why certain conditions and actions led to others. What were the causes of the Northwest Rebellion?)
- take *historical perspectives* (understanding the "past as a foreign country," with its different social, cultural, intellectual, and even emotional contexts that shaped people's lives and actions. How could Canadian Prime Minister John A. Macdonald compare "Chinamen" to "threshing machines" in 1886?)
- understand the *ethical dimension* of historical interpretations (this cuts across many of the others: how we, in the present, judge actors in different circumstances in the past; when and how crimes and sacrifices of the past bear consequences today; what obligations we have today in relation to those consequences. What is to be done today, about the legacy of aboriginal residential schools?)

From the outset, assessment concerns were a high priority for the HT Project: teachers would be justifiably reluctant to adopt learning objectives without the requisite means or guidance for evaluating student achievement. The HT Project's tools consisted of assessment rubrics for classroom-based student projects, along with exemplars of student work at a variety of levels (see http:// historicalthinking.ca/resources). Therefore, they were intended to be used as discrete tasks or models of tasks rather than comprehensive assessments of historical thinking. These assessment tasks provided a foundation for the current exploration of a design process for valid and reliable assessment of historical thinking.

We chose to work within the framework of a single one-hour test that could easily be administered within one class period. Standing alone, such a test cannot provide a comprehensive assessment of all components of historical thinking in all history topics. Yet, it can provide a building block for multiple assessments during the course of a year, and as a module that can be expanded for a summative course assessment. Test-time constraints, reliability considerations, and scoring efficiency led us to include short answer and multiple-choice items, as well as constructed response questions.

Any assessment team aiming to measure competencies in historical thinking immediately faces two fundamental challenges. First, historical knowledge (the subject matter or topics of history) is mutually interdependent with historical thinking. One cannot be said to understand history by virtue of understanding "causation" in the abstract: "causation" obviously demands "causes of what?" Nor can one be said to understand causation by memorizing "the five causes of

World War I." So the question of how, and how much, to distinguish the assessment of historical thinking from that of historical knowledge is ever-present in the design process. Second, the practices of history depend so much on reading and writing that instruments designed to target historical thinking may largely be measuring reading and writing skills and text-based analysis without utilizing historical thinking (see Reisman, this volume).

An Approach to the Assessment of Historical Thinking

The National Research Council (2001, pp. 44 ff.) proposes an "assessment triangle" as a way to conceive of three interdependent cornerstones of assessment—cognition, observation, and interpretation—which give rise to three questions (cf. Ercikan, 2006; Ercikan & Seixas, 2011):

1   What is the model of students' historical thinking (or *cognition*) that is targeted by the assessment?
2   What tasks will enable *observations* of students' responses or products, to provide evidence of students' historical thinking?
3   How will the observations be *interpreted* as evidence of students' historical thinking?

While the HT Project model of historical thinking comprises six concepts, in order to attain good measurement from a one-hour test, we focused on only three of the six concepts: evidence, perspective taking, and the ethical dimension. Explained below, these three concepts provide the foundation for the test's model of historical cognition.

Historical Thinking Concept—Evidence

The analysis of primary sources is universally accepted as fundamental to the discipline of history and to the pedagogy of historical thinking. If there is one common starting point, this is it. We define "evidence," following the work of the HT Project, as the cognitive processes required to use primary source documents as evidence for claims about what happened in the past. In order to make valid historical inferences from the traces left by unreliable, personally-interested, historically-situated, professionally-compromised individuals and institutions, students need to read them in view of the authors' perspectives and purposes. Also, students need to consider the historical context in which they were written. Finally, they need to be able to read between and among documents, piecing together, through contrast and corroboration, a larger picture than any one of the documents could provide. This is not to suggest a lock-step formula or algorithm for analyzing sources, but rather, a series of considerations that must be kept in mind.

The signal failure in reading documents in this way is to read them as presenting information, as one would read a phonebook or a textbook. One turns to the latter *because* they are expected to provide reliable information to people in our positions (telephone users and students, respectively)—that is the purpose for which they were produced; if they fail to do so, they get tossed into the recycling. In contrast, the *unreliable* primary source document may be highly *useful* in revealing the intentions of its author and the unspoken assumptions of her times. This understanding is built into the term "trace" as applied to sources from the past (see Lee & Ashby, 2000; Seixas, 1996; Wineburg, 1991).

Historical Thinking Concept—Perspective Taking

The concept of perspective taking evolved from the term that was at one point ubiquitous in British history education: historical empathy. The problem with the term "empathy" is its connotation of emotional involvement (Ashby & Lee, 1987; Davis, Yeager, & Foster, 2001). When students take historical perspectives, they articulate the potential depths of difference between our current beliefs, values, and motivations and those of earlier peoples. Their statements show that they recognize the temporal distance between themselves and the objects of their study.[1] They explain the beliefs, ideas, values, motivations, and actions of people in the past *as related to the historical context* in which they lived. Moreover, they recognize that a variety of potentially incommensurable perspectives can co-exist within the same historical moment.

Competency in taking historical perspectives overlaps with using evidence: analyzing a source involves inferring the perspectives of its author(s) in their historical moment; and articulating the perspectives of people in a particular moment demands analyzing sources to provide evidence for claims about those perspectives.

Historical Thinking Concept—the Ethical Dimension

The ethical dimension of history is far less discussed in the history education literature than is either the use of primary source evidence or taking historical perspectives. If the use of primary source evidence is ubiquitous in definitions of history curriculum and pedagogy, the ethical dimension is virtually absent in the Anglophone literature outside of the Canadian context (see, e.g., Monte-Sano & Reisman, forthcoming). Yet, there is ample debate among historians and philosophers of history about the implicit and explicit ethical judgments entailed by doing history (see, e.g., Carr, Flynn, & Makkreel, 2004; Fay, 2004). The ethical dimension can be seen, however, where history education meets citizenship education (as in the current Quebec curriculum, Duquette, this volume), and even more so where curricula adopt the frameworks of "historical consciousness," as has the new national Swedish curriculum (Eliasson, Alvén,

Rosenlund, & Rudnert, 2012; Eliasson, Alvén, Yngvéus, & Rosenlund, this volume). There are several distinct but complementary aspects. First, there is the problem of making ethical judgments about actions that took place in a more or less distant past. While history would become a limp and pallid discipline without the condemnation of Nazi exterminators, Southern U.S. slaveholders, and Belgian imperialists, all such judgments need to recognize the historical context in which actors were operating. The simple application of today's ethical standards as universal and transhistorical dicta risks presentism. Striving for complexity, caution, and contextualization is thus a virtue in the pursuit of both the heroes and villains of the past. Second, the ethical dimension involves assessing the implications for today of sacrifices and injustices of the past: these may range from the minimum of memorial obligations to the maximum of restitution and reparation. Temporal distance is a key factor to be considered: the further away the events are, and the more tenuous the causal chains between them and their legacies today, the weaker the argument for maximal forms of obligation. "Temporal distance" is, of course, a malleable and subjective term: "memories" of chronologically distant events are always available for whipping into an emotional presence.

Competency within the ethical dimension, defined in this way, is conceptually related to, and dependent upon, competence in historical perspective taking. Both rely on negotiating the historical distance between the objects of our study and us. Indeed, the conceptual links among the concepts suggest the appropriateness of test items that target all three.

From Cognition Model to Observation and Interpretation

For each of the three historical thinking concepts, we generated a Cognition and Observation Table arraying components of the concept with observable behaviors that could demonstrate mastery of the concept, and the corresponding tasks that could generate those behaviors (see Appendix 1). We used the same tables to determine to what extent and what kinds of student responses would provide evidence of students' historical thinking. These resulted in a set of scoring rubrics for all the items, which we discuss below.

The Test

History assessments are generally designed to test students' knowledge of particular historical eras and geographic areas at the same time that they measure students' thinking competencies. Even a test that does not aim to measure factual knowledge must still take it into account, as students need enough understanding of historical context to make sense of the test questions. We designed the test on the topic of Canadian policies towards Ukrainian "enemy aliens" under the War Measures Act of 1914. While students taking the test had recently studied World

War I as part of British Columbia's Grade 11 Social Studies curriculum, none of them had spent any time on these particular events.

The choice of the World War I internment was also shaped by the relevance of the ethical dimension of historical thinking in understanding this event. This was an incident that created significant debates about the violation of human rights, the treatment of ethnically identified minorities, and the appropriate responses to recent demands for recognition and restitution.

The test begins with basic information, presented in six bullet points, on the World War I internment of 8,579 "enemy aliens," mainly Ukrainian immigrants from the Austro-Hungarian Empire. Then there are excerpts, approximately 100 words each, from five primary sources with titles and brief captions that include information about the author, date, and context (Wineburg & Martin, 2009). Each excerpt is followed by one to three questions, either multiple-choice or short answer. Finally, two constructed-response questions ask students to use all of the documents to write paragraph responses (see Appendix 2).

Choosing Sources and Framing Questions

The five sources worked individually and also in relation to each other for assessing the three historical thinking concepts. Moreover, using the sources to construct assessment items required working with three nodes: the document text, the cognition model, and the wording of the question. What elements of the cognition model could be examined with the source, and what questions would enable students to demonstrate competency in those elements? As suggested above, these three were mutually interdependent: there was not a 1–2–3 sequence, but rather mutually determined adjustments and revisions.

A fundamental feature of the test was the series of document excerpts written at an appropriate level of vocabulary and syntax, related to the culminating questions. These requirements demanded considerable editing of the sources, in order to provide highly focused nuggets whose interpretative potential lay relatively close to the surface. Precedents for using a series of documents in an assessment exercise on a large scale include the paradigmatic U.S. Advanced Placement Document-Based Questions (College Board, 2014; Matts & Charap, 2012), Cambridge history examinations, New York State Regents exams in Grades 10 and 11, and, in Canada, the paragraph and essay questions of the Begbie Canadian History Contest (Hou, n.d.).

The first source was from an interview with Reverend Father Moris printed in the Calgary *Daily Herald* in 1899.

> As for the Galicians [Ukrainians] I have not met a single person in the whole of the North West who is sympathetic towards them. They are, from the point of view of civilization, 10 times lower than the Indians.

They have not the least idea of sanitation. In their personal habits and acts, [they] resemble animals, and even in the streets of Edmonton, when they come to market, men, women, and children, would if unchecked, turn the place into a common sewer.

The document initially required our own explicit analysis. For today's sensibilities, the *Daily Herald* text contains extreme language about an entire group of immigrants. It embodies a nineteenth century hierarchy of "civilization," where "Indians" are low and "Galicians" even lower. Yet, the very fact that it was spoken by a religious leader and published in a newspaper suggests that it was both acceptable at the time, and widely, if not universally, shared by Canadians who had been in Canada for longer. Thus, while it is not a credible report of the "Galicians" way of living, it is useful, indeed, highly efficient, as a trace of the attitudes of established Canadians at the time.

This analysis of the document suggested that it would be useful for questions examining students' competence in making plausible inferences about the assumptions of the authors of the text. Such a question had to be able to capture the error of students reading the source as reliable information about "Galicians" or their impact on Canada. Each of the distractors (a, b, and d) signals that error.

This source would be useful for a historian today, because it

a. describes the personal habits of Galician immigrants to Canada.
b. compares how Galicians and Indians lived at this time.
c. reveals the attitudes of some Canadians towards Galician immigrants to Canada.
d. helps to understand conditions on the streets of Edmonton.

Without follow-up opportunity for students to explain their answers, multiple-choice questions that could provide evidence of student thinking proved difficult to construct. One problem was writing plausible distractors that anticipated the answers that less sophisticated historical thinkers might arrive at. A solution (which we did not attempt) might be to experiment with the question stem posed as a constructed response question, asking students at different levels of competence in historical thinking to generate plausible distractors.

The second document was an excerpt from a 1916 report by Mr. G. Willrich, an external inspector of the internment camps, who described the prisoners as ". . . good, sturdy, inoffensive men, able and willing to work, most of them desirous of becoming Canadian citizens. . . ." After providing a caption with a substantial description of the author's position, we asked students to explain in one sentence, "why Mr. Willrich describes Ukrainians so differently from Father Moris (Document 1)." Like the multiple-choice item above, it prompts students to think about the perspective of the author of the document. Unlike earlier items, it asks students to compare evidence from two contrasting documents, thus furthering the step-by-step building of an evidence base upon which they will build the two longer constructed-response items at the end of the test.

Constructed-response items like this one demand scoring criteria for interpreting student responses. These scoring criteria were developed *a priori*, using the Cognition and Observation tables, and subject to revision through pilot testing. The Willrich question had a three-point scale (2, 1, 0).[2] Two points were given if the "student presents an explanation of the perspective of Willrich or Father Morris and their motivations, in light of their positions, purposes and/or contexts, based on the documents." One point was given for partial explanations of the differences. The student was given zero points if no answer was given, or the answer was incorrect. Subsequent item response theory based analysis indicated, however, that our scoring criteria failed to discriminate well between score levels 1 and 2 (Ercikan, Seixas, Lyons-Thomas, & Gibson, 2012).

Having explicitly exposed a contention in viewpoints with the first two documents, three more documents followed, each with one or two multiple-choice or short constructed response questions. They comprised a letter signed by six Ukrainian newspaper editors protesting internment, a speech by Canada's Minister of Justice defending the internment as a humanitarian measure aimed at relief for Ukrainians unable to find work, and a letter from a 9-year-old girl to her interned father, describing the hardships of living without him.

Like those that followed each of the first two documents, the items asked students about the implicit and explicit views and assumptions of the authors and potential uses of the documents by historians. They also introduced ethical concerns, with words like "blame" (e.g., "Whom did the newspaper editors think was to blame?") and "justify" (e.g., "Did Doherty believe that the internment of Austrians was justified?"). These ethical concerns, however, are all couched in the perspectives of the documents—asking students to interpret their points of view. Only with the last two constructed-response items did we require students to deliberate about whether the internment policies were justified. The first asked, "Was the Canadian government justified in its policies towards Ukrainians during World War I? Discussing the contrasting perspectives in the documents, explain why or why not."

Scoring was based on a four-point scale (0, 1, 2, 3). A score of 3 was given if the "student discusses at least two contrasting perspectives in the documents, accurately explaining how each is relevant to the justifiability or unjustifiability of the policies, and in each case referring to the author's position and situation (conditions)." A score of 2 was given for doing the same with only one perspective; a score of 1 for a "general statement of belief, with no use of sources for evidence." Again, the scoring criteria were derived from cognitive demands, for this question, from all three historical thinking concepts.

Discussion and Conclusion

We started from definitions of three of the six historical thinking concepts, as defined by the Historical Thinking Project. We restated these in terms of what students who understood each of these would be able to do. Next, we defined sample tasks that would enable them to demonstrate each of these abilities. The development of the task model—actual questions about a substantive historical topic, in a variety of question formats in a test that could be administered within one classroom period—forced us to emphasize some of the sample tasks and to abandon others. It also forced us to come to terms with the interdependence of the three concepts of historical thinking. This interdependence is neither surprising nor undesirable. However, it makes it impossible to make claims about students' competencies with regards to the three concepts independently. We based the initial development of our interpretation—the scoring and coding—on *a priori* definitions of progression in using the historical thinking concepts. In the analysis of students' responses to the test items, we gained new insights about confounding factors in the cognition model and, more so, in the tasks themselves. Students' responses helped to reveal several characteristics of the documents that either supported their reading of the sources competently as traces of the past, making inferences in view of the time they were written and the position of their authors, or alternatively, reading them uncritically as reliable reports simply conveying information.

First, we expected that the foreignness of some ideas (such as Father Moris') would be helpful for students in establishing a critical distance from the text. Indeed, with comments like, "harsh!" they indicated this distance. But that distance was not necessarily an opening for all students to make well-grounded observations about the social context that allowed ideas like Moris' to be expressed publicly. Systematic teaching of such documents as opportunities to enter into a foreign environment could set marginal students up for a higher level of performance.

Second, not only the foreignness of the ideas, but the complexity of the position held by the author of the document is an important factor in students' readings. Katie Domytryk, the internee's daughter who wrote the letter to her father, and Mr. Willrich, the American government representative empowered to inspect the Canadian camps, occupy two ends of a simple/complex continuum. It was easier to read the child's statement, in part because of the simplicity of vocabulary and sentence construction, but even more because this is a position about which students had more prior understanding.

Third, we expected that the contrasting views among documents would create dissonance that could be resolved by reading them as traces, rather than as information. Some students managed to circumvent such a reading by interpreting them uncritically, as reliable reports, by stringing them together, temporally, into a seamless narrative, even if it meant confusing their chronological order.

Making the analysis process more complex, we uncovered many instances where the same student performed at different levels in respect to the same cognitive demand, even in response to the same document. This finding raises cautions about assigning students to particular levels of competence in historical thinking on the basis of limited numbers of test items. As well, it points to the desirability of ongoing assessment over multiple occasions.

Each of these difficulties points to the problems of any assessment research that is not tied to instructional practice. Even though the test was administered in classes that were completing a study of World War I, the students had not received instruction in the competencies that we set out to assess, nor were they familiar with some of the terms (e.g., internment, enemy alien, Ukrainian) included on the test. It would be a different exercise had the students been immersed in classrooms where these were part of the curriculum. Even some algorithmic steps for approaching documents, repeated a number of times over the course of a year (or, even better, several years) might make a substantial difference in how students approach the problems we put in front of them.

Notwithstanding these challenges, the architecture of this one-hour test provides a promising task model for the design of assessments of historical thinking (see also Reisman, this volume). The key features are (1) a genuine problem of historical interpretation, shaped around one of the historical thinking concepts (in this case, the ethical dimension), (2) a series of five (more or less) excerpts of primary source documents (100 words, more or less) relevant to the problem and appropriate to student reading levels, (3) short answer and/or multiple-choice questions following each of the excerpts, helping students to scaffold their thinking about the historical events as they provide evidence of their competence in addressing these smaller items, and (4) one or two longer constructed response items on the problem (1, above) that allow students to work with multiple sources.

While other assessments of historical thinking have used documents and test items to generate students' responses, this model is distinguished by having multiple sources, whose analysis builds cumulatively. This structure provided opportunities for students to analyze single documents. It also provided opportunities to use multiple documents, without students facing all of them in one onslaught.

There are many directions to go from here. Other tests might target ethical controversies in history that arouse more emotionally charged responses among the test-takers, particularly where their own identities are at stake (see van Boxtel, Grever, & Klein, this volume). Any of the three concepts we omitted—cause and consequence, continuity and change, or historical significance—might provide the basis for items on new tests, using the approach we have presented here. Designing items for these concepts will pose some of the same opportunities, challenges, and issues, as well as some new ones. We look forward to engaging them.

Notes

1 The notion of historical distance has been problematized recently. See Phillips (2011) and the entire Theme Issue of *History and Theory* in which it appears.
2 See Ercikan et al. (2012) for a description of the scoring training and procedures.

References

Ashby, R., & Lee, P. (1987). Children's concepts of empathy and understanding in history. In C. Portal (Ed.), *The history curriculum for teachers* (pp. 62–88). London, UK: Falmer.

Carr, D., Flynn, T. R., & Makkreel, R. A. (Eds.). (2004). *The ethics of history*. Evanston, IL: Northwestern University Press.

College Board. (2014). Exam information: history and social sciences. www.apcentral. collegeboard.com

Davis, O. L., Yeager, E. A., & Foster, S. J. (Eds.). (2001). *Historical empathy and perspective taking in the social studies*. Oxford, UK: Rowman & Littlefield.

Eliasson, P., Alvén, F., Rosenlund, D., & Rudnert, J. (2012, January). *Historical consciousness in Sweden*. Paper presented at the Assessment of Historical Thinking Conference of the Historical Thinking Project, Toronto, ON.

Ercikan, K. (2006). Developments in assessment of student learning. In P. A. Alexander & P. H. Winne (Eds.), *Handbook of educational psychology* (2nd ed., pp. 929–953). Mahwah, NJ: Lawrence Erlbaum.

Ercikan, K., & Seixas, P. (2011). Assessment of higher order thinking: the case of historical thinking. In G. Schraw & D. H. Robinson (Eds.), *Assessment of higher order thinking skills* (pp. 245–261). Charlotte, NC: Information Age.

Ercikan, K., Seixas, P., Lyons-Thomas, J., & Gibson, L. (2012, April). *Designing and validating an assessment of historical thinking using evidence centered assessment design*. Paper presented at the American Educational Research Association, Vancouver, BC.

Fay, B. (2004). Historians and ethics: A short introduction to the theme issue. *History and Theory, 43*(4), 1–2.

Hou, C. (n.d.). Begbie Canadian History Contest. www.begbiecontestsociety.org/

Lee, P., & Ashby, R. (2000). Progression in historical understanding ages 7–14. In P. Stearns, P. Seixas, & S. S. Wineburg (Eds.), *Knowing, teaching, and learning history: National and international perspectives* (pp. 199–222). New York, NY: New York University Press.

Matts, T., & Charap, L. (2012, January). *Large-scale assessment of history in the United States*. Paper presented at the Assessment of Historical Thinking Conference of the Historical Thinking Project, Toronto, ON.

Monte-Sano, C., & Reisman, A. (forthcoming). Understanding history. In E. M. Anderman & L. Corno (Eds.), *Third handbook of educational psychology*. Mahwah, NJ: Lawrence Erlbaum.

National Research Council. (2001). *Knowing what students know: The science and design of educational assessment*. Pellegrino, J., Chudowsky, N., and Glaser, R. (Eds.). Washington, DC: National Academy Press.

Peck, C., & Seixas, P. (2008). Benchmarks of historical thinking: First steps. *Canadian Journal of Education, 31*(4), 1015–1038.

Phillips, M. S. (2011). Rethinking historical distance: From doctrine to heuristic. *History and Theory, 50*(4), 11–23.

Seixas, P. (1996). Conceptualizing the growth of historical understanding. In D. Olson & N. Torrance (Eds.), *Handbook of education and human development: New models of learning, teaching, and schooling* (pp. 765–783). Oxford, UK: Blackwell.

Seixas, P. (2010). A modest proposal for change in Canadian history education. *International Review of History Education, 6,* 11–26.

Wineburg, S. S. (1991). On the reading of historical texts: Notes on the breach between school and academy. *American Educational Research Journal, 28*(3), 495–519.

Wineburg, S. S., & Martin, D. (2009). Tampering with history: Adapting primary sources for struggling readers. *Social Education, 73*(5), 212–216.

APPENDIX 1

Cognition and Observation Table for *Evidence*

Student understanding	Observable behaviors	Tasks that could generate observable behaviors
1. Understands how history is an interpretation based on inferences from primary sources; Understands that traces, relics and records (primary sources) are not necessarily accounts.	Makes justifiable inferences from primary sources (both traces and accounts); Distinguishes between accounts and traces (primary sources).	Presented with an account and a trace: "what can you learn from these? How are they different?"
2. Asks questions that turn primary sources into evidence for an inquiry, argument or account.	Formulates questions to interpret a source; Interprets relevant information in support or against an argument.	Presented with a primary source: "write two questions that this source would help to answer." Presented with a series of the questions: "which would the source help to answer?"
3. Reads sources in view of the conditions and worldviews at the time when it was created (contextualization).	Articulates the role of material conditions (including technologies) and worldviews (context of the source) in interpreting events, actions, and motivations.	Presented with sources from situations foreign to our own (e.g., sultans killing their brothers, witches being burned, child labor), explain actions in terms of belief systems and conditions.

(Continued)

(Continued)

Student understanding	Observable behaviors	Tasks that could generate observable behaviors
4. Infers the conscious purposes of sources' authors/creators as well as their assumptions (sourcing).	Authors' purposes and assumptions are taken into account when interpreting sources.	Presented with source(s) and basic information about the author's background, use both to identify purposes and assumptions of the author.
5. Validates inferences from a single source with inferences from other sources (primary and secondary) and expresses degrees of certainty (corroboration).	Verifies and evaluates validity of inferences.	Presented with a single source and questions, what other documents/ sources would help to corroborate inferences/ interpretations?

APPENDIX 2

The Test's Five Primary Sources with Item Types and Two Final Constructed Response Items

Document 1: Attitudes towards Ukrainians 1899:
An interview with Reverend Father Moris in the Calgary *Daily Herald* 27 January 1899:
• Followed by three multiple-choice questions.

Document 2: American Report on the Internment of Enemy Aliens in Canada:
Under the terms of the 1907 Hague Convention, neutral governments were permitted to inspect the treatment of prisoners of war being held in enemy camps. American government representative **G. Willrich** reported on prisoners of war being held in a Canadian internment camp, 29 December 1916.
• Followed by two short answer questions.

Document 3: Signed Letter from Ukrainian Newspaper Editors:
This letter, signed by six Ukrainian Canadian newspaper editors, was published in the *Manitoba Free Press* (Winnipeg) 17 July 1916.
• Followed by two multiple-choice questions.

Document 4: Reasons for Internment:
A speech by the Honorable C. J. Doherty, Canada's Minister of Justice, House of Commons, 22 April 1918
• Followed by one short answer question.

Document 5: Letter from Child to Interned Father:
Katie Domytryk, 9, to H. Domytryk, internee #1100, arrested in Edmonton, March 1916, father of four.
• Followed by one multiple-choice question.

Final Constructed Response Questions:
Was the Canadian government justified in its policies towards Ukrainians during World War I? Discussing the contrasting perspectives in the documents, explain why or why not (one paragraph).

Does today's Canadian government have an obligation to make amends for internment of the Ukrainian Canadians during WWI? Why or why not? [Scaffolding was provided for students here.]

8

MATERIAL-BASED AND OPEN-ENDED WRITING TASKS FOR ASSESSING NARRATIVE COMPETENCE AMONG STUDENTS

Monika Waldis, Jan Hodel, Holger Thünemann, Meik Zülsdorf-Kersting, and Béatrice Ziegler

Introduction

Narrativity is considered as a structural principle of historical thinking and learning (Baumgartner, 1997). In order to understand the (deep) structure of historical narratives or perform historical reconstruction as a coherent narrative, narrative competence is necessary. In recent years, history educators throughout Austria, Germany, and Switzerland have developed several competency models describing core aspects of historical thinking (Gautschi, 2009; Körber, Schreiber, & Schöner, 2007; Pandel, 2005). However, the conceptualization of narrative competence remains vague and there is a lack of empirically valid criteria by which narrative performance can be assessed. This paper presents a model of historical thinking which distinguishes among four different sub-operations of narrative competence and reports on a study designed to test this model empirically.[1] The task design and scoring procedures used in this study have broader implications for assessments of historical thinking.

Theoretical Background

In their attempt to define the specific nature of historical learning and thinking, many history educators and researchers follow Jörn Rüsen's definition of creating meaning through experiencing time in the form of a historical narrative (Rüsen, 2008, p. 62). Rüsen stresses the active reconstruction of history as the core of engagement with history and the past. However, other approaches emphasize the independence of de-constructive (i.e., analytic) acts for the purpose of historical orientation (Hasberg, 2013) or emphasize the interaction between synthetic (constructive) and analytic (deconstructive) processes. Building on Rüsen's "disciplinary matrix" of historiography (Rüsen, 1993, p. 162), Hasberg and Körber (2003) describe two basic operations of historical thinking: the ability to develop historical narratives and the ability to comprehend and critically question the (deep) structure of existing historical narratives for recognizing and developing one's own notions of and attitudes towards the past.

Based on the theoretical contributions of Rüsen (1983, 1993, 2004), Jeismann (1978, 2000), Gautschi (2009), and Hasberg and Körber (2003), we define narrative competence as the interaction among four corresponding sub-operations, all of which apply to both synthetic and analytic processes:

- A historical thought process begins with formulating historical questions. They are characterized by temporality in "that they take into account the connection between the interpretation of the past, an understanding of the present, and a future perspective" (Thünemann, 2013, p. 147; see Thünemann, 2010, pp. 50–51). The choice of historical questions leads to the construction of a perspective from which the past can be seen. Ideally, historical questions reveal both: the inquirers' epistemological interest, which is influenced by the present, and his/her underlying desire for orientation in the present and in the future.
- In a second sub-operation, based on historical sources and accounts, factual historical analyses are developed or reviewed in terms of the guiding question: how did a historical event most probably take place? The choice of historical facts must be substantiated by references to historical sources and has to take multiple perspectives into account. Historical facts remain falsifiable.
- A third sub-operation focuses on developing or reviewing factual historical judgments. The process of forming such judgments establishes logical (e.g., causal, temporal, modal) relationships among factual-analytical findings.
- The—forever temporary—endpoints of historical thinking are historical value judgments. Rüsen refers to this sub-operation of historical thinking as "historical orientation" (Thünemann, 2013, p. 147–148; see Jeismann, 2000, p. 64; Rüsen, 2008, pp. 67–68; Schönemann, Thünemann, & Zülsdorf-Kersting, 2011, pp. 66–68). Historical value judgments, which always ought to be preceded by factual historical judgments, are meant to reflect the norms, premises, and perspectives of historical evaluation.

These four operations of historical thinking draw on different forms of knowledge and can have both analytical and synthetic features (Hodel, Waldis, Zülsdorf-Kersting, & Thünemann, 2013, p. 126; Zülstorf-Kersting, 2010, p. 46). This chapter explains a design for assessing historical thinking empirically on the basis of this model.

Research Questions

Given the central role of narrative in defining historical thinking competence, our study investigated the structure and quality of student narratives in response to a history assessment task. It aimed to provide an empirical method to gain insights into students' historical thinking competence. We pursued two main directions in studying such narratives: First, we identified the central elements indicative of historical thinking following our above model. This approach aimed to determine how narrative *structures* (i.e., the presence of the above sub-operations) reflect competent thinking and how such thinking can be evidenced. Second, we assessed the subject-specific *quality* of student narratives and how such assessment allows one to evaluate narrative competence. Our main research questions were:

1   Which sub-operations of historical thinking are evident in student texts?
2   How many texts in our sample provide evidence of all four thought operations, or rather in which of these texts is one or are several categories of historical thinking missing?
3   Can such texts be assessed qualitatively in terms of previously defined feature-related criteria and, if so, which quality features are evident?
4   Is there a connection between the occurrence of historical sub-operations and the qualitative assessment of texts?
5   Considering the writing context: to what extent do the topics or the writing prompts influence the narrative performance demonstrated in the students' texts (e.g., occurrence of elements of historical thinking and the quality features of student texts)?

Method

Instruments: To assess students' historical thinking, a task that asked students to produce a historical narrative based on a selection of sources was developed. Two thematic test booklets were devised: (1) "Trade Relations between Japan and Europe" during the sixteenth and seventeenth centuries, and (2) "The Nazi Boycott of Jewish Businesses" in 1933. Whereas the first topic is seldom taught in schools, the latter is usually integrated into the broader topic of "National Socialism and World War II." Both test booklets followed the same structure: Part I contained some general questions assessing subject interest, academic self-concept in history, and epistemological beliefs about history. Part II included selected historical sources and accounts that illuminated different aspects of each topic accompanied by three-step directions for the students to follow: (1) Please scan the material; (2) formulate at least three questions about the material; (3) choose three items from the material and decide whether these are historical sources or accounts. The third task highlighted one aspect of dealing with historical materials. Part III invited students to write a text using the materials provided. Three types of text were suggested, each oriented toward real-world writing scenarios for young people and each with a clear target audience: (1) Please prepare a text that could be used for a panel discussion; (2) write an article for your school newspaper; or (3) write a "blog entry." Part IV asked students to reflect on their writing process with closed-ended questions and to provide some personal details (age, sex, educational status of students' families measured with the "Book"-item, first language, etc.).

Sample: The sample included 193 students from nine classes from three different towns (Aarau, Münster, and Osnabrück) in Switzerland and Germany. The teachers (and classes) participating in the test were either known personally to the researchers or contact was established by a trusted source. There were four grade 9 classes, three grade 10, and two grade 11 classes. Thus, students were 15 to 17 years old. With one exception, the test classes belonged to the highest track. 53.8% of the students were female; 58.6% of students' families owned more than a hundred books, which indicated a rather high educational background; 82.8% of students spoke German as their mother tongue.

Test administration: Students were tested within a regular 90-minute history class. The tests were conducted by the authors of this article and their research staff. Students received the test booklet at the beginning of the lesson and were allowed to work through it at their own pace. Half of the students in each class completed the "Japanese" test booklet, the other half the "National Socialism" test booklet.

Analysis of open-ended student texts: The handwritten student texts were copied into a digital file. The original spelling and punctuation were preserved. Data analysis involved two methods: content analysis (Mayring, 2007) and high-inference rating (Clausen, Reusser, & Klieme, 2003):

Content analysis: A categorizing procedure was adopted to identify the argumentative pattern and constituent elements of each narrative. The coding unit was the sentence. Following our model presented above, four sub-operations of historical thinking were distinguished and coded: (1) dealing with historical questions; (2) dealing with historical facts; (3) dealing with factual historical judgments; and (4) dealing with historical value judgments. After piloting the four categories on empirical material, we changed "(2) dealing with historical facts" (a code that was not manageable) to the code, "referring to historical materials" where students' narratives refer explicitly to any sources or accounts provided. Table 8.1 shows the categories applied.

The first coding step was followed by a second step, in which a generalizing code called "text focus" was applied to the entire text to identify its main message, such as (1) developing a historical question, (2) developing a historical analysis, (3) developing a historical judgment, (4) developing a historical value judgment, or (5) no clear main message.

Student narratives were coded by three qualified student teachers from the University of Osnabrück. Several codes could be allocated to a single sentence. Before their coding assignment, the student teachers received specific training,

TABLE 8.1 Historical thinking: Categories, descriptors, and indicators

Category	Description	Indicators/Examples
Dealing with historical questions	Asking historical questions aimed at establishing a fact, a factual judgment, or a value judgment	Direct questions, such as "Why is Japan willfully obstructive?" Sentence beginnings, such as "I ask myself . . ., we need to ask . . ., I am surprised that . . ." Indirect questions such as "Whether x actually influenced y . . . would require further research."
Referring to historical materials	Identifying references to historical materials	Citations or paraphrases indicating a specific source/account. References that reveal the use of concrete information contained in the materials. For instance, "As Hitler's statements about the situation of Jewish shop owners show . . ."
Dealing with factual historical judgment	Describing a relationship using an argumentative pattern	Occurrence of argumentative patterns, such as causal (x was the reason for y), instrumental (x was a means for achieving y), attributional (x was part of y, belonged to), comparative (x was similar to y), etc. Example: "One reason why the Japanese were hostile to the Portuguese, is that they were stingy, what has made them hated by the Japanese."
Dealing with historical value judgment	Assessing historical facts or circumstances from a present-day perspective. Formulating conclusions serving present and future orientation	Judgmental statements such as "For these ancestors we should be honestly ashamed." This code in particular was conceived in broad terms by also subsuming sentences containing judgmental adjectives.

during which additional student texts from five other classes were used to develop and apply the coding scheme, and to examine inter-rater reliability. After intensive training, the three coders achieved satisfactory inter-rater reliability values (percentage agreement ≥ .80; Cohen's Kappa ≥ .75) in applying the categories described in Table 8.1. The application of the general code "text focus" was carried out by consensus between coders. This means that the decision for a particular code was based on comprehensive discussion between the three.

High-inference rating: A third step consisted of high-inference, expert ratings, to assess seven quality features identified in the literature as significant for historical narratives (Bergmann, 1997; Hartung, 2013; Pandel, 2010; Rüsen, Fröhlich, Horstkötter, & Schmidt, 1991; Schönemann, Thünemann & Zülsdorf-Kersting,

2011). These aspects are linked to our above model: the "quality of making historical references" as a part of factual historical analysis; "factual correctness" as a part of factual historical analysis and historical judgment and "normative cogency" as a part of historical value judgment. Ratings applied to an entire narrative. The narratives were rated using a four-point ordinal scale from 0 to 3 indicating different quality levels. This approach enabled the inclusion of information scattered across a text or spanning several sentences in the overall assessment. Three history education researchers (Jan Hodel, Holger Thünemann, and Meik Zülsdorf-Kersting) served as rating experts. The rating was conducted using a partial sample consisting of 52 randomly selected student narratives. To determine rater reliability, a generalizability coefficient Ep^2 was calculated, taking into account the estimated variance components of text, rater, and a residual component (Webb, Shavelson, & Haertel, 2006). On balance, reliability proved to be satisfactory to good, with values of $\geq .68$ for each quality feature (See Table 8.2).

TABLE 8.2 Expert ratings: reliability values for the rating of individual quality features

Quality feature	Questions for assessing individual quality features	Ep^2
Quality of making historical references	Are there references to several materials (with author references, title, material number) that substantiate the core statement(s) of the narrative?	.87
Coherence of historical thinking	Is there evidence of joined-up historical thinking, which supports and amounts to a coherent and convincing overall narrative statement?	.99
Linguistic cohesion	Does the narrative have a sophisticated linguistic structure, does it contain numerous cohesive features (e.g., conjunctions, topic-comment links, interrelated terms and concepts, etc.), and a line of argument of high quality?	.77
Factual correctness	Are the statements consistently correct and empirically cogent?	.76
Normative cogency	Are value judgments substantiated and does such substantiation include both explanations of the standards applied and place-specific reflection?	.72
Terminological clarity	Instead of using everyday terms, does the writer make correct use of technical terms and categories occurring in the materials, or of other technical terms, and is terminological reflection evident?	.77
Dealing with concepts	Is there evidence of an elaborated, abstracting, and well-structured approach to naming historical actors (individuals, groups, e.g., priests, Jewish traders, Nazis) and institutions (government, NSDAP)?	.68

Notes: $n = 52$ texts. The variance components to determine generalizability coefficients Ep^2 were calculated by SPSS "varcomp" command using REML procedure.

Results

Text Length and Text Type

186 students from a total of 193 students wrote a narrative text. Text length varied between one sentence and 33 sentences. The average length was 11.4 sentences (SD = 5.74). 16.1% of students wrote a text for a panel discussion, 29.0% wrote a blog, 34.7% wrote a student newspaper article, and 19.7% chose no explicit text format. There was no association between text types and the chosen topic.

Students' Historical Thinking: Categorization Results

Below we consider whether and how far historical thinking was evident in the student narratives investigated. Table 8.3 shows that four fifths of the texts contained one or several references to materials and that most texts included factual historical and value judgments. Asking historical questions was less frequent; approximately half of the texts contained no historical question.

In this respect, two aspects of the narratives studied were considered: first, instances of creating historical meaning; second, the combination of such instances. 36.6% of the texts combined a historical question, a factual judgment, and a value judgment, 31.2% contained factual judgments and value judgments. Evidence of other category combinations or the use of only one category was found in a smaller number of texts: historical question and value judgment (7.5%), historical question and factual judgment (4.3%), value judgment (9.1%), factual judgment (6.5%), historical question (2.2%), and no elements of historical thinking (2.7%).

TABLE 8.3 Evidence of historical thinking in narratives (frequency and percentages)

Number of sentences	*References to materials* Number of texts (in %)	*Historical questions* Number of texts (in %)	*Factual historical judgments* Number of texts (in %)	*Value judgments* Number of texts (in %)
0	36 (19.4)	92 (49.5)	40 (21.5)	29 (15.6)
1	41 (22.0)	24 (12.9)	33 (17.7)	37 (19.9)
2	46 (23.8)	26 (14.0)	38 (20.4)	32 (17.2)
3	41 (21.2)	25 (13.4)	29 (15.6)	23 (12.4)
4	15 (7.8)	5 (2.7)	24 (12.9)	21 (11.3)
5	5 (2.6)	5 (2.7)	9 (4.8)	19 (10.2)
6	1 (0.5)	2 (1.1)	5 (2.7)	10 (5.4)
More than 6	1 (0.5)	7 (2.2)	8 (4.3)	15 (8.1)
Total texts	*186 (100.0)*	*186 (100.0)*	*186 (100.0)*	*186 (100.0)*

Determining the overarching "text focus" revealed that a considerable number of narratives amounted to a value judgment (37.6%). A further 22.6% focused on developing historical facts. 13.9% of the texts focused on the development of historical judgments. Evidence for shaping the argument with a view to developing a historical question was found in only a few texts. In 15% of the texts, the resulting overall statement lacked an unequivocal focus. 5.4% of the texts showed no evidence of historical questions, historical judgments, or value judgments. As a rule, such texts consisted of one to two sentences.

Quality Features: High Inference Ratings

The high inference ratings by experts of six quality features were conducted on a partial sample of 52 survey sheets, which were drawn randomly from the overall sample. Table 8.4 lists the descriptive characteristics and the correlations between the quality aspects. The mean values of each category indicate that *normative cogency* is assessed most critically compared to the other categories. Thus, student narratives frequently fell short of quality standards in this respect. By comparison, *linguistic cohesion, quality of making historical references*, and *factual correctness* were rated more positively. Quality features were systematically correlated, except for the relationship between normative cogency and quality of making historical references.

Correlations between quality features and sub-operations of historical thinking in Table 8.5 show the correlations between high-inference, expert-rated quality features and sub-operations of historical thinking. As suspected, the *quality of making historical references* coincided with the number of references to materials. Moderate correlations were found between historical questions, factual judgments, value judgments, and the expert-rated *coherence of historical thinking*. *Normative cogency* was linked both to the frequency of asking historical questions and to the statement of value judgments, but not to the frequency of factual judgments. Overall, the correlations between quality features and the categories of historical thinking met expectations.

Making Sense of History: National Socialism Versus Japan

Below we discuss to what degree the topic of the test booklets—National Socialism (core curriculum) versus Japan (non-core)—was related to the frequency of the four historical thinking operations and the quality features studied. Univariate variance analyses of the differences between the occurrence of various categories, such as the number of references to materials, the number of texts with historical questions, and factual judgments, revealed no significant topic-related difference. However, historical value judgments were more frequent in student narratives about National Socialism than about Japan [$M_{\text{Japan}} = 2.28$,

TABLE 8.4 Descriptive characteristics and quality feature correlations

	M (SD)	Min./Max.	Quality of references	Coherence of historical thinking	Linguistic cohesion	Normative cogency	Terminological clarity	Factual correctness
Quality of references	1.07 (.75)	0/2.67	–					
Coherence of historical thinking	0.91 (.71)	0/2.33	.44**					
Linguistic cohesion	1.12 (.67)	0/2.67	.39**	.89**				
Normative cogency	0.38 (.56)	0/2.00	–.09	.43**	.50**			
Terminological clarity	0.58 (.58)	0/2.00	.38**	.77**	.80**	.49**		
Factual correctness	1.40 (.79)	0/3.00	.42**	.81**	.80**	.40**	.71**	
Dealing with concepts	.47 (.48)	0/1.67	.46**	.63**	.68**	.24	.60**	.58**

Notes: 0 = does not apply/non-existent; 1 = does rather not apply/hardly recognizable; 2 = somewhat applies/recognizable; 3 = applies completely/clearly recognizable; n = 52. Pearson correlation r, $p < .05*$, $p < .01**$.

TABLE 8.5 Correlations between quality features and the frequency of historical thinking

	Number of materials	Historical questions	Factual historical judgment	Historical value judgment
Quality of references	.69**	.07	.45**	.24
Coherence of historical thinking	.42**	.47**	.37**	.38**
Linguistic cohesion	.40**	.35*	.35*	.37**
Normative cogency	−.16	.40**	−.07	.41**
Terminological clarity	.39**	.23	.29*	.15
Factual correctness	.41**	.31*	.35*	.29*
Dealing with concepts	.32*	.04	.40**	.13

Note: Correlative findings based on Pearson's r, $p < .05*$, $p < .01**$.

$SD = 3.11$; $M_{\text{National Socialism}} = 3.56$, $SD = 3.11$ ($F = 11.39$, $df = 184$, $p < .01$)]. The topic-related difference is significant. As regards text-focus distribution, dealing with historical facts ranked first in narratives about Japan, followed by value judgments and factual judgments, whereas the overall statement of more than half of the narratives about National Socialism (26.3% of all texts) amounted to value judgments, while the other text focuses were considerably less frequent. The varying distribution of the text focuses by topic is significant (chi² = 19.22, $p < .01$). By contrast, no topic-related differences between the combinations of historical thinking operations were found. Nor did the univariate variance analyses of the dependency between quality features and topic reveal any statistically significant differences.

Influence of Text Format on the Narrative Performance

The choice of text format coincides with statistically significant differences as regards the number of references ($F_{3, 185} = 4.88$, $p < .01$) and the frequency of value judgments ($F_{3, 185} = 5.89$, $p < .01$). More references to historical materials were found in contributions to student newspapers ($M = 2.40$, $SD = 1.50$) than in blog texts ($M = 1.69$, $SD = 1.15$) or in texts with an unspecific format ($M = 1.42$, $SD = 1.37$; Bonferroni Post-Hoc-Test, $p < .05$). Historical value judgments were more frequent in panel discussion texts ($M = 3.83$, $SD = 3.50$) and blog texts ($M = 3.62$, $SD = 2.72$) than in texts with an unspecific format ($M = 1.55$, $SD = 1.79$; Bonferroni Post-Hoc-Test, $p < .05$). The various text formats differed significantly as regards the coherence of historical thinking, linguistic cohesion, terminological clarity, and factual correctness (Table 8.6).

TABLE 8.6 Mean, standard deviation, and *F*-statistic for multivariate analysis of variance investigating differences of quality features according to text format

	Panel discussion	Blog	Student newspaper	Unspecified text format	ANOVA F-statistic	Bonferroni Post-Hoc-Test
	M (SD)	M (SD)	M (SD)	M (SD)	F, p	p < .05
Quality of references	1.10 (.76)	1.24 (.83)	1.05 (.76)	.83 (.65)	.59 n.s.	–
Coherence of historical thinking	1.43 (.74)	.62 (.42)	1.18 (.65)	.43 (.74)	5.89**	PD > B, UTF SN > UTF
Linguistic cohesion	1.52 (.54)	.96 (.43)	1.33 (.58)	.63 (.90)	4.28**	PD > UTF SN > UTF
Normative cogency	.62 (.65)	.51 (.68)	.30 (.49)	.17 (.32)	.27 n.s.	–
Terminological clarity	1.20 (.79)	.38 (.38)	.68 (.50)	.27 (.49)	5.58**	PD > B, UTF
Factual correctness	1.81 (.92)	1.15 (.60)	1.70 (.64)	.87 (.91)	4.24*	SN > UTF
Dealing with concepts	.57 (.63)	.36 (.32)	.58 (.51)	.37 (.51)	.92 n.s.	–

Notes: Bonferroni Post-Hoc-Test: $p < .05$.

Discussion

The student narratives investigated in our pilot study are very heterogeneous. One case in point is text length, which varies from one to 33 sentences. Considerable differences also exist with regard to structure and content. We attempted to categorize the texts in terms of their narrative structure and to assess their quality, so as to obtain empirically supported insights into students' historical competence. Of particular interest was whether the topic (core curriculum: National Socialism; non-core: Japan) and the writing prompt (contribution to panel discussion, blog, or student newspaper) were associated with the competencies evident in the texts. Details on these two factors provide insight into the genesis of historical student narratives and are likely to be important for developing future tests.

Analysis first considered the number of references to historical materials and how students approached historical questions, factual judgments, and value judgments on the level of the "sentence" (the basic coding unit). Such aspects were evident in most texts and missing only in a few cases. Equally, references to historical materials occurred in most texts, suggesting that students used the sources and documents provided. Since narratives include more than just information gathered on any single sub-dimension, expert ratings (by history education researchers) were used to determine the occurrence of the key quality features (which refer to a text as a whole). Expert-rated features exhibited rather low scores, with none of the features attaining or exceeding a mean value of 1.4 (between 1, "hardly recognizable," and 2, "recognizable"). This quality-related finding points to the untapped potential of history education, particularly as regards developing both historical understanding and individual competencies through writing processes. Thus, the low scores for normative cogency suggest that students urgently need to be taught how to construct well-founded value judgments. This concern seems even more pressing given that the vast majority of texts (84.4%) include value judgments and that more than half (64.5%) contain more than one value judgment. Quality ratings provided no evidence that confirmed the assumption that the careful deduction and substantiation of value judgments was less frequent and less painstaking in narratives about the "Nazi Boycott," due to the familiarity and over-determined (that is, a widely shared consensus of opinion that appears not to need careful, evidence-supported argument) status of this topic, than in narratives about Japan. Over-determined value judgments and a lack of critical reflection were equally frequently found in student narratives about Japan. However, historical thinking scores indicate that value judgments are more frequent in texts about National Socialism. Thus, whereas the topics were treated using differently structured patterns of argument, the quality of these arguments seems equally low.

The absence of significant differences between the quality of texts about "National Socialism," a topic firmly anchored in the school curriculum and in historical culture, and those about "Trade Relations between Japan and Europe" suggests that previous knowledge has only a marginal influence on grade 9–11 student narratives. Nevertheless, caution seems warranted. Possibly, the unfamiliar task format, which required students to produce a historical narrative including historical sources and accounts, prevented students writing about National Socialism and drawing on their previous knowledge from developing a more sophisticated argumentative structure than those writing about Japan. Another reason could be that students were already so familiar with the historical facts, factual judgments, and socially desirable value judgments about National Socialism (Meseth, Proske, & Radtke, 2004) that they considered close scrutiny of the sources and accounts no longer necessary for a cogent narrative. Future studies using material-based, open-ended writing tasks to understand narrative competence need to take into account that such an overly familiar topic as National Socialism possibly is of limited value in encouraging an investigative-exploratory use of materials in a test situation, that is, to enabling students to demonstrate their narrative competence.

Our pilot study provides insights about how larger samples of student texts might be dealt with. Instead of adopting a hermeneutic approach to interpreting student texts (Barricelli, 2005), we used a categorizing approach, aimed at stocktaking, and a qualifying approach, aimed at high-inference quality assessment by experts. However, the narratives still await exhaustive analysis. While we have certain notions of the narrative linkages permitted by the selected materials, and of the structural and propositional logic underlying those materials, content-related patterns of argument still need to be identified. Moreover, it would be interesting to work out typical sense-making patterns or the levels of causal explanations for history (Voss & Carretero, 2000).

Using open-ended, material-based writing tasks in future surveys involves considering whether using such a large number of materials (four and seven respectively), as in the pilot study, is both necessary and feasible. Restricting future studies to a few materials might limit the variance of argumentative structures, and thereby facilitate content determination and comparative assessment. Besides, the results of the pilot study as regards the influence of the text format suggest that task formulation requires careful consideration. Thus, using the "blog" as a format to satisfy methodological requirements, such as making explicit references to materials, proved misleading. "Casual" blog-style texts could not compete against "serious" narratives written for panel discussions and student newspapers. This finding is problematic for comparative analyses. Overall, our pilot study strongly indicates that both materials selection and task formulation present considerable challenges and require careful consideration.

Using source-based, open-ended writing tasks to understand historical competence in the area of "large-scale assessment" will probably remain complex. We are convinced, however, that this approach will send a strong message to practitioners, not only to encourage doing history in this way but also to use the diagnostic potential inherent in individual narratives for school-based processes of understanding.

Note

1 The main results of this study have already appeared in a German-speaking Journal for Didactics of Social Sciences (Hodel, Waldis, Zülsdorf-Kersting, Thünemann, 2013). For the purpose of this article, data analysis was expanded.

References

Barricelli, M. (2005). *Schüler erzählen Geschichte. Narrative Kompetenz im Geschichtsunterricht.* Schwalbach/Ts., Germany: Wochenschau Verlag.

Baumgartner, H. M. (1997). Narrativität. In K. Bergmann, K. Fröhlich, & A. Kuhn (Eds.), *Handbuch der Geschichtsdidaktik. 5. Auflage* (pp. 157–160). Seelze-Velber, Germany: Kallmeyer.

Bergmann, K. (1997). Personalisierung, Personifizierung. In K. Bergmann, K. Fröhlich, & A. Kuhn (Eds.), *Handbuch der Geschichtsdidaktik, 5. Auflage* (pp. 298–300). Seelze-Velber, Germany: Kallmeyer.

Clausen, M., Reusser, K., & Klieme, E. (2003). Unterrichtsqualität auf der Basis hochinferenter Unterrichtsbeurteilungen. Ein Vergleich zwischen Deutschland und der deutschsprachigen Schweiz. [Using high-inference ratings to assess quality of instruction. A comparison between Germany and the German speaking part of Switzerland.] *Unterrichtswissenschaft, 31*(2), 122–141.

Gautschi, P. (2009). *Guter Geschichtsunterricht. Grundlagen, Erkenntnisse, Hinweise.* Schwalbach/Ts., Germany: Wochenschau Verlag.

Hartung, O. (2013). *Geschichte Schreiben Lernen. Empirische Erkundungen zum konzeptionellen Schreibhandeln im Geschichtsunterricht.* Berlin, Germany: Lit-Verlag.

Hasberg, W. (2013). Jutta oder Johanna—oder wer macht hier Geschichte(n)? Grundlegende Bemerkungen zur Narrativität historischen Lernens. *Zeitschrift für Didaktik der Gesellschaftswissenschaften/Journal for Didactics of Social Sciences, 4*(2), 55–82.

Hasberg, W., & Körber, A. (2003). Geschichtsbewusstsein dynamisch. In A. Körber (Ed.), *Geschichte—Leben—Lernen. Bodo v. Borries zum 60. Geburtstag* (pp. 177–200). Schwalbach Ts., Germany: Wochenschau Verlag.

Hodel, J., Waldis, M., Zülsdorf-Kersting, M., & Thünemann, H. (2013). Schülernarrationen als Ausdruck historischer Kompetenz. *Zeitschrift für Didaktik der Gesellschaftswissenschaften/Journal for Didactics of Social Sciences, 4*(2), 121–145.

Jeismann, K.-E. (1978). Grundfragen des Geschichtsunterrichts. In G. C. Behrmann, K.-E. Jeismann, & H. Süssmuth (Eds.), *Geschichte und Politik. Didaktische Grundlegung eines kooperativen Unterrichts* (pp. 76–107). Paderborn, Germany: Schöningh.

Jeismann, K.-E. (2000). Geschichtsbewusstsein als zentrale Kategorie der Didaktik des Geschichtsunterrichts. In K.-E. Jeismann (Ed.), *Geschichte und Bildung: Beiträge zur Geschichtsdidaktik und zur Historischen Bildungsforschung* (pp. 46–72). Paderborn, Germany: Schöningh.

Körber, A., Schreiber, W., & Schöner A. (Eds.). (2007). *Kompetenzen historischen Denkens. Ein Strukturmodell als Beitrag zur Kompetenzorientierung in der Geschichtsdidaktik.* Neuried, Germany: Ars Una.

Mayring, P. (2007). *Qualitative Inhaltsanalyse. Grundlagen und Techniken.* Weinheim/Basel, Switzerland: Beltz.

Meseth, W., Proske, M., & Radtke, F. O. (2004). *Schule und Nationalsozialismus. Anspruch und Grenzen des Geschichtsunterrichts.* Frankfurt/Main, Germany: Campus.

Pandel, H.-J. (2005). *Geschichtsunterricht nach PISA. Kompetenzen, Bildungsstandards und Kerncurricula.* Schwalbach/Ts., Germany: Wochenschau Verlag.

Pandel, H.-J. (2010). *Historisches Erzählen. Narrativität im Geschichtsunterricht,* Schwalbach/Ts., Germany: Wochenschau Verlag.

Rüsen, J. (1983). *Historische Vernunft. Grundzüge einer Historik I: Die Grundlagen der Geschichtswissenschaft.* Göttingen, Germany: Vandenhoeck & Ruprecht.

Rüsen, J. (1993). *Studies in Metahistory.* Pretoria, South Africa: Human Sciences Research Council.

Rüsen, J. (2004). Historical Consciousness: Narrative Structure, Moral Function and Ontogenetic Development. In P. Seixas (Ed.), *Theorizing Historical Consciousness* (pp. 61–85). Toronto, ON: University of Toronto Press.

Rüsen, J. (2008). *Historisches Lernen. Grundlagen und Paradigmen, 2. Auflage.* Schwalbach/Ts., Germany: Wochenschau Verlag.

Rüsen, J., Fröhlich, K., Horstkötter, H., & Schmidt, H. (1991). Untersuchungen zum Geschichtsbewußtsein von Abiturienten im Ruhrgebiet. In B. von Borries, H.-J. Pandel, & J. Rüsen (Eds.), *Geschichtsbewußtsein empirisch* (pp. 221–344). Pfaffenweiler, Germany: Centaurus.

Schönemann, B., Thünemann, H., & Zülsdorf-Kersting, M. (2011). *Was können Abiturienten? Zugleich ein Beitrag zur Debatte über Kompetenzen und Standards im Fach Geschichte*, 2. Auflage. Berlin, Germany: Lit Verlag.

Thünemann, H. (2010). Geschichtsunterricht ohne Geschichte? Überlegungen und empirische Befunde zu historischen Fragen im Geschichtsunterricht und im Schulgeschichtsbuch. In S. Handro & B. Schönemann (Eds.), *Geschichte und Sprache* (pp. 49–59). Berlin, Germany: Lit Verlag.

Thünemann, H. (2013). Historische Lernaufgaben. Theoretische Überlegungen, empirische Befunde und forschungspragmatische Perspektiven. *Zeitschrift für Geschichtsdidaktik, 12*, 141–155.

Voss, J. F. & Carretero, M. (2000). *Learning and Reasoning in History: International Review of History Education*. London, UK: Routledge.

Webb, N. M., Shavelson, R. J., & Haertel, E. H. (2006). Reliability Coefficients and Generalizability Theory. In C. R. Rao (Ed.), *Handbook of Statistics*, Vol. 26 (Volume on Psychometrics; pp. 81–124). Amsterdam, The Netherlands: Elsevier.

Zülsdorf-Kersting, M. (2010). Kategorien historischen Denkens und Praxis der Unterrichtsanalyse. *Zeitschrift für Geschichtsdidaktik, 9*, 36–56.Table 8.2 (Continued)

COMMENTARY

Historical Thinking: In Search of Conceptual and Practical Guidance for the Design and Use of Assessments of Student Competence[1]

Josh Radinsky, Susan R. Goldman, James W. Pellegrino

The four papers in this section all attempt to clarify the nature of historical thinking for purposes of assessing students' disciplinary competence. Each details the design of assessments and their interpretive use, spanning educational contexts from classroom practices to international assessments. These papers make valuable contributions to the field, highlighting many conceptual and practical considerations needed to advance the assessment of historical thinking.

Our discussion is divided into three parts. Part 1 presents three conceptual frames regarding the nature of assessment and assessment design, providing an interpretive language for discussing the four chapters. Part 2 applies these frames to the chapters as a way to interpret the specifics of each case. Part 3 highlights challenges that remain in conceptualizing and operationalizing the assessment of historical reasoning.

Part 1: Three Conceptual Frames

We suggest three conceptual frames for analyzing the contributions of the chapters in this section: (1) the "C-I-A"; (2) assessment as evidentiary reasoning; and (3) evidence-centered design.

The "C-I-A": Curriculum, Instruction, and Assessment

Assessment does not and should not stand alone in the educational system. Rather, it is one of three coordinated components—curriculum, instruction, and assessment. *Curriculum* refers to knowledge and skills in subject matter areas that teachers teach and students are supposed to learn. It generally consists of a scope of content in a given subject area and a sequence for learning. *Instruction* refers to methods of teaching and the learning activities used to help students master the content and objectives specified by a curriculum. *Assessment* is the means used to measure the outcomes of education and students' achievements with regard to important competencies. Assessment may include large-scale formal methods (e.g., state or national assessments) or less formal classroom-based procedures (e.g., quizzes, class projects, and teacher questioning). Ideally, an assessment should measure what students are actually being taught, and what is taught should parallel the curriculum one wants students to master. Aligning the three components is often a challenge; each chapter in this section addresses this challenge in a different way.

Assessment as Evidentiary Reasoning

Assessment enables educators to learn about what students know and can do, but cannot offer a direct window into a student's mind. An assessment is a tool designed to observe students' behaviors, in order to produce data that can be used to draw reasonable inferences about what students know. In the process of generating and interpreting evidence to support inferences about what students know, all assessment procedures operate from a chain of reasoning about learning. This is true for classroom quizzes, standardized achievement tests, computerized tutoring programs, and even the conversation between student and teacher as they work through a problem together or discuss the meaning of a historical text.

This process of reasoning from evidence has been portrayed as a triad of three interconnected elements: the *assessment triangle* (Pellegrino, Chudowsky, & Glaser, 2001). The vertices represent three key elements underlying any assessment: a model of student *cognition* and learning in the domain of the assessment; a set of assumptions and principles about the kinds of *observations* that will provide evidence of students' competencies; and an *interpretation* process for making sense of the evidence. For effective and valid assessment, the three elements must be in synchrony.

The assessment triangle provides a useful framework for analyzing the underpinnings of assessments to determine how well they accomplish intended goals, for designing assessments, and for establishing their validity (e.g., Marion & Pellegrino, 2006). Each of the elements of the triangle must make sense on its own, and must connect meaningfully to each of the other two to lead to an effective assessment and sound inferences. Central to this process are theoretically grounded and empirically supported understandings of how students learn, what students know as they develop competence, and how students' performances reflect these competencies. Such considerations are reflected differently in each chapter in this section.

Evidence-Centered Design

The design of an actual assessment is a challenging endeavor that must be guided by theory and research about cognition in context, as well as practical prescriptions regarding the processes that lead to productive and potentially valid assessments for particular contexts of use. Design is always a complex process that applies theory and research to achieve near-optimal solutions under multiple constraints, some of which are outside the realm of science. Assessment design is influenced in important ways by variables such as its purpose (e.g., to assist learning, to measure individual attainment, or to evaluate a program); the context in which it will be used (e.g., classroom, district, or international-comparative); and practical constraints (e.g., resources and time).

Recognizing that assessment is an evidentiary reasoning process, it is useful to consider this process of creating assessments as *evidence-centered design* (Mislevy & Haertel, 2006; Mislevy & Riconscente, 2006). The process starts by defining the claims that one wants to be able to make about student knowledge in a disciplinary domain, such as particular historical thinking abilities, epistemological stances, or recall of historical facts. It is critical that these claims about disciplinary-learning targets be specified as precisely as possible, using verbs that afford assessment, rather than vague, high-level cognitive superordinate verbs such as "know" and "understand." Example verbs might include *compare, describe, analyze, elaborate, explain, predict,* or *justify.* Guiding this process of specifying claims is a body of theory and research on domain-specific knowing and learning.

Each claim about a student's mastery of some aspect of disciplinary thinking must also be linked (by warrants or rules of interpretation) to the forms of evidence that would provide support for such a claim. The *evidence statements* associated with given claims capture the features of students' performances that would substantiate the claims. This includes which features need to be present and how they are weighted—what matters most and what matters least or not at all. The tasks need to allow students to "show what they know" in a way that is as unambiguous as possible. The precision that comes from elaborating these claim-evidence statements pays off when designing assessments, because it is clear what forms of evidence the task design needs to produce if it is to support the intended range of claims. These criteria determine the inferences about student cognition that are permissible and sustainable from a given set of assessment tasks or items. The chapters in this section differ in the ways they balance these criteria, and in their approaches to incorporating evidence into assessment design.

Part 2: Consideration of the Four Chapters

Our comments on the chapters reflect our analysis from the perspective of each of these three conceptual frames: C-I-A, evidentiary reasoning, and evidence-centered design. Key questions are what we want students to know and be able to do as learners of history, and how the knowledge and skills develop over time with appropriate curriculum and instruction. Assessment serves the function of making explicit—to students and their teachers, among others—the nature of what is expected of students, and the types of performances that are associated with the development of competence and expertise.

The C-I-A Frame: Addressing the Alignment of Curriculum, Instruction, and Assessment

All four papers mention curricular concerns that should inform assessment in some way, and this in itself is an important contribution. Körber and Meyer-Hamme point out the assessment challenges created by the lack of curricular alignment across districts and countries, leading to the need for assessments that are topically "self-contained." Similarly, Waldis et al. connect curricular concerns with assessment concerns in discussing possible implications of students' differential familiarity with specific historical topics for the assessment of particular competencies. They found that students tended to jump to the evaluative and short-circuit the evidentiary aspects of historical thinking for topics that were highly familiar to them (or "over-determined").

VanSledright more specifically frames such curricular concerns as issues of the ecological validity of assessments, and models an approach for developing ecologically-valid assessment items for a particular historical topic. VanSledright also links assessment to instruction, arguing for the importance of formative assessments that "can be used by both [students and teachers] to make more robust daily decisions that enhance historical thinking and understanding" (p. 88). He highlights the importance of *opportunities to learn* in the assessed constructs, a key issue in the C-I-A relationship (Gresalfi, 2009; Moss, Pullin, Gee, Haertel, & Young, 2008).

Going further, Seixas et al. point to "the problems of any assessment research that is not tied to instructional practice" (p. 113). The findings of their study are used to suggest instructional strategies that might help develop particular historical thinking practices (e.g., p. 112: "Systematic teaching of such documents as opportunities to enter into a foreign environment could set marginal students up for a higher level of performance"). Indeed, their program of work is couched in the assumption that assessments should inform instruction.

Taken together, these chapters suggest a continuum: from awareness of ways curriculum and instruction might impact the design of assessments to more integrated considerations of *how* curriculum, instruction, and assessment might more productively inform one another in educational design and practice.

The Evidentiary Reasoning Frame: Addressing the Three Components of the "Assessment Triangle"

The "assessment triangle" hinges on an explicit model of domain cognition, i.e., historical thinking. Each paper articulates such a domain model, laying out the forms of knowledge and the reasoning practices that define the domain of history for the proposed assessments. These models are used in each paper to specify the scope of what is assessed, including what is *not* in the current scope of the investigation.

Across the four papers, there are clear overlaps among the domain models; many of the constructs can be easily articulated to one another. At the same time, there appears to be a continental difference: the two chapters by North American researchers (VanSledright and Seixas et al.) are grounded in models of historical thinking that are informed primarily by the work of North American researchers in a cognitive research tradition following Sam Wineburg, and by the North American academic-standards movement. In contrast, the two chapters by European researchers (Körber and Meyer-Hamme, and Waldis et al.) are grounded more squarely in a model of historical thinking that is based on Jörn Rüsen's (2004) foundational work on narrative competencies.

These traditions are certainly not incompatible, and Seixas' (2004) edited volume, *Theorizing Historical Consciousness* (with a chapter by Rüsen), provides a useful reference for articulating these domain models to one another. Still, it is notable that the chapters do not more thoroughly cite a common base of literature. A diversity of frameworks is certainly a desirable thing; however, careful articulation of these frameworks to one another is an essential step in moving the field forward. The international research and education communities interested in the assessment of historical thinking must draw on a coherent and consistent common base of theoretical and empirical work. Other parts of the world not represented in these four papers need to be integrated into this conversation as well, if the kind of international-comparative assessment described by Körber and Meyer-Hamme is indeed a goal.

There are also differences across chapters as to what constitutes the domain in terms of epistemological knowledge, content knowledge, and the practices of historical analysis and reasoning. Such differences can have substantial consequences with respect to how the assessment development process unfolds. The more clarity there is about the elements of the domain analysis, the easier it is to specify the claims one wishes to make about what students are supposed to be able to do and the scope of those performances—the types of materials, the types of activity, the specific cognitive processes, and sociocultural practices—as well as the types of evidence that would support claims that students have mastered the desired competencies under consideration. Again the diversity of models can be productive, but where there are overlaps, clarity will support better assessment design.

Each paper's domain model is mapped to student performances that could serve as evidence of key competencies, though this is done at very different levels of detail. VanSledright's model names a set of "procedural organizing concepts" (evidence, accounts, significance, context, and causation) and "strategic thinking capabilities" (careful reading, identifying and attributing accounts, perspective assessing, reliability judging, and corroborating evidence) that work together to construct historical accounts. Körber and Meyer-Hamme's "FUER" model consists of four competencies: devising historical questions, synthesis and analysis of historical statements ("re-constructive competence"), perspective-taking ("orientation competence"), and "Sachkompetenz," a broad constellation of concepts and categories that make up the domain of historical cognition, procedures, and epistemology. The model incorporates three levels of mastery for each of these four dimensions (aconventional, conventional, and transconventional), constituting an ambitious framework to inform assessment design.

A key challenge for such global models is the alignment of each competency with the kinds of observations that can be used to assess them. Körber and Meyer-Hamme focus on the assessment of "re-constructive competence," proposing three types of tasks for eliciting and evaluating different aspects. While the authors point to the need for an empirical base for validating such models and items, the process of interpreting actual student performances (the third leg of the triangle) remains unclear. The key question for an assessment item like their proposed story-construction task (p. 98) is how students' stories would be scored as evidence of particular constructs within the FUER model.

Waldis et al. map aspects of students' narrative performances to aspects of their domain model, which incorporates four "sub-operations." In the study, they correlate evidence of these sub-operations with a separate evaluation of quality of the students' narratives, broken down into specific "qualities" and "quality features." While interesting and relevant, these correlations between quality features and sub-operations do not explicate the evidentiary reasoning for assessment. Interpretation of these findings needs a clearer articulation of the claims to be made based on students' narratives, including how each scoring process yields evidence in support of particular claims.

Seixas et al. use the "assessment triangle" explicitly, to attempt to specify this process of aligning student performances with aspects of their model. As this chapter shows, this specification is important for more than validation of assessments: it also serves to clarify and nuance the domain model itself. As noted on p. 112, "[i]n the analysis of students' responses to the test items, we gained new insights about confounding factors in the cognition model and, more so, in the task items themselves." Like VanSledright, examples of possible answers to each item are articulated to those aspects of the domain model that would (and would not) be made visible.

The Evidence-Centered Design (ECD) Frame: Addressing the Purposes, Contexts of Use, and Practical Constraints Shaping Assessment Design

A unique and valuable contribution of these four chapters is the opportunity to gain insight into the process of designing historical-thinking assessments. The ECD framework highlights design decisions as valuable opportunities to make the evidentiary logic of an assessment clearly visible.

Several important design challenges are described in these chapters, and the authors leverage them differently to highlight key assessment issues. All four describe aspects of the envisioned contexts of use for each assessment that constrain and shape the design: the amount of time and effort required of teachers and students (Seixas et al., VanSledright, Waldis et al.); considerations of historical topics likely to be covered in the curriculum (Körber & Meyer-Hamme, VanSledright, Waldis et al.); and considerations of text difficulty in the selection of sources (Seixas et al., Waldis et al.).

At a finer level of detail, specifying the design details of the assessment tasks and items has particular value. Körber and Meyer-Hamme's proposed structure for a narrative-construction task (Figure 6.1) suggests a large number of design decisions that would need to be made in applying this template to the construction of rubrics for scoring students' work. Waldis et al. explore assessment possibilities of multiple genres of writing tasks (panel discussion, article, and blog), and map examples of writing to competencies, but do not design a scoring scheme for making assessment decisions. VanSledright focuses on the design of *weighted multiple-choice items* (WMCs), specifying the rationales for particular types of answers and distractors, and the logic of the weighting of the answers in several examples. At this level of detail the deeper challenges of this work become clear: for example, the logic of VanSledright's specific weighting decisions invite debate and challenge.

Seixas et al. most closely approximate an ECD analysis, in that the focus of the design discussion is specifically on the value of the evidence that each item would produce. They point to important issues related to the interactivity of different test items with each other, the ways a test can build toward more complex evidence of mastery, and limitations of their approach. Still, the "architecture" of the 1-hour test described on p. 113 remains a fairly general design guide, and key issues for an ECD analysis remain to be articulated, including (most importantly) the design of detailed guides for the interpretation of students' work in light of the model.

Part 3: Challenges for Future Research and Development

Several tensions emerge in these chapters, as well as challenges for the field as the development of assessments of historical thinking continues to evolve.

Content Versus Historical Thinking Practices

The four chapters agree on the need to move away from conceptions of history as static bodies of dated events, and on the importance of a citizenry versed in historical thinking practices. Yet, all four recognize that engaging in (and assessing) historical thinking necessarily involves some historical content. The Waldis et al. findings suggest that familiarity with a historical topic may change the competencies that students make evident in an assessment. The resolution of exactly how to incorporate historical content into assessments depends, in part, on the purposes of the assessment and the claims for which evidence is sought.

At one end of the spectrum of purposes is VanSledright, who is explicit about the formative purpose of his assessment development work. These assessments target only content and practices that students have had opportunities to learn. At the other end of the spectrum, Körber and Meyer-Hamme discuss the design of large-scale assessments in which the fairness of the assessment across a wide range of students and curricula is of paramount importance. They advocate assessment of historical thinking using facts that are unfamiliar, in assessments that are "self-contained," with all the facts students need to know embedded in the assessment itself.

Somewhere between the two is classroom-based summative assessment, as reflected in the Seixas et al. chapter. Their content is drawn from historical periods that students had studied, but the assessment dives deeply into particular incidents. The issue of studied-versus-unknown content in assessments of historical thinking needs to be explicitly considered in interpreting the observed performances, to support claims about what students know and can do. These chapters offer useful models of clearly articulating different logics for this consideration.

Literacy Demands of the Assessments

The literacy demands of an assessment are a necessary set of considerations in the design of assessment tasks. This applies to production as well as comprehension. Have students been provided with opportunities to learn to write like historians as well as to read like historians (cf. De La Paz, 2005; Monte-Sano, 2011; Reisman, 2012)? Using an ECD process, the literacy demands would be addressed in the design of the assessment task models (Mislevy & Riconscente, 2006).

Comprehension: Authentic Historical Documents Versus Adapted Materials

Not unsurprisingly, adapting source texts has been a serious bone of contention among historians, history teachers, and assessment developers. On the one hand, students need to be able to access the content in order to reason with it. If documents are too complex or contain high proportions of vocabulary or syntax from bygone ages, students will simply not read the material and it will not be possible to obtain observations of their historical thinking. Accordingly, designers may justify the use of extracts or adapted materials that do the "translations" for the students. On the other hand, if students are never confronted with historical documents that they have to struggle to make sense of, they will develop neither strategies (cognitive and interpersonal) for dealing with complex and challenging traces of the past nor the confidence to tackle them. Students' development as historical thinkers will be dependent on the presence of document translators. This issue is explicitly addressed only by Seixas et al. It is an area that needs a great deal more attention, especially regarding ways in which instructional supports can assist students in tackling challenging texts when reading like a historian (cf. Goldman, 2012; Goldman & Snow, in press; Reisman, 2012; Schoenbach, Greenleaf, & Murphy, 2012).

Production: Constructed Responses Versus Multiple Choice

The assessment tasks that were featured in the chapters varied from those with high production demands (e.g., essay writing) to those with lower production demands (e.g., multiple-choice items). Several issues rest on these choices. First, essays are difficult to score, especially if the assessment developers have no exemplar responses. Rubric development is time-consuming, and reliability across scorers is often difficult to obtain without clear criteria. The Waldis et al. chapter presented the tip of the iceberg of this process, and their experience is typical (cf. De La Paz, 2005; Monte-Sano & De La Paz, 2012). The scoring issue is less complicated for short-answer constructed responses, but unless the criteria for reasoning are clear, reliability issues are just as problematic. Also, short-answer responses may not afford students rich opportunities to demonstrate historical reasoning. Students are also often able to demonstrate more sophisticated reasoning orally than in written form. Thus, the literacy demands of written production may mask the historical thinking and reasoning that students can do.

In contrast to the high-output demands of constructed responses, multiple-choice items do not require students to produce language. They do, however, require comprehension—at least for the more well-constructed multiple-choice items like those of Seixas et al. and VanSledright. Even here the comprehension demands of items with lengthy alternatives can sometimes obfuscate the historical thinking the item was intended to assess. We find VanSledright's approach to weighted alternatives a provocative one. However, we suspect that many readers, ourselves included, could argue with some of the weighting decisions.

What seems called for in efforts to develop multiple-choice alternatives are the rigorous kinds of evaluation techniques that VanSledright, Körber and Meyer-Hamme, and Seixas et al. discuss. These need to be conducted with individuals who reflect different levels in the development of expertise with respect to historical thinking. We speculate that what more knowledgeable students of history see as clear distinctions among various alternatives are much more difficult to see for those less knowledgeable. Thus, there is a strong need to validate assessments on the populations for whom they are intended.

Developmental Issues and Learning Progressions in Historical Thinking

The question of whether alternative tasks or items tap the "same" historical thinking competencies across a wide range of individuals raises a larger set of issues regarding the development of historical thinking practices, and how they are introduced and then deepened through successive learning experiences. We know from the literature on expertise (e.g., Ericsson, 2006) that hundreds to thousands of hours of practice are needed to achieve expert status. This implies the need to coordinate the teaching of historical thinking within and across grades, with an eye toward making visible the processes of interpretation of the historical record and construction of historical narratives. To date, we know of little work that has attempted to examine this issue or trace out such progressions (but see Goldman et al., 2009).

In the context of the assessment triangle and the ECD process, this would mean unpacking the domain model into student models that are developmentally appropriate for a given age range of students. For example, while we might want 7 year olds to be aware that different people have different perspectives on events, the cognitive model would differ for the performance we expect from a 17 year old. The four chapters in this section do not address the issue of such progressions, nor the developmental level of the participants in their studies. This is an important direction for this work going forward.

Assessment development in any disciplinary domain is a challenging endeavor. We applaud the efforts of these authors to specify the domain of historical thinking for purposes of assessment, and their articulation of design models and cases. While they share a common goal, it is clear that there is far from a consensus view of the domain and how to assess student competence. These cases are instructive, and offer the opportunity for further dialogue about how to meet the conceptual and practical challenges in the assessment of historical thinking.

Note

1 Acknowledgments: The preparation of this commentary was supported, in part, by Project READI, a multidisciplinary, multi-institution collaboration aimed at research and development to improve complex comprehension of multiple forms of text in literature, history, and science. The authors, while thinking on matters of assessment of historical thinking, have benefitted from discussions with their READI colleagues. Project READI is supported by the Institute of Education Sciences, U.S. Department of Education, through Grant R305F100007 to the University of Illinois at Chicago. The opinions expressed are those of the authors and do not represent views of the Institute or the U.S. Department of Education.

References

De La Paz, S. (2005). Effects of historical reasoning instruction and writing strategy mastery in culturally and academically diverse middle school classrooms. *Journal of Educational Psychology, 97*, 139.

Ericsson, K. A. (2006). The influence of experience and deliberate practice on the development of superior expert performance. In K. A. Ericsson, N. Charness, P. Feltovich, and R. R. Hoffman (Eds.), *Cambridge handbook of expertise and expert performance* (pp. 685–706). Cambridge, UK: Cambridge University Press.

Goldman, S. R. (2012). Adolescent literacy: Learning and understanding content. *Future of Children, 22*(2), 89–116.

Goldman, S. R., Britt, M. A., Greenleaf, C., Lee, C. D., Brown, M., Magliano, J., . . . George, M. (2009). *Reading for understanding across grades 6–12: Evidence based argumentation for disciplinary learning.* Funded July, 2010 by Institute for Educational Sciences, U.S. Department of Education, Grant # R305F100007.

Goldman, S. R., & Snow, C. (in press). Adolescent literacy: Development and instruction. In A. Pollatsek & R. Treiman (Eds.), *The Oxford Handbook of Reading.* New York, NY: Oxford University Press.

Gresalfi, M. S. (2009). Taking up opportunities to learn: Constructing dispositions in mathematics classrooms. *The Journal of the Learning Sciences, 18*(3), 327–369.

Marion, S. F., & Pellegrino, J. W. (2006). A validity framework for evaluating the technical quality of alternate assessments. *Educational Measurement: Issues and Practice, 25*(4), 47–57.

Mislevy, R. J., & Haertel, G. D. (2006). Implications of evidence-centered design for educational testing. *Educational Measurement: Issues and Practice, 25*(4), 6–20.

Mislevy, R. J., & Riconscente, M. M. (2006). Evidence-centered assessment design: Layers, concepts, and terminology. In S. Downing & T. Haladyna (Eds.), *Handbook of test development* (pp. 61–90). Mahwah, NJ: Erlbaum.

Monte-Sano, C. (2011). Beyond reading comprehension and summary: Learning to read and write in history by focusing on evidence, perspective, and interpretation. *Curriculum Inquiry, 41*(2), 212–249.

Monte-Sano, C., & De La Paz, S. (2012). Using writing tasks to elicit adolescents' historical reasoning. *Journal of Literacy Research, 44,* 273–299.

Moss, P., Pullin, D., Gee, J., Haertel, E., & Young, L. (Eds.). (2008). *Assessment, equity, and opportunity to learn.* Cambridge, UK: Cambridge University Press.

Pellegrino, J. W., Chudowsky, N., & Glaser, R. (Eds.). (2001). *Knowing what students know: The science and design of educational assessment.* Washington, DC: National Academies Press.

Reisman, A. (2012). Reading like a historian: A document-based history curriculum intervention in urban high schools. *Cognition and Instruction, 30,* 86–112.

Rüsen, J. (2004). Historical consciousness: narrative structure, moral function, and ontogenetic development. In P. Seixas (Ed.), *Theorizing historical consciousness* (pp. 63–85). Toronto, ON: University of Toronto Press.

Schoenbach, R., Greenleaf, C., & Murphy, L. (2012). *Reading for understanding: How Reading Apprenticeship improves disciplinary learning in secondary and college classrooms.* Hoboken, NJ: John Wiley.

Seixas, P. (Ed.). (2004). *Theorizing historical consciousness.* Toronto, ON: University of Toronto Press.

PART III
Large-Scale Assessment of Historical Thinking

9

A LARGE-SCALE ASSESSMENT OF HISTORICAL KNOWLEDGE AND REASONING

NAEP U.S. History Assessment

Stephen Lazer

Introduction: NAEP

In the United States, the National Assessment of Educational Progress (NAEP), also known as *The Nation's Report Card,* is the only ongoing, nationally representative survey of student achievement in a variety of academic areas. NAEP is a group-score assessment for which individual student results are neither reported nor computed. The central goals of the assessment are to measure what students know and can do and to track trends in achievement. The assessment is based on matrix-sampling approaches, in which samples of students take portions of a long aggregate assessment. NAEP samples support national- and state-level reporting in mathematics, science, reading, and writing. Smaller student samples allow for national and regional reporting in subjects such as U.S. History, Geography, Civics, Technology and Engineering, Literacy, and the Arts. In most subjects, assessments are conducted in grades 4, 8, and 12.

This chapter is intended to provide readers an overview of the NAEP U.S. History Assessment. The next section will describe the content and skills *Framework* for the NAEP U.S. History Assessment. This will be followed by a discussion of the opportunities for and limitations in assessing historical thinking in NAEP. The following section includes examples of the sorts of test questions included in NAEP. The final section in his chapter discusses future challenges facing NAEP, and a brief conclusion.

The NAEP U.S. History *Framework*

The *Framework* describing the content and skills to be measured in the NAEP U.S. History Assessment was first written for use in 1994. While it has been updated over the past 20 years, the basic elements of the *Framework* remain intact, and NAEP has continued to report data on the same trend lines begun in 1994.

The *Framework* has a number of key distinguishing characteristics. The document instructs developers to create questions that cover four thematic areas. While distributions of assessment time by chronological categories are also included in the *Framework,* it is the thematic areas that serve as the primary organizing scheme and define subscales on which the assessment results are estimated and reported.[1] The areas are:

- Change and Continuity in American Democracy: Ideas, Institutions, Events, Key Figures, and Controversies
- The Gathering and Interactions of Peoples, Cultures, and Ideas
- Economic and Technological Changes and Their Relationship to Society, Ideas, and the Environment
- The Changing Role of America in the World (NAGB, 2013).

The authors of the *Framework* also faced a decision common to all designers of history assessments: how to balance the roles played by content knowledge on the one hand, and inquiry, analytic, and reasoning skills on the other. They clearly believed in the importance of reasoning skills:

> Students need historical reasoning skills to enable them to examine evidence, analyze cause and effect, and appreciate how complex and sometimes ambiguous the explanation of historical events can be. Historical study must encourage students to think and judge evidence responsibly, independently, imaginatively, and critically. In developing critical-thinking skills, students should engage in debates and consider alternative viewpoints or possibilities of historical movements and their causes.
>
> (NAGB, 2013, p. 5)

However, the authors of the *Framework* did not believe that testing reasoning skills obviated the need to assess content knowledge. They called for an assessment that measured both, but not necessarily in separate test questions. In other words, the assessment was designed to include questions that measure prior knowledge, those that focus on analytic and interpretive skills, and those that jointly measure reasoning and knowledge.

This belief in the relatedness of content knowledge and historical reasoning skills is also shown in the *Framework's* definition of two modes of knowing and thinking about history.

> Historical study requires specialized ways of knowing and thinking, habits of mind, and cognitive processes that typify historians' approaches to the past. These habits of mind require almost simultaneous exercise of

lower- and higher-order cognitive skills, such as recall, analysis, judgment, application, and evaluation. This assessment identifies and defines the cognitive processes of historical knowing and thinking as follows:

- **Historical Knowledge and Perspective** If Knowing and understanding people, events, concepts, themes, movements, contexts, and historical sources; sequencing events; recognizing multiple perspectives and seeing an era or movement through the eyes of different groups; and developing a general conceptualization of U.S. history.
- **Historical Analysis and Interpretation** If Explaining issues, identifying historical patterns, establishing cause-and-effect relationships, finding value statements, establishing significance, applying historical knowledge, weighing evidence to draw sound conclusions, making defensible generalizations, and rendering insightful accounts of the past (NAGB, 2013, p. 32).

The remainder of the chapter covers the assessment that was developed to meet the *Framework*. The next section discusses key design decisions developers faced in constructing the NAEP assessment.

Assessing Historical Knowledge and Skill in NAEP: Opportunities, Limitations, and Key Design Decisions

Large-scale survey assessments, in general, and NAEP, in particular, offer a unique set of opportunities for assessment designers. They also pose a particular set of challenges. Some of these opportunities and challenges are related to the way in which group-score assessments are structured; others are specific to the measurement of history.

For example, all history tests that produce scores at the individual student level face a key and in some ways irresolvable tension between domain coverage and test length. In tests that include explicit measurement of content knowledge as one of their goals, reliable test scores necessitate including questions on the different themes, regions, and periods covered in the course of study. This tends to lead to a large number of questions, each taking a fairly short time to complete. Even in tests that focus on reasoning skills and provide extensive stimuli for students to use in showing these skills, context matters. Being able to interpret primary sources from one era may not predict ability to do the same if the sources are from hundreds of years earlier or later. Reading graphs and tables of quantitative data may or may not correlate with ability to interpret a political cartoon.

The situation is made even more complicated in assessments that use extended performance tasks taking substantial time to complete. The use of such questions almost certainly allows for measurement of reasoning skills not otherwise accessible. But at the same time, they place pressure on domain coverage and score reliability. Therefore, the designer of a high-stakes history test is faced with imperfect choices. She can either create a very long test (which is not likely feasible at younger grades and creates fatigue issues at all levels), focus on content coverage by including a large number of short items, or concentrate on the measurement of the sorts of reasoning skills that necessitate extended performance tasks, thus creating challenges for reliability. Most history tests are compromises among these goals.

Matrix-sampled assessments, such as NAEP, have flexibility in addressing this particular set of problems. An NAEP U.S. History Assessment is not a collection of parallel forms. It is rather a single long assessment, in which individuals complete only short portions. Consider the grade 8 U.S. History Assessment. It is made up of 250 minutes of testing. However, rather than giving a test in excess of four hours to respondents, the assessment is divided into ten 25-minute blocks. Individuals take two of these blocks, and are therefore tested for 50 minutes. The blocks are paired in a design that ensures that each block is paired with all other blocks (and with one block twice) and appears an equal number of times in both positions. Fifty total booklets are created.

By creating and administering a long aggregate assessment, NAEP can solve some of the problems facing other programs. Most history tests in the United States are what one might call "broad survey assessments," in which a large number of unrelated items are used to cover an array of history content and skills. In fact, much of the NAEP assessment itself could be characterized in this way. However, the assessments at grades 8 and 12 also include "thematic blocks," in which students read materials and answer questions in a single topical area (in one case, for example, students read and react to a series of materials about the Great Depression; NCES, 2013a). These blocks are intended to ensure that NAEP measures of student achievement balance the ability to work across the domain with the ability to work in focused areas. In an individual student test, time spent on a thematic unit would necessarily come at the expense of content coverage or longer test length. In NAEP, thematic blocks can simply be added to the matrix. The aggregate assessment gets longer, but individual testing time does not.

This relates to another singular advantage of group-score assessments, particularly in content-rich areas like history: in aggregate, they can include more questions than could a test yielding individual scores. In addition, because of the ability to expand aggregate assessment length without a concomitant increase in individual testing time, NAEP can use a far higher proportion of open-ended questions than is common in American standardized history testing. As Table 9.1 shows, the NAEP assessment at grade 8 includes 166 total items, of which 48 are open ended (NCES, 2013b).

NAEP's use of student sampling also allows for the use of large numbers of open-ended items that require human scoring. A NAEP national sample is composed of approximately 10,000 students at grades 8 and 12 (and fewer at grade 4). Roughly 2,000 take any single item. Thus for grade 8 NAEP, scoring about 96,000 responses to open-ended items allows us to estimate what

TABLE 9.1 NAEP distribution of items by item type: 2010 U.S. History Assessment

	Multiple-choice	Short open-ended	Extended open-ended	Total
Grade 4	63	28	4	95
Grade 8	118	37	11	166
Grade 12	110	36	13	159

national and regional populations know and can do in U.S. history. For purposes of comparison, if all U.S. eighth-graders (roughly 4 million students) took the entire 250 minutes of NAEP, and each completed all the open-ended questions, one would need to score 192 million responses. This would almost certainly be financially and logistically intractable.

NAEP also gathers contextual data that aids in the understanding of student results. In addition to content testing, NAEP administers survey questionnaires to students, teachers, and school administrators. Responses to these instruments let analysts relate data on instructional approaches, student interests, and school policy to student performance. For example, questions asking students and teachers about use of primary source documents in history instruction can be used to track the relationship between different levels of use of these materials and achievement.

While much in the structure of NAEP allows for rich assessment of history, there are also factors that limit the sorts of instruments the program can use. NAEP is low-stakes for students, who do not even know until a week or two before testing that they will be included. In addition, there is no national U.S. history curriculum. For these reasons, students cannot and do not prepare for NAEP. This has led designers to avoid the use of lengthy tasks that pose motivational issues or that require study and preparation ahead of time; extended response items on NAEP are meant to be completed in 5–10 minutes. NAEP does not include the types of long essay questions seen on some other tests.

There is a related reason that NAEP developers have avoided lengthy essay responses such as those used in the Advanced Placement program (AP). The goal of NAEP is to gather data on what students know and can do. Students presented with a very long single task might not be able to engage it at all, which means NAEP would have little usable data for that student. Even in a group-score assessment, such data holes are suboptimal. The thematic blocks described above are attempts to gain the sort of in-depth focus an AP Document-Based Question (DBQ) requires. However, unlike the DBQ, in which students interpret a large number of documents in a single essay, NAEP thematic blocks ask a series of questions about a related set of documents. Additionally, NAEP designers chose to use a fairly large amount of scaffolding in which complex tasks were separated into explicit pieces for students. NAEP designers believe that these shorter open-ended questions provide excellent measurement of a range of key skills.

However, there were those who participated in the original design phase who viewed the long on-demand history essay as a key practice, and saw its absence in NAEP as an unfortunate limitation.

Even these short open-ended items pose an issue for NAEP: they have omission rates far in excess of multiple-choice questions. It is unclear whether this is a result of low motivation or the fact that students cannot guess answers on open-ended questions that do, in many cases, require specific content knowledge. It is likely that both factors contribute. Whatever the causes, it is worth noting that while NAEP gains construct-relevant data from the extensive use of constructed-response items, it loses response data. Table 9.2 shows these omission rates (NCES, 2013b).

The heavy inclusion of open-ended items in NAEP leads to an additional challenge: they add complication to accurate reporting of trends in student achievement. To measure changes in student performance, NAEP uses common blocks of items over time. To ensure that the trends are based on a representative measure of the construct, open-ended questions are included in the blocks that are reused. If they are to be a measure of progress, common items must be scored in the same way from year to year. To ensure this, NAEP uses a trend scoring approach in which papers from previous administrations are seeded into a current year scoring. If the newer scoring differs from earlier years by more than an allowable amount, raters are retrained and scoring is conducted again. Note that this trend scoring must check more than rater agreement rates, since even modest differences in the average scores given to common papers can translate into a spurious change in average performance.

NAEP faces special challenges at grade 4 because of a characteristic of the American educational system. In most of the country, U.S. history is not studied as a course before grade 5. Children do study history and "social studies" at younger grades, but in most places, early instruction is influenced heavily by the so-called expanding environments approach. Content knowledge and reasoning skills are taught, but the geographic context expands as students get older; at kindergarten, first, and second grades, history and social studies classes focus on family, school, neighborhood, and community. By third grade, comparisons with other communities are included. The focus of fourth-grade history or social curricula in most of the nation is the state. U.S. history as a national subject is

TABLE 9.2 Average percentage of students omitting different types of test items: 2010 U.S. History Assessment

Item Type	Grade 4	Grade 8	Grade 12
Multiple-Choice	1.59	0.75	0.67
Short Open-Ended	6.76	7.85	9.43
Extended Open-Ended	8.70	5.86	6.74

first commonly taught in grade 5 (Zarrillo, 2012). So, while historical skills and regional content are taught before grade 5, the same content is not taught nationally.

In addition, before grade 4 in most states, U.S. history is not taught as an independent subject, but as part of an integrated curriculum that includes geography and civic education. Thus, the amount of actual historical content covered is limited, and the amount of content common across states is even more constrained. There is, to be sure, some common U.S. content taught, often around shared national events such as holidays. Most students are taught something about the historical context of the Fourth of July or Martin Luther King Day. However, it remains true that the subject being assessed in the grade 4 NAEP is not taught as a subject in most of the nation.

This situation leads to two questions: Why assess U.S. history at grade 4 at all? If we do decide to assess, how should we assess history in the absence of a common set of content or skills learning expectations? The first question is fairly easily answered. The goal of NAEP is not to give grades to students, or to evaluate the effectiveness of specific schools. It is rather to measure what students know and can do at key grade levels set in the legislation that governs NAEP, and this remains an important goal, even if we cannot measure against a set of common national teaching goals. The skills and content students acquire in early grades prepare them for the study of U.S. history in the later grades and subjects.

The question of how to measure competency in a subject that has not yet been taught is a good deal trickier. One approach would have been to focus the assessment solely on skills measurement, and supply all the content students needed in the form of stimulus for the questions. There are a number of questions on the assessment that do just that: students are asked to read documents or interpret tabular and graphical data displays. However, relying on such a skills-based approach alone would violate the spirit of the *Framework* that calls for integrated measurement of knowledge and skills. Therefore, designers have tried to bring content to the grade 4 assessment in a number of ways.

One approach was especially interesting: Some questions called for application of content knowledge but provided a choice of the content to be used in responding, thus allowing students to use their content knowledge based on local curricula in the assessment. For example, in one question, students were given a list of major American historical figures, including George Washington, Thomas Jefferson, Sojourner Truth, and Sitting Bull. They were asked to provide a list of key facts about one of these people (most students would have learned about at least one of these figures; NCES, 2013b). In a test designed to provide individual scores, such choice would almost certainly be problematic. In NAEP, comparability issues associated with choice do not have the same psychometric implications.

Even given these attempts to bring content to the grade 4 assessment, there was in the opinion of designers simply less to cover at that grade than at the other levels. While the grade 8 and 12 assessments are each, in aggregate, 250 minutes long, the grade 4 assessment is only 150 minutes. In addition, grade 4 does not include thematic blocks.

The following section includes example tasks from the NAEP U.S. History Assessment. They are chosen to show some of the variety of types of reasoning tasks that have been included in the assessment, and also illustrate different periods and historical themes covered in the assessment. Note that literally hundreds of released NAEP U.S. History exercises can be accessed at the NAEP website: nces.ed.gov/nationsreportcard/.

Example Tasks from the NAEP U.S. History Assessment[2]

Grade 4

For the two-question sets shown in Figure 9.1, students were asked to interpret a simple map and apply what one might call general historical knowledge to the stimulus. In other words, they were asked to read a stimulus and then to apply prior knowledge to responding to the questions. The items were both designed to measure the *Economic and Technological Change* theme, and in the *Historical Analysis and Interpretation* cognitive area.

Students found these two questions of moderate difficulty. The first question was scored on a three-point scale, and 28 percent wrote answers that were awarded full credit (that is, they answered both parts of question 1 correctly). An additional 56 percent were awarded partial credit (that is, were able to identify one job accurately). The second question in the set proved somewhat harder. While 59 percent were able to identify one reason why towns were located near rivers, only 15 percent were able to identify multiple reasons.

As was mentioned above, the grade 4 assessment focuses largely, though not exclusively, on the reasoning skills of students. One key skill at all grades is the interpretation of primary historical sources. The item in Figure 9.2 requires students to interpret a diary from the nineteenth century and identify specific ways in which the writer's life was different than that of children today.

Students found this question of moderate difficulty. The responses were scored on a three-point rubric. Thirty-five percent received the highest score on their response, while another 14 percent received partial credit.

Grade 8

At grade 8, the content requirements of the assessment become more pronounced. Most students will have had U.S. history in grade 5 and will be taking it again at grade 8. Additionally, the stimuli used are that much more complex. However, as with grade 4, the extent to which external content knowledge is required varies across items, and thus use of scaffolding in questions continues.

The following question refers to the map below.

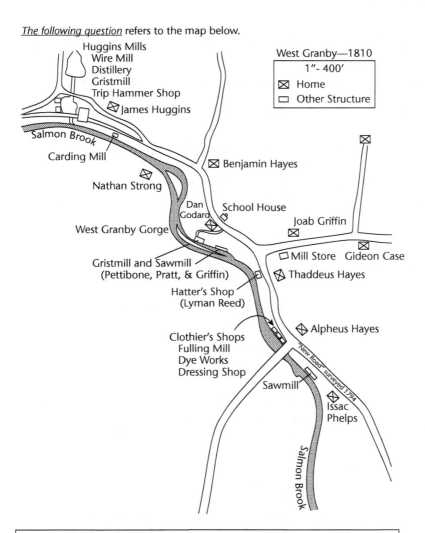

Huggins Mills
Wire Mill
Distillery
Gristmill
Trip Hammer Shop
⊠ James Huggins

West Granby—1810
1"- 400'
⊠ Home
☐ Other Structure

Salmon Brook

Carding Mill

⊠ Benjamin Hayes

Nathan Strong ⊠

Dan Godard ⊠
School House ⬦

Joab Griffin
⊠

West Granby Gorge

⊠

⊠

Gristmill and Sawmill
(Pettibone, Pratt, & Griffin)

☐ Mill Store   Gideon Case

☐ ⊠ Thaddeus Hayes

Hatter's Shop
(Lyman Reed)

⬦ Alpheus Hayes

Clothier's Shops
Fulling Mill
Dye Works
Dressing Shop

"New Road" surveyed 1794

Sawmill

⬦
Issac
Phelps

Salmon Brook

1. List TWO jobs you might have had if you had lived in West Granby in 1810, and then describe the kinds of work you would have done for each job.

Job 1.

Job 2.

2. Why do you think that many towns were located near streams and rivers like Salmon Brook? Give two reasons.

1.

2.

FIGURE 9.1 Grade 4 item set on map of West Granby, Connecticut

The following question is about the portion of the diary of Elizabeth Fuller shown below. Elizabeth was 14 years old in 1790 when she wrote this diary. She lived in Princeton, Massachusetts.

October 4	Mr. Pope was here, bought a pair of oxen from Pa. Mr. Keys at work here.
October 7	Very pleasant today. I have to work very hard.
October 11	I washed today.
October 12	Pa got in his corn. Mr. Joseph Eveleth died last night.
November 11	Timmy went to mill.
November 24	We baked two ovensfull of pies. Mr. Nathan Perry here this eve.
November 25	Thanksgiving today we baked three ovensfull of pies. Mr. Nathan Perry here this eve.
November 27	Mr. Gregory killed our hogs today.
December 4	I minced the link meat.
December 16	John Brooks here killing our sheep. A severe snow storm.
December 17	Very cold. I made sixteen dozen candles.

4. Explain one important way that Elizabeth Fuller's days were different from the lives of children today.

FIGURE 9.2 Grade 4 item involving a diary

The question in Figure 9.3 asked eighth graders to interpret pie charts, and explicitly requires application of content knowledge to the interpretation. More specifically, the pie charts show changes to patterns of immigration. Students are asked first to correctly interpret the pie charts, and then provide historical reasons for the changes.

Sixty-five percent of students received partial credit, which meant they were able to accurately interpret the data but not to give a historical explanation for those changes. Only 15 percent were awarded full credit (that is, answered both parts of the question correctly). Therefore, the explanation of the difference was quite difficult.

It is worth noting that because of the greater content focus at grade 8, the assessment also contains some more traditional item types. For example, one question asked students to explain the debate at the U.S. Constitutional Convention that occurred between large and small states over how representation in the national legislature should work, and then describe the "Great Compromise" that resolved this debate.

This question was very hard for students, with only 6 percent of responses receiving the highest score category, and another 24 percent receiving some level of partial credit. Also, likely because of the demand for explicit content knowledge, over 20 percent of students omitted this question.

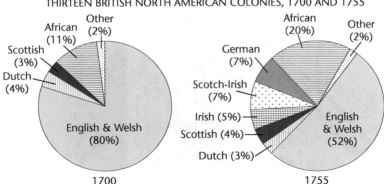

DISTRIBUTION OF ETHNIC AND RACIAL GROUPS WITHIN THE
THIRTEEN BRITISH NORTH AMERICAN COLONIES, 1700 AND 1755

3. Part A. Using the information in the charts above, identify the most significant changes in the colonial population between 1700 and 1755.

Part B. Explain why these changes occurred.

FIGURE 9.3 Grade 8 item involving interpretation of pie chart data

Grade 12

At grade 12, the questions require both more content knowledge and more sophisticated skills than at earlier grades. Additionally, twelfth graders are expected to be able to read a range of authentic materials from U.S. history.

Figure 9.4 shows a question that asks students to interpret a political cartoon and provide a historical context. Note that this is measuring a thematic area many students find difficult: the changing role of the United States in the world. In addition, reading and interpreting political cartoons tends to bring its own challenges.

This question proved extremely hard: 63 percent of students wrote responses that were awarded no credit, and another 19 percent either omitted the question or wrote off-task responses.

The assessment also includes questions in which twelfth-graders are asked to interpret tabular data and provide historical explanations for the patterns shown in the data. Specifically, in one case students were asked to interpret simple quantitative data showing an average increase in farm size, and then identify an invention that helped cause this change. The question calls for both stimulus interpretation and application of prior knowledge, and uses scaffolding. Both approaches are common in NAEP.

This question was at a moderate level of difficulty. Twenty-nine percent of students were able to both read the table accurately and give an historical explanation for the pattern, while another 45 percent were able to do only the former.

The following question refers to the cartoon below.

Cartoon by Louis Dalrymple.

Part A: Describe the type of foreign policy that the policeman in the cartoon represents.

Part B: Give one specific example of this type of foreign policy from the period that the cartoon shows.

FIGURE 9.4 Grade 12 item on a political cartoon

NAEP Assessments in the Future

The current NAEP U.S. History Assessments were initially developed in 1992 and 1993, and administered in 1994. While blocks of items have been released and replaced, the basic structure of the assessment has remained unchanged since then. It remains a pencil-and-paper test made up of a combination of multiple-choice and open-ended questions.

However, after the 2014 assessment, NAEP U.S. History will almost certainly move to digital delivery, and this will allow substantial changes to the assessment content. For example, much modern history, of course, exists on film and video. Including these dynamic stimuli in the assessment is an obvious way to take advantage of technology-based assessment. Even for static stimulus, technology delivery provides a low-cost way to use color.

Perhaps even more important, technology-based delivery will open up assessment of key skills that can now only be measured through fairly poor proxies. In the future, we will be able to assess student abilities to work with reference materials, such as textbooks, atlases, and archives. For example, we can require students to navigate among easily accessible and varied sources—text, image, video, or audio—to respond to questions. History educators often say that knowing all the facts is not what is important, but rather knowing how and where to find them is crucial. Technology-based history assessments will allow us to measure just that.

Perhaps further out are the uses of history simulations and games in assessment. While a discussion of the specifics is beyond the scope of this chapter, suffice it to say that immersive environments may allow us measurements not currently possible, including the assessment of collaboration. Of course, such measures will pose real challenges for NAEP. Because students do not and will not prepare for NAEP, the "rules of the game" will need to be simple and intuitive enough that students can pick them up in a single sitting.

Technology delivery affords other possibilities as well. Given the difficulty of NAEP for certain students, use of adaptive testing seems appropriate. By targeting items to students at different levels, we might be able to drive down the high levels of omission we currently see on open-ended questions. However, little, if any, adaptive testing has been done in assessments of history, and the context and content richness would seem to pose real problems for this approach. Much study will be needed before NAEP considers such a change.

Perhaps more likely is the use of artificial intelligence (AI) scoring of student-produced responses. This would have the dual advantages of driving down costs and easing trend measurement. To do this, however, AI systems will need to improve their ability to score content.

Finally, there is one way in which the movement to technology delivery will force NAEP to question initial assumptions. In an era when the facts of history can all be found online, the extent to which measurement of factual knowledge needs to remain part of NAEP may change. We stress the term *may*, in that it is far from certain that content knowledge will become unimportant. Historians will still use familiar content to set up typologies and analogies that help students make sense of new and unfamiliar content. Furthermore, the automaticity that comes with recall may remain important. However, since the stuff of history can all be found on the Internet, we may want to add measurement of students' abilities to find the information they need quickly and efficiently, and to tell good sources from untrustworthy ones.

Whatever changes technology brings, NAEP designers should always remain conscious of the distinct advantages of a group-score assessment. NAEP can and should continue to measure in ways not practical in individual-score tests. It should strive to adapt its measures to the way the children of tomorrow will learn history.

Summary and Conclusions

The current version of the NAEP U.S. History Assessment was first operational in 1994. Doing a national assessment in the absence of a national curriculum posed—and continues to pose—real challenges. These challenges are most pronounced at grade 4. However, matrix sampling gives NAEP opportunities to do things other assessments cannot. Perhaps greatest among these is inclusion of a large number of discrete open-ended questions, covering a broad array of skills. NAEP has not used the traditional extended essay, but has rather relied on shorter items that focus on the application of content to reasoning tasks. These items would be effective on individual score tests as well, and could allow for enhanced measurement of thinking skills, without the coverage pressures usually associated with extended essays.

Moving forward, NAEP will need to consider how measurement can be changed and updated when the assessment moves to technology delivery. This will certainly necessitate changes to the assessment *Framework,* or a new *Framework* entirely.

Notes

1 The NAEP composite scale in U.S. History is a weighted average of the four subscales, in which the weighting varies by grade.
2 All the sample questions in this section and related data can be found at the following web site: http://nces.ed.gov/nationsreportcard/itmrlsx/search.aspx?subject=history

References

National Assessment Governing Board (NAGB). (2013). *U.S. History Framework for the 2014 National Assessment of Educational Progress.* Washington, DC: National Assessment Governing Board.

National Center for Education Statistics (NCES). (2013a). *Nation's Report Card Website, Released Items.* http://nces.ed.gov/nationsreportcard/itmrlsx/search.aspx?subject=history

National Center for Education Statistics (NCES). (2013b). *Nation's Report Card Website, Technical Documentation on Instruments.* http://nces.ed.gov/nationsreportcard/tdw/instruments/

Zarillo, J. J. (2012). *Teaching Elementary Social Studies: Principles and Applications.* Fourth Edition. Boston, MA: Pearson Education.

10

ASSESSING HISTORICAL THINKING IN THE REDESIGNED ADVANCED PLACEMENT UNITED STATES HISTORY COURSE AND EXAM

Lawrence G. Charap

Introduction

The past two decades have witnessed a controversial expansion of high-stakes testing at many levels of the U.S. education system. Most of these efforts have occurred in the core subjects of English and mathematics; fewer attempts have been made to enact large-scale tests in history and social studies, subjects in which states, districts, and schools mandate a variety of different courses and sequences for students through middle and high school years. The College Board's Advanced Placement (AP) courses and exams are thus nearly unique in providing a uniform assessment experience to American and international high school students in the fields of United States, European, and World History. This chapter describes how recently announced changes to these courses and exams could affect the way millions of high school students and teachers experience the study of the past.

Goals of the Advanced Placement Program in United States History

The AP program is one of the world's largest and best-known programs for providing high school students with the opportunity to undertake college-level coursework. Students who take AP courses expect to engage in a rigorous learning experience that mirrors a college survey-level course in the discipline. Near the end of the academic year in May, students take an internationally administered AP exam in their subject; a qualifying score allows them to receive college credit from participating institutions or placement standing to proceed to intermediate coursework in the discipline. The program has seen tremendous growth over the past decade: over 400,000 students took the AP U.S. History Exam alone in 2012, a nearly twofold expansion from 2002.[1]

The AP experience is the product of a relationship between an outline of topics, contained in an *AP Course Description* published by the College Board for each course; a syllabus developed by individual AP teachers; and that course's AP exam. A Development Committee of college and high school educators approves the exam questions and the assembled exam, whose specific content changes every year. The exam questions follow the scope and content of the *AP Course Description,* which outlines the topics students might expect to study in the college-level survey course. For AP U.S. History, for example, the *AP U.S. History Course Description* (until the debut of the redesigned course in fall 2014) specifies over a hundred possible topics in 28 different historical periods that appear in the typical yearlong introductory college course in American History. The *Course Description* also specifies how topics will appear on the exam by area (e.g. political history, social history, diplomatic history) and chronology (e.g. 1914 to the present).

Any high school course that is meant to give students advanced placement or credit for college work must meet the expectations of postsecondary institutions that the experience is comparable to their own survey course. It is therefore crucial that students are exposed to questions on the AP exam that reflect the kinds of tasks that students will encounter in their freshman year of college, especially rigorous essay writing. In recent years the exam has included a Document-Based Question (DBQ), two free-response essay questions, and between 80 and 100 multiple-choice questions (Hacsi, 2004; Rothschild, 1999). The DBQ and free-response essay questions take between 30 and 60 minutes for students to complete. The DBQ asks students to construct a plausible argument about the historical significance of between 6 and 10 related primary source documents. Other essay questions ask students to use their knowledge to develop and defend a historical argument on various aspects of U.S. history. Student essays are read and scored by trained college and high school faculty at a weeklong event each June.

The AP exams in history also contain multiple-choice questions. These allow test designers to easily cover the sweep of U.S. history, both chronologically and topically, and help to ensure high reliability (the likelihood that candidates taking different forms of the same examination will receive the same scores). Multiple-choice questions allow an appropriate level of difficulty and discrimination among students at different performance levels. Furthermore, the reuse of some number of multiple-choice questions across different years allows a statistical equating process that ensures scores are comparable over time, accounting for the naturally occurring differences in exam difficulty by comparing cohorts' performances.

After each exam administration, student scores on the different components of the AP exam are combined into a composite score. The aggregate data from these scores, in tandem with equating data, are then used to establish cut points for AP grades that reflect the performance of college freshmen on similar questions and allow comparability with earlier exam administrations. Students receive AP scores between 1 and 5, where 5 means "extremely well qualified for subsequent college-level work in the discipline," and 1 means the College Board makes "no recommendation" for advanced standing. In this way, students' demonstrated proficiency in college-level history knowledge and skills can be used by colleges and universities in making decisions about credit and/or placement into intermediate coursework.

Critiques of AP and High-Stakes Assessment Models in History

AP courses and exams are offered every year at a wide variety of high schools and to students with diverse backgrounds and prior experiences in history. Because AP courses do not model a particular survey course at any one college or university (which vary widely by institutions; see Townsend, 2003), *AP Course Descriptions* have traditionally been silent about teaching methods, or how deeply students need to know about the topics that might appear on the AP exam. The possibility that AP exams might ask about any historical fact or individual leads many teachers to feel a pressure to cover as many topics as possible in their AP course, an approach sometimes disparaged as "mile wide and inch deep" learning.

This situation has led researchers on student teaching and learning to express concerns about the quality of AP instruction. A study undertaken by the National Research Council (2002) on Advanced Placement courses in math and science found that the breadth of many AP science courses pressured teachers to spend insufficient time on major topics in their courses and to emphasize the memorization of disconnected facts (pp. 156–157). AP history courses have been criticized on similar grounds. Wineburg (2006) noted a divide between AP U.S. History classrooms in which students engaged in vigorous classroom discussions and investigation into the past, and those in which teachers felt pressured to race through every historical topic in order to adequately prepare their students for the possible range of content they might encounter on the exam. AP history teachers surveyed by the College Board describe the pressures they face in similar terms.

A deeper criticism of AP history concerns the exams' use of multiple-choice questions. Rothstein (2004) and Wineburg (2004), for example, challenge the use of multiple-choice questions to assess authentic historical knowledge on high-stakes history exams, including AP. Because large-scale testing primarily seeks to discriminate between students at different ability levels, Wineburg argues, the multiple-choice questions on these tests are primarily intended to ensure that few students will perform well on them. A second criticism of multiple-choice testing is that it poorly reflects the types of historical thinking and understanding valued by the discipline (Breakstone, Smith, & Wineburg, 2013). Similarly, Willingham (2003), summarizing studies of memory and student learning, concludes that presenting students with facts out of historical context results in shallow comprehension and poor long-term retention. These studies suggest that "drilling" for student recall on multiple-choice tests ironically makes students less prepared to learn and remember historical facts. Finally, another critique of AP history assessments faults the Document-Based Question for including too many tasks (making an argument, analyzing evidence, and synthesizing information) to be sure what the single score given on these essays says about a student's understanding of history (Breakstone et al., 2013). This echoes previous independent research showing that AP students perform poorly at the heart of the DBQ task: the rigorous analysis of primary source documents (Wineburg, 2001; Young & Leinhardt, 1998).

Setting Curricular Goals

Over the past decade, the College Board has responded to these and similar criticisms of Advanced Placement by seeking to redesign AP courses and exams to align with best practices in teaching and learning. In place of the model outlined above, in which the topic list in the *Course Description* only generally corresponds to the content and tasks contained in the AP exam, AP courses are now being planned using the methodology of Understanding by Design (Wiggins & McTighe, 2005) to integrate curricular goals with assessment design. In this model, the curriculum must define the key understandings students will develop about a domain, and then describe ways to elicit evidence of student learning within that domain. The AP history courses (U.S., European, and World History) are among the first AP courses to benefit from the new approach.

The effort to redesign AP history had to begin with a curriculum framework that explained at what depth students needed to learn about historical facts, while also making clear how students should articulate skills and habits of mind that show evidence of authentic historical understanding. Beginning in 2006, the College Board asked panels of scholars and expert teachers to join Curriculum Development and Assessment Committees ("CDACs") for each AP history course that would create new curriculum framework documents and assessment models. These groups first agreed upon the historical thinking skills that all redesigned AP history exams would measure. In addition to such skills as engaging with primary and secondary source materials and persuasively using evidence to make a historical argument, these panels identified broader historical habits of mind, such as an awareness of historical context, continuity and change over time, periodization, and historical causation (see Figure 10.1).

Groups of historians and teachers then created a *Curriculum Framework* for each AP history course that defined its scope and identified major course themes. For AP U.S. History, these themes included topics that would span the 500+ years covered by a college-level survey course in American history, such as "identity," "power and politics," and "work, exchange, and technology." The *Curriculum Framework* then describes the goals of the course in a set of learning objectives

Skill Type	Historical Thinking Skill
I. Chronological Reasoning	1. Historical Causation
	2. Patterns of Continuity and Change over Time
	3. Periodization
II. Comparison and Contextualization	4. Comparison
	5. Contextualization
III. Crafting Historical Arguments from Historical Evidence	6. Historical Argumentation
	7. Appropriate Use of Relevant Historical Evidence
IV. Historical Interpretation and Synthesis	8. Interpretation
	9. Synthesis

FIGURE 10.1 Historical thinking skills assessed by questions on the redesigned AP History exams

that are organized around significant developments within these themes in different historical periods (College Board, 2014). For example, under the theme of "identity," one learning objective states that students should be able to "[e]xplain how conceptions of group identity and autonomy emerged out of cultural interactions between colonizing groups, Africans, and American Indians in the colonial era." All AP U.S. History exam questions will now be designed to measure student understanding of the course's learning objectives.

The *Curriculum Framework* also contains a detailed course outline, organized chronologically, that presents the topics, events, and patterns that are required knowledge (and thus potentially assessable) for the AP exam. Instead of a "laundry list" of names, dates, and events, historical topics are presented in a narrative form explaining the significance of various events in different historical periods. Most crucially, the framework presents the required topics in conceptual terms, allowing teachers a variety of ways in which to illustrate them without worrying that neglect of other, optional topics will harm student exam scores. For example, an understanding of U.S. antebellum reform movements is required by the course, but whether to teach in depth about one specific reformer (for example, Charles G. Finney) or a utopian reform group (such as Brook Farm) is left to the discretion of the teacher. In both cases, these illustrative examples can be drawn upon by students in the written sections of the AP exam, but are not subject to assessment in multiple-choice questions, as described below.

Redesigning Written Assessment Tasks

In order for teachers to have the instructional flexibility needed to improve students' depth of understanding and historical thinking skills, the structure and nature of the AP exam had to change along with the course's curriculum. In particular, exam questions were needed that would assess student understanding of the learning objectives laid out in the course's *Curriculum Framework*. The emphasis on development of historical thinking skills in the curriculum warranted the creation or realignment of exam tasks that assess students' ability to reason about the past in ways authentic to the discipline of history.

A starting point in history assessment design is the research literature exploring the best practices of history teaching and learning, along with a consideration of how these could be coupled with effective assessment strategies (e.g. Leinhardt, Beck, & Stainton, 1994; Pace, 2004; Seixas, 2011; Stearns, Seixas, & Wineburg, 2000; Wineburg, 2001). The emerging work in this field validates the use of assessment tasks reflecting facility with the disciplinary practices of history, such as writing well-supported historical arguments, accurately interpreting historical evidence, and the use of authentic primary and secondary sources (cf. New York State Education Department, 2013; Stanford History Education Group, 2012; VanSledright, 2014). These also reflect the expectations of higher education faculty that a history survey course should center on persuasive interpretation of historical evidence (College Board, 2010; Townsend, 2003). A focus on writing in response to historical texts also aligns with broader trends in K-12 education in the United States, such as the widespread adoption of the Common Core State Standards for English Language Arts, and their emphasis on the sophisticated analysis of primary and secondary source texts drawn from history and social studies (Council of Chief State School Officers, 2010). Similarly, the National Council for the Social Studies' recent *College, Career, and Civic Life (C3) Framework for Social Studies State Standards* helps history and social studies teachers ground their teaching in discipline-specific practices of literacy, learning, and assessment (National Council for the Social Studies, 2013).

To develop assessment tasks aligned with the goals for the redesigned course, the U.S. History CDAC worked in consultation with the administrators of the AP exams, Educational Testing Service, as well as researchers in educational and cognitive psychology and assessment. The CDAC decided that the DBQ and essay questions, long central to assessments of historical understanding in college classrooms, would remain as critical components of AP exams. However, to answer criticisms that these long writing questions were murky about exactly which skills they measured, they will be written to target one or more of the historical thinking skills defined in the *Course Description*. Scoring rubrics for the written questions will reflect an alignment with the various historical thinking skills elicited by the question. A question asking about continuity and change over time, for example, will have a rubric awarding students points for their use of this skill, as well as other points for accurately using historical evidence, writing a thesis statement, and synthesizing information.

In addition, to address the concern of Breakstone et al. (2013) that the DBQ and essay questions on the AP exam demand a "complex orchestration of skills" that do not permit clear insight into how a student reasons historically, each AP U.S. History exam will now feature four "short answer questions" that require students to write for 10–12 minutes on significant problems in U.S. history.

These questions focus on student use of one of the particular historical thinking skills defined in the *Curriculum Framework*. For example, a question might ask students to choose whether the Northwest Ordinance, the Missouri Compromise, or the Mexican-American War marked the beginning of the sectional crisis that led to the Civil War (and then support their choice), as a way to assess proficiency in the skill of historical periodization. In this way, the questions are much more targeted to particular thinking skills than in past AP history exams.

Redesigning Multiple-Choice Questions

The limitations of multiple-choice questions have led some critics to conclude that they cannot assess sophisticated historical thinking: in the words of Breakstone et al. (2013, p. 54), expecting them to be able to measure deep historical understandings "is like using a pocket-knife to do surgery." Moreover, in this view, most multiple-choice exam questions are both *disconnected* (asking students about a variety of disparate topics at different times and places in history) and *shallow* (asking students to simply recall knowledge without understanding its significance). On the other hand, the main goal of the Advanced Placement Program—to ensure that students who are capable of advanced work can place out of introductory courses in college—mitigates against completely eliminating the use of multiple-choice questions on the AP history exams. College and university faculty need to have confidence in the reliability and validity of AP exam results in order to give students credit and placement for their AP scores, and as explained above, multiple-choice questions are a critical source of AP exams' overall reliability.

Recognizing the critiques of multiple-choice questions, the redesigned exam does reduce the importance of multiple-choice questions: both the number (55 questions, down from 80) and weight (40%, down from 50%) of multiple-choice questions have decreased. In addition, the range of assessable content in this section has been narrowed to include only the content specified in the *Curriculum Framework,* as explained above. Only a small number of individuals, for example, are named in the *Curriculum Framework*'s topic outline, meaning that multiple-choice questions will not ask students to recall minutiae about non-named individuals. Of course, since true understanding of historical phenomena often requires deep investigation into specific individuals, groups, and phenomena, some of these are still present in the framework, as "illustrative examples." Students can (and should) continue to learn about these and other historical facts beyond those named in the framework, in order to have a broader understanding of American history. However, they will not need to worry that they will be penalized for not knowing details about every possible historical fact and figure.

To address the concern that multiple-choice questions are often disconnected, the redesigned AP history exams organize the multiple-choice questions into sets of 2 to 5 questions on a given historical topic. More significant, however, is the organizing principle behind each set. All of the questions in a set now relate to one or more pieces of stimulus material (historical sources). The stimulus material can be drawn from written primary texts (excerpts from letters, editorials, song lyrics), visual culture (cartoons, paintings), secondary sources (historians' arguments, taken from books or journal articles), or data (maps, charts, graphs). These sources are not ones that test-takers have necessarily encountered before, allowing the creation of an almost limitless number of item sets. However, these sources must still relate to the learning objectives for AP U.S. History, as laid out in the *Curriculum Framework*.

In the context of examining a particular source material, test-takers are asked a series of questions that probe their understanding of the historical significance of the stimulus. Questions might ask students to place the stimulus material in context—asking what contemporary event a letter relates to, for example, or what political group a cartoonist most likely agreed with. They might also ask about the most likely causes or effects of the stimulus material, or about how the views in a source compare to those of similar actors in other historical periods.

Figure 10.2 illustrates how two questions might be asked around the same stimulus material, in this case, a short paragraph by the historian James Patterson

---

Questions 1–2 refer to the excerpt below.

"Economic growth was indeed the most decisive force in the shaping of attitudes and expectations in the postwar era. The prosperity of the period broadened gradually in the late 1940s, accelerated in the 1950s, and soared to unimaginable heights in the 1960s. By then it was a boom that astonished observers. One economist, writing about the twenty-five years following World War II, put it simply by saying that this was a 'quarter century of sustained growth at the highest rates in recorded history.' Former Prime Minister Edward Heath of Great Britain agreed, observing that the United States at the time was enjoying 'the greatest prosperity the world has ever known.' "

James T. Patterson, historian, *Grand Expectations: The United States, 1945–1974*, published in 1996

1. One significant result of the economic trend described in the excerpt was the

(A) rise of the sexual revolution in the United States.
(B) decrease in the number of immigrants seeking entry to the United States.
(C) rise of the Sun Belt as a political and economic force.
(D) decrease in the number of women in the workforce.

2. Many of the federal policies and initiatives passed in the 1960s address which of the following about the economic trend described in the excerpt?

(A) Affluence had effectively eliminated racial discrimination.
(B) Pockets of poverty persisted despite overall affluence.
(C) A rising standard of living encouraged unionization of industrial workers.
(D) Private industry boomed in spite of a declining rate of federal spending.

FIGURE 10.2 Stimulus material and multiple-choice questions on the redesigned AP U.S. History Exam

on the post-World War II period of prosperity in the United States. Question 1 asks test-takers to accurately connect Patterson's arguments to later developments in the United States. Question 2 asks test-takers to place the text into the context of contemporary political developments in the 1960s.

Additional questions that follow this model ask about continuity and change over time, or about analogous developments in other time periods. Most notable about these questions, however, is what they do *not* ask. First, since the main goal of the exam is assessing students' *historical* knowledge, questions cannot primarily ask students whether or not they comprehend the passage (questions that could presumably be answered correctly by students who have not taken American history). Second, these questions seek to avoid asking test-takers to simply recall historical facts in isolation from the text being examined.[2] Finally, no questions will simply assess student comprehension of a text or passage independent of its historical context. In this way the redesigned multiple-choice questions seek to reward, wherever possible, students who can *both* correctly understand a piece of historical evidence *and* interpret it in its proper historical context.

Pilot Administrations, Validation, and Teacher Training

In Fall 2010, a group of higher education history faculty was surveyed to confirm that the approach of the proposed AP U.S. History *Curriculum Framework* met their expectations for survey-level courses and that they would continue to grant credit or placement for successful performance on the redesigned exam (College Board, 2010). Next, pilot questions in the new exam format were administered to high school students to assess how well the new multiple-choice and short answer questions elicited evidence that they were engaged in historical reasoning in responding to these questions. Students were asked to engage in a "think-aloud" exercise in which they described the process through which they answered the questions. Many of the students used similar terms to explain how they had tried to reason historically about the questions. As one put it, the new questions "make the connection between [the reading] and other events in history. It's not something you can just read a question and say oh, that's definitely wrong. You have to think about what's going on in the question so you have to—it requires a lot of thinking" (College Board, 2012). These and similar responses during the interviews supported the proposition that the questions measure intended historical thinking skills.

The AP U.S. History CDAC (now the Development Committee), working on behalf of the College Board, has since approved hundreds of items that are being piloted for statistical purposes and assembled into forms for exam administration. Several full forms of the redesigned AP U.S. History exam have been piloted to determine how the exam performs on such indicators as performance discrimination and reliability. Another purpose of these full-form pilots was to determine whether students had sufficient time to respond to all questions, given the dramatically increased amount of reading included on the redesigned exam. Exam readers trained in applying the rubrics for the new questions scored these pilot exams beginning in May of 2012. Some minor changes to the exam design and format were made as the result of the findings of these pilot administrations, namely, an increase in the weighting and number of multiple-choice questions and increases in time for several other sections. With these changes, the College Board gained increased confidence in the reliability and timing of the U.S. History exam design, without sacrificing its validity, and will begin administering the redesigned U.S. History exam for all students beginning in May 2015.

Samples of the new types of questions are contained in the *AP United States History Course and Exam Description* (College Board, 2014). Since teachers began instruction in the new course in September 2014, during the summer of that year the College Board published one of the pilot exam forms for use as a practice exam, with rubrics, scoring commentaries, and sample student responses for each question. Other teacher support efforts included AP workshops and Summer Institutes, the publication of curricular pacing and planning guides, and the creation of tools such as syllabus development guides and interactive online events. These efforts emphasize research-based best practices for history professional development, which focus on learning to read and write with authentic historical sources (e.g. Monte-Sano, 2008, 2011).

Implications for Teachers and Practitioners

The redesign of the AP U.S. History curriculum and exam are perhaps the most significant changes to the Advanced Placement Program courses in history since the program's inception in 1956 (cf. Rothschild, 1999). Teachers who are familiar with AP will need to prepare students for new models of multiple-choice questions, short answer questions, and skills-based rubrics for essays and DBQs. However, the use of learning objectives to constrain the content of the course will also provide much-desired guidance to teachers and students about what content might be assessable on the exam. Teachers who use released AP exams and scored essays with their students should benefit from the ability to use short answer questions with smaller historical tasks, providing models of how to develop proficiency in those skills in instruction. In addition, a more focused exam design should allow teachers to receive more precise score reporting data after each exam administration, allowing them to work on improving their instruction in areas where their students have scored poorly.

The creation of the redesigned AP U.S. History course and exam provided a number of important lessons for history curriculum and assessment design. The goal of having students investigate the past in a deeper, more meaningful fashion led to a curriculum that emphasized flexibility and constrained breadth through the use of learning objectives tied to the development of historical thinking skills. At the same time, the goal of more meaningfully assessing student understanding of historical events led to an exam design that abandoned disconnected recall-based multiple-choice questions in favor of multiple-choice and writing questions that ask students to analyze evidence and use other historical thinking skills. Most significantly, both components—the curriculum and the assessment—had to be constructed simultaneously to meet the larger goals of fostering and measuring in-depth student understanding of the past. In order to promote a more engaging, meaningful style of history instruction, educators must consider how to use new forms of assessment that reward in-depth historical reasoning.

It is hoped the integrated approach to curriculum and instruction in the redesigned course and exam will help AP teachers place the development of historical thinking skills and deep inquiry at the heart of their instruction. These changes should allow AP teachers to create even more engaging learning experiences that help students to become apprentice historians, adept at using the tools and habits of minds employed in the discipline and well prepared for success in their continuing study of the past.

Notes

1 "AP Program Participation and Performance Data," at http://research.collegeboard.org/programs/ap/data/participation/2012
2 In practice, questions that do not directly assess understanding of the passage could not be entirely excluded from the multiple-choice section and are mixed into the sets, but they cannot amount to more than 20% of the multiple-choice section total.

Author note: The author wishes to thank Allison Thurber, Thomas Matts, and two outside reviewers for their comments and feedback.

References

Breakstone, J., Smith, M., & Wineburg, S. (2013). Beyond the bubble in history/social studies assessments. *Phi Delta Kappan, 94*, 53–57.
College Board. (2010). *Fall 2012 AP U.S. history higher education validation study.* http://media.collegeboard.com/digitalServices/pdf/ap/Fall2010-AP-USHistory-HigherEd-Validation-Study.pdf
College Board. (2012). *AP U.S. history pilot exam think-aloud study.* (Unpublished research). New York, NY: College Board.
College Board. (2014). *AP United States history course and exam description and curriculum framework.* http://media.collegeboard.com/digitalServices/pdf/ap/ap-course-exam-descriptions/ap-us-history-course-and-exam-description.pdf
Council of Chief State School Officers. (2010). *Common core state standards for English language arts and literacy in history/social studies, science, and technical subjects.* Washington, DC: National Governors Association Center for Best Practices, Council of Chief State School Officers.
Hacsi, T. A. (2004). Document-based question: What is the historical significance of the advanced placement test? *Journal of American History, 90*, 1392–1400.
Leinhardt, G., Beck, I. L., & Stainton, C. (1994). *Teaching and learning in history.* Hillsdale, NJ: Lawrence Erlbaum.

Monte-Sano, C. (2008). Qualities of historical writing instruction: A comparative case study of two teachers' practices. *American Educational Research Journal, 45,* 1045–1079.

Monte-Sano, C. (2011). Beyond reading comprehension and summary: Learning to read and write in history by focusing on evidence, perspective, and interpretation. *Curriculum Inquiry, 41,* 212–249.

National Council for the Social Studies. (2013). *The college, career, and civic life (C3) framework for social studies state standards: Guidance for enhancing the rigor of K-12 civics, economics, geography, and history.* Silver Spring, MD: NCSS.

National Research Council. (2002). *Learning and understanding: Improving advanced study of mathematics and science in U.S. high schools.* Washington, DC: National Academy of Sciences.

New York State Education Department. (2013). *Regents exam in U.S. history and government.* www.nysedregents.org/

Pace, D. (2004). The amateur in the operating room: History and the scholarship of teaching and learning. *American Historical Review, 109,* 1171–1192.

Rothschild, E. (1999). Four decades of the advanced placement program. *The History Teacher, 32,* 175–206.

Rothstein, R. (2004). We are not ready to assess history performance. *Journal of American History, 90,* 1381–1391.

Seixas, P. (2011). Assessment of historical thinking. In P. Clark (Ed.), *New possibilities for the past: Shaping history education in Canada* (pp. 139–153). Vancouver, BC: UBC Press.

Stanford History Education Group. (2012). *Beyond the bubble.* http://beyondthebubble. stanford.edu/

Stearns, P. N., Seixas, P., & Wineburg, S. (Eds.). (2000). *Knowing, teaching, and learning history: National and international perspectives.* New York, NY: NYU Press.

Townsend, R. B. (2003). *Teaching the introductory survey: Insights from the College Board's AP survey.* http://apcentral.collegeboard.com/apc/public/homepage/46835.html

VanSledright, B. (2014). *Assessing historical thinking and understanding: Innovative designs for new standards.* New York, NY: Routledge.

Wiggins, G., & McTighe, J. (2005). *Understanding by design: Expanded 2nd edition.* Alexandria, VA: Association for Supervision and Curriculum Development.

Willingham, D. (2003). *Ask the cognitive scientist: Students remember . . . what they think about.* www.aft.org/newspubs/periodicals/ae/summer2003/willingham.cfm

Wineburg, S. (2001). *Historical thinking and other unnatural acts: Charting the future of teaching the past.* Philadelphia, PA: Temple University Press.

Wineburg, S. (2004). Crazy for history. *Journal of American History, 90,* 1401–1414.

Wineburg, S. (2006). A sobering big idea. *Phi Delta Kappan, 87,* 401–402.

Young, K. M., & Leinhardt, G. (1998). Writing from primary documents: A way of knowing in history. *Written Communication, 15,* 25–68.

11

HISTORICAL CONSCIOUSNESS AND HISTORICAL THINKING REFLECTED IN LARGE-SCALE ASSESSMENT IN SWEDEN

Per Eliasson, Fredrik Alvén, Cecilia Axelsson Yngvéus, and David Rosenlund

Introduction

In 2011, comprehensive schools in Sweden received a new curriculum for all subjects. This change is attributed to the growing concern over deteriorating results observed not only in international tests but also in the students' performance in higher education. Since the former curriculum was vague, the ambition was to construct one with fewer central aims, with clear core content, and with understandable knowledge requirements for each subject (Prop. 2008/09:87, 2008).

Sweden has a tradition of national tests in Swedish, English, and Mathematics. With the addition of tests in Geography, History, Religion, and Civics in 2013, most subjects in compulsory school now have national tests in grades six and nine in order to increase consistency in grading these subjects. Malmö University was responsible for constructing the national test in history for grade nine, administering it in April 2013 to 21,000 students.

The History Curriculum

"Man's understanding of the past is interwoven with beliefs about the present and perspectives of the future. In this way, the past affects both our lives today and our choices for the future" (Lgr11, 2011, p. 163). This first sentence of the Swedish history curriculum for grades one through nine summarizes the aim of history education: the development of the student's historical consciousness. Historical consciousness is defined in terms of three different competencies: Students should be able (1) to use a historical frame of reference; (2) to critically examine, interpret, and evaluate sources as a basis for creating historical knowledge; (3) to reflect upon their own and others' use of history. An additional competence, aiming to enhance the other three, is using historical concepts to analyze how historical knowledge is organized, created, and used.

The aim of the new history curriculum is the development of a historical consciousness through self-reflective history learning (von Borries, 2011). The essential competence of historical consciousness is a narrative competence, which divides into three competencies: experience connected to content, interpretation connected to form, and historical orientation connected to function (Rüsen, 2004). One way to interpret the new curriculum is thus to look at the competencies students should develop as they attempt to operationalize this narrative competence: First, the frame of reference that involves various perspectives of the past and what separates it from the present, which demands a competence to experience the past as history; second, the competence to examine, interpret, and evaluate sources as a basis for creating historical knowledge, which is necessary for a meaningful interpretation of the past; third, the ability to reflect upon their own and other people's uses of history, which makes students understand the function of historical narratives for individual orientation in life and shows them how different actors in society use history as a means to influence people's perception of the past, their orientation in the present, and, subsequently, their orientation in the future; and last, the competence to use historical concepts. This last competence is introduced already in the first school years with timelines and time concepts. In grades seven through nine, there is continuity and change, explanation, criticism of sources, and identity. These concepts are the tools with which the first three competencies are developed (see Table 11.1).

The history education curriculum is organized chronologically and, for grades seven through nine, spans from ancient civilizations to present times. It specifies what historical processes, events, and persons history education should deal with, such as the Industrial Revolution or the Holocaust. Accordingly, it also influences the content of the test—the events or processes the test tasks should deal with.

Students' competencies when dealing with this core content are assessed using the knowledge requirements and are graded as F (fail), E (pass), C, and A (high pass) to indicate how well the student has achieved the requirements.

TABLE 11.1 Curriculum competencies and concepts in relation to historical consciousness as narrative competence

	Competence with related concepts		
	Experience	*Interpretation*	*Orientation*
Curriculum competence	To use an historical frame of reference	To use sources to create history	To reflect on the uses of history
Concepts	Causes—Consequences Continuity—Change	Sources, interpretation	Similarities and differences, identity

Construction of tasks

Multiple-choice (MC) questions are the most common item types in large-scale assessments (Grant, 2006), but current research, though limited, shows that they are unsuitable for testing more complex discipline-based thinking (Kuechler & Simkin, 2010; Reich, 2009). The knowledge requirements in the Swedish curriculum ask for reasoning, and it is questionable whether historical reasoning can be assessed using MC questions. Consequently, constructed response (CR) tasks are used to assess students' competencies for the higher levels of knowledge requirements.

To ensure alignment with curriculum, the construction of test tasks began with a theoretical analysis of the curriculum and a definition of the cognitive process necessary for meeting each of the knowledge requirements. Tasks were developed in accordance with these definitions and piloted with students. The empirical findings led to adjustments of the tasks; these adjustments included several types of scaffolds to direct the students' thinking in the right direction, thus making the tasks more reliable as instruments for assessing targeted student competencies. The CR tasks also have a rubric defining the three stages of progression (levels E, C, and A). By showing students the qualities required on each level, assessment is made more transparent. The subsections below present three sample tasks from the test and the distribution of performance at these levels on three tasks are described in Table 11.2.

Sample Task 1: Sweden's Democratic Development— Assessing the Competencies to Use a Historical Frame of Reference and Historical Concepts

The historical thinking concepts of causation, continuity, and change are central in the knowledge requirements. Causation is explicitly stated in the part of the requirements related to the competence to use a historical frame of reference, and continuity and change are related to the competence to use historical concepts. They are assessed in the same task, "Sweden's Democratic Development," which stresses a trend in politics that is one of the four lines of development (also including how cultures interact, migration, and people's living conditions) that structure the content of the curriculum. It is accompanied by three pictures

TABLE 11.2 Percentage of students at different levels

Tasks	Grade			
	F (fail)	*E (pass)*	*C*	*A*
Task 1: Causation	27%	45%	23%	6%
Task 1: Continuity and Change	38%	38%	18%	5%
Task 2	22%	37%	28%	13%
Task 3	46%	29%	18%	7%

showing the eighteenth century Swedish king Gustavus III, the all-male and all-white Swedish Government in 1918 (elected by a male electorate), and a more mixed Swedish government from 2010 (elected by universal electorate), respectively. The task asks the students to use the concepts of continuity and change to describe how and to explain why the democratic situation had changed in Sweden between the three time periods. With respect to curricular alignment, this task design combines knowledge requirements with three historical periods.

An example of change across the three time periods could be the different degrees of democracy in the process of appointing the government in Sweden. Examples of continuity, such as the continuous role of patriarchal structures throughout the three time periods, are expected to be less common since earlier trials had shown it was more difficult to reason about continuity than it was for change. An understanding of change and continuity is linked to the understanding of historical frameworks and the ways in which past and present are connected (Dawson, 2004).

The students are also asked to reason about the causes of the continuity and change elements they discuss in their answers. Causation is included in the task for two reasons: First, it is an issue of validity since it is part of the curriculum. And second, taking the causes of elements of continuity and change into consideration would make the task more historically relevant (Lee & Shemilt, 2009). This approach makes it possible for students to show their knowledge in two of the curriculum's competencies in one task; however, it might be more difficult for students to incorporate the aspects into one answer. Nevertheless, the advantages are twofold: it saves time because students have one less answer to write and it shows the teachers how the different competencies in the curriculum can be combined to make the subject of history less fragmented.

The test results show this task is neither among the most difficult nor the easiest ones. However, it is clear that using the concepts of continuity and change proved more difficult than reasoning about their causes. A possible explanation for this is that these concepts are new to most teachers in Sweden and have not been used extensively in classes.

A level E answer requires students to apply concepts in a basic, functional way. This was operationalized in this task as an application of continuity and change, where students could describe either an element of continuity or an element of change. This is an example from one student: "One way the democratic situation has changed is that it is not the king that has the power, now it is elected politicians."

Level A requires students to apply concepts in a well-functioning way. In this context, it means students must describe elements of continuity and of change and should support their answers with several historical examples. One student, having described changes in the democratic situation in Sweden between the time periods indicated by the photos, uses the two concepts in the following manner:

> The reason why it was not a democracy in Sweden during time period (TP) 1 is that Sweden was still a monarchy at the time. The reason there were

no women in the government in TP2 was that women did not qualify as citizens at the time and had no suffrage and were, because of that, not eligible for government. Something continuous is that there have always been men at the top, never women. A cause could be that women have not been citizens for as long as men have. In this area, there are both continuity and change because in TP1 & 2 there were only men ruling and only men that could vote. In 2010, TP3, women had become citizens and got the vote, which brought change to the democratic situation.

The student gives examples of both continuity and change regarding the patriarchal structure in Swedish politics and reasons about possible causes of changes within this structure. The competence to use these two elements in the same context is an example of Level A knowledge.

Sample Task 2: Olof Palme's Speech—Assessing the Competence to Reflect upon Uses of History

When reasoning about how the past is used, students must identify why a certain historical event might be utilized in the present. It is important to see uses of history within coherent narrative frameworks linking past to present (Shemilt, 2009). Students must discuss the extent to which a particular use of this event might be effective, given the assumed intent of the user.

There are several tasks in the test aiming to assess students' competence to reflect upon uses of history. Three such tasks concern the use of the Industrial Revolution at the opening ceremony of the Olympic Games in London 2012, the use of the Kristallnacht as a comparison to the Behring Breivik terrorist acts in Norway in 2011, and the use of Lenin's name for an award given to artists or writers considered rebellious and critical of society. These are all examples of present uses of history.

Another task that focuses on a past use of history concerns the Christmas speech of former Swedish Prime Minister Olof Palme in 1972. In his speech, Palme equated the US bombings of Hanoi with atrocities committed prior to the events in Vietnam. Among the atrocities Palme used in the speech were Guernica, Treblinka, and Sharpeville. In the task's introduction, students are informed that Palme gave a speech in 1972 that was related to US bombings in Vietnam in December that year. The students are also informed that Palme used historical events in the speech and that they can read an excerpt from the speech attached to the task. The task asks students to explain why Palme chose those particular events when commenting on the bombings. From a validity aspect, the task is thus very close to the formulation in the curriculum.

Considering the share of students passing this task, it seems to have a level of difficulty lower than the one concerning causation and continuity and change, possibly because it supplies students with parts of the contextualization needed to solve it.

Level E requires students to give one plausible reason for Palme's use of the historical examples mentioned in the speech. The following is a level E student's response: "He is trying to show that the USA is no better than the Nazis; bombing a city kills a lot of innocent people, just like the Nazis did."

The student provides us with a plausible reason why Palme chose to use the historical examples. Level A requires students to explain why the historical examples are more or less effective in the given context. One level A student reasoned about Palme's motives for using history in his speech and why he used these events in particular:

> The reason that Palme mentioned these events of tragic genocide was because they are known and give the listener an emotional connection to the speech. The listener gets angry at the United States for repeating it. Five of these historical examples happened during WW2, and Palme used them because the United States was involved and therefore aware of them. However, I think he should have mentioned the bombings of Hiroshima and Nagasaki as the bombing of Hanoi is a repetition of this, but without the atomic bombs.

The student presents a plausible argument why Palme saw the events as significant for his aim. In addition, the student suggests a historical event even more relevant than the ones Palme used. This competence to reason around the effectiveness awarded this student the highest level, A, on this task.

Sample task 3: What Can We Say About the Future? Assessing the Competence to Use a Historical Frame of Reference

The competence of temporal orientation (relating past, present, and future to each other) is a central part of historical consciousness (Rüsen, 2005; Seixas, 2004; Shemilt, 2009). It is integrated into the knowledge requirements related to the competence to use a historical frame of reference. This aspect of historical thinking is assessed in the task "What can we say about the future—with the help of history." This task has the most complex instructions in the test due to the complexity of the expected cognitive procedure. The student is asked to imagine that she/he is supposed to appear on a news program as a historian. The issue at stake is the effects the worsening economic conditions might have on future emigration from Sweden. The question in the program is "Can higher unemployment rates lead to a rise in emigration from Sweden?"

Two pictures accompany the task: The first shows people embarking a boat in the 1880s with a caption saying "In the 1880s, unemployment was high in Sweden and many emigrated from Sweden, e.g., to the USA." The second shows a bread queue of unemployed people in the early 1930s with a caption saying "In the 1930s, unemployment was high in Sweden but there were not many that emigrated from Sweden." Students need to identify what in these time periods is significant in relation to possible future emigration. To solve the task, they must first have content knowledge about the processes portrayed in the pictures. Second, they must identify which part of their knowledge is significant in relation to the issue at hand, and they must refer to this knowledge when they reason about possible future emigration in Sweden. The cognitive process students have to engage in is, from a validity aspect, very close to the definition of temporal orientation in the curriculum.

Progression in this task starts from singular statements concerning the future based on references to one of the historical time periods and the present. The next level of progression requires arguments for increasing and decreasing emigration based on simple references to both historical periods and to the present. The most advanced level requires arguments for increasing and decreasing emigration based on not only references but also the context of the two time periods and the present.

The task results indicate that a larger share of the students had difficulty reaching level E compared to other tasks in the test. However, the share of students that reached level A was equal to that for the other tasks.

Central to the assessment of this task is that the students use knowledge of the past to warrant their discussion of the future. On the E-level, one student first described the situation in the example from the nineteenth century and then argued that emigration rates will not be changed in the future "because we have, after all, much greater possibilities than in the nineteenth century to get allowances so we can survive."

On the A-level, one student reasoned about possible future emigration from Sweden as follows:

> Looking back on the depression of the 30s, one can see that there were not many that emigrated. That could be caused by the unemployment that was high in other places than Sweden: there had been a crash on the stock market in the USA that had spread to many parts of the world. The situation was not better in other countries compared to Sweden. What we can see is that emigration from Sweden is influenced by the situation in Sweden relative to the one in other places. Because of the fact that unemployment can have different consequences and because of the fact that we have to take into account the situation in other countries in the present in order to evaluate how a higher unemployment might affect Sweden. . . . And at the moment, it does not look very good in many places around the world, which points to a situation similar to the one in the 1930s.

This answer was assessed as level A because the student used both contrasting historical time periods to explain the logic of economic emigration from Sweden in relation to larger international contexts.

Assessment Scoring Instructions

School teachers themselves grade the national tests. The scores are used for statistical analyses and for support in setting student grades for the entire course. For teachers to be able to consistently assess the students' answers to the CR tasks, a comprehensive booklet with assessment instructions is provided together with the test material.

To ensure as reliable assessments as possible, both the construction of the tasks and their scoring instructions demand a certain chain of logic, similar to what John Biggs called a constructive alignment (Biggs, 1999). The alignment for a task takes its starting point in one or more of the four competencies in the curriculum and leads (via the core content and the knowledge requirements) to the construction of the task and its specific scoring instructions.

Sample Task 3, previously discussed, is designed after this idea of alignment to make it possible for students to show their competence in using a historical frame of reference and the core content migration within and between countries.

The knowledge requirements make it possible to assess the ability to use a historical frame of reference. For level A, for instance,

> Students can study some trends where cultures interact in migration, politics, and living conditions and describe **complex** relationships between different time periods. Students also give some possible extrapolations of these trends and justify their reasoning by applying **well-developed and well-informed** references to the past and the present.
>
> (Lgr11, 2011, p. 171)

This requirement demands reasoning about how trends in the past influence the present and the future. Sample Task 3 concerns the trend of migration. Two steps are taken to determine what to look for when evaluating responses to a specific task. The first is to decide what should be assessed in the students' reasoning according to the knowledge requirements: what are they supposed to show proof of? These are called aspects of the assessment. In Sample Task 3, students should reason about an extrapolation of a trend and, to support their reasoning, refer to the past and the present. The response thus contains the following aspects:

- The way in which students refer to the periods specified in the task, other historical periods, and contemporary life.
- The way in which students place their examples in a historical context.

Using student responses from trials, it is possible to concretize the expressions of progression (in bold, above) in the knowledge requirements. This is the second step. Accordingly, progression levels can be based on empirical studies of learners in the domain. This facilitates the identification of competent and

TABLE 11.3 Task specific rubric for the task "What can we say about the future?"

The student shows knowledge at E-level	The student shows knowledge at C-level	The student shows knowledge at A-level
In simple and to some extent informed references the student makes one description of a reasonable extrapolation about migration in the future. The student makes a reference to one of the historical examples and the present in order to explain the extent of the migration in the future.	In developed and relatively well-informed references the student makes two descriptions of reasonable extrapolations about migration in the future. The student makes a reference to both of the historical examples and the present in order to explain the extent of the migration in the future.	In well-developed and well-informed references the student makes two descriptions of reasonable extrapolations about migration in the future. The student makes a reference to both of the historical examples and the present in order to explain the extent of the migration in the future. The historical examples are put in their historical context.

less competent performances and the description of progression for grade nine students. Hence, the progression, realized in the task-specific rubric (Table 11.3), can be identified in the student responses.

The task-specific rubric is included in the assessment scoring instructions. It is complemented by the aspects of assessment and typical student responses taken from the task trials. These responses correspond to different levels in the rubric. The responses are also commented upon, and the passages in the responses that correspond to particular requirements in the rubric are pointed out clearly. Nevertheless, the rubric remains relatively open to interpretation.

Currently, there is no statistical inter-rater reliability test that evaluates differences in teacher grading with the use of assessment scoring instructions. This will be included in statistical analyses of the test in 2014.

Test Results

A comparison between the national test results and the final course grades for grade nine shows that students received higher final course grades than grades on the national test (See Table 11.4). One possible explanation for this is that there are discrepancies between teachers' interpretations of the curriculum and the test constructors' interpretations. To reduce this risk, the tasks of the test are continuously tested and revised by practicing and experienced teachers that form an expert panel to strengthen the tasks' validity. Another plausible explanation is that, since the national test is but one of several opportunities for the teachers to assess student performance, students had the chance to achieve better results on occasions other than the national test. Another possibility is of course that teachers are grading their students more generously in their own assessments.

TABLE 11.4 Distribution of students' test grades and final grades

	Grade					
	F	E	D*	C	B*	A
National test in history 2013	16.5%	26.0%	23.2%	19.2%	9.1%	6.1%
Final grade in history 2013	4.7%	27.0%	19.5%	24.3%	14.0%	9.6%

*The grades B and D are derived from the number of A's, C's and E's the student had achieved. If the student had achieved most, but not all, of the knowledge requirements for A the grade is B, so B and D are not described in the knowledge requirements. They could therefore not be used in assessment of single tasks but only as a test grade after scoring the whole test.

The tasks assessing the historical frame of reference are the ones causing the students the most problems. The best results are on the tasks concerning handling historical sources. The discrepancy between these competencies may be due to the tasks involving sources drawing on more of a generic logical skill than a distinctive historical knowledge. If so, the tasks involving sources require revision.

Girls performed better on the test than boys, and students whose first language is Swedish performed better than students studying Swedish as a second language. The latter is probably because developed reading and writing skills are necessary to understand what is required in the test.

The value of Cronbach's Alpha is 0.919, which indicates a reasonable degree of internal consistency in the test (Muijs, 2011). This means that a student who does well on a difficult question also succeeds with other difficult questions of the same sort and, consequently, that a student who fails to solve one question also fails with other similar questions.

Consequences and Conclusions

The introduction of compulsory national tests in history has had great consequences for teachers and students. Some teachers voice the apprehension that a national test will compromise the possibilities of a complex and multifaceted history education. They are afraid all focus will be on preparing for this one test. Nevertheless, the national test has also generated a lot of positive feedback for being legitimate and helpful. Research shows that external tests influence teachers' practices in teaching, assessment, and collegial deliberations (Cimbricz, 2002; Grant, 2006; Vogler & Virtue, 2007). In questionnaires answered by teachers in connection to the national test, 75 percent report it has enhanced discussions with colleagues about learning, 80 percent consider the test helpful in interpreting the curriculum, and 80 percent find it helpful in interpreting the knowledge requirements and their expressions of progression. Teachers' reactions show that the test matters and provides support in grading.

A positive reaction is also that the government has decided to introduce a similar history test in upper secondary schools in 2015, and the assignment to construct it has been given to Malmö University.

This chapter has related some of the thought processes and challenges involved in constructing a large-scale assessment test for history. A major challenge is the construction of complex tasks that combine several different cognitive processes to create a test that is both possible to realize on a large scale and valid to curriculum requirements. The challenges of validity are addressed by a construction process involving theoretical analyses of the curriculum, continual trials of tasks on students and teachers, and adjustments in the form of scaffolding to direct student thinking towards curriculum requirements, also making the tasks more reliable. Assessment instructions provided for teachers also clarify the validity of the tasks.

One of the main reasons for introducing a national test is to increase consistency in grading. This requires clear scoring instructions. Student responses yield much evidence that the assessment criteria are met by students, but in several different ways. This means that scoring instructions must point out aspects for assessment without mentioning specific content. The challenges of reliability are addressed by rubrics for the CR tasks, and the scoring instructions also consist of commented, authentic examples of student answers concretizing the expressions of progression in the knowledge requirements.

The main challenge is constructing a test that meets the complex requirements of the national curriculum, which has the main objective of developing historical consciousness. The national test shows how it is possible both to interpret the competencies of the curriculum as historical thinking processes and to operationalize them in tasks. In conclusion, the historical thinking approach has proven useful in concretizing and assessing the competencies required by the new curriculum. Furthermore, the approach can be successfully used in large-scale assessment of history education.

References

Biggs, J. (1999). *Teaching for quality at university.* Society for Research into Higher Education. Buckingham, England: Open University Press.

Cimbricz, S. (2002). State-mandated testing and teachers' beliefs and practice. *Education Policy Analysis Archives, 10*(2), 1–21.

Dawson, I. (2004). Time for chronology? Ideas for developing chronological understanding. *Teaching History, 117,* 1–21.

Grant, S. G. (2006). *Measuring history: Cases of state-level testing across the United States.* Greenwich, CT: Information Age Publishing.

Kuechler, W. L. & Simkin, M. G. (2010). Why is performance on multiple-choice tests and constructed-response tests not more closely related? Theory and an empirical test. *Decision Sciences Journal of Innovative Education, 8,* 55–73.

Lee, P., & Shemilt, D. (2009). Is any explanation better than none? Over-determined narratives, senseless agencies and one-way streets in students' learning about cause and consequence in history. *Teaching History, 137,* 42–49.

Lgr11 (2011). *Curriculum for the compulsory school, preschool class and the recreation centre.* www.mah.se/historia9

Muijs, D. (2011). *Doing quantitative research in education with SPSS.* (2nd ed.) London: Sage.

Prop. 2008/09:87. (2008). *Tydligare mål och kunskapskrav för grundskolan.* www.regeringen. se/sb/d/10003/a/117269

Reich, G. A. (2009). Testing historical knowledge: Standards, multiple-choice questions and student reasoning. *Theory & Research in Social Education, 37*(3), 325–360.

Rüsen, J. (2004). Historical consciousness: Narrative structure, moral function, and onto-genetic development. In P. Seixas (Ed.), *Theorizing historical consciousness* (pp. 63–85). Toronto, ON: University of Toronto Press.

Rüsen, J. (2005). *History: narration, interpretation, orientation.* New York, NY: Berghahn Books.

Seixas, P. (2004). Introduction. In P. Seixas (Ed.), *Theorizing historical consciousness* (pp. 3–20). Toronto, ON: University of Toronto Press.

Shemilt, D. (2009). Drinking an ocean and pissing a cupful. In L. Symcox & A. Wilschut (Eds.), *National history standards: the problem of the canon and the future of teaching history.* Charlotte, NC: Information Age Publishing.

Vogler, K. E., & Virtue, D. (2007). "Just the facts, ma'am": Teaching social studies in the era of standards and high-stakes testing. *The Social Studies, 98*(2), 54–58.

von Borries, B. (2011). How to examine the (self)-reflective effects of history teaching. In H. Bjerg, C. Lenz, & E. Thorstensen (Eds.), *Historicizing the uses of the past* (pp. 281–301). London, England: Transaction.

COMMENTARY

Assessment of Historical Thinking in Practice

Susan M. Brookhart

Introduction

The three chapters in this section describe large-scale history assessments in the United States and Sweden. The theme of the commentary is connecting the three assessments and their conceptions of historical thinking with the classroom, because all three assessment programs rest on the assumption that students will—or at least should—learn historical thinking in school. This chapter will address three issues:

- The nature of "historical thinking"
- The purpose of the assessment program
- Decisions about test construction.

The Nature of "Historical Thinking"

All three definitions of historical thinking stand in stark contrast to a view of history as an accumulation of historical facts and concepts. Lazer (this volume) explains that the *National Assessment of Educational Progress (NAEP) U.S. History Framework* specifies two ways of knowing and thinking about history: (1) historical knowledge and perspective and (2) historical analysis and interpretation. Charap (this volume) lists a set of nine historical thinking skills in four areas (see Figure 10.1, p. 165). Eliasson and colleagues (this volume) describe "historical consciousness," a slightly different approach to historical thinking in that it emphasizes the identity of the one doing the historical thinking (the student). Table C3.1 presents a comparison of the elements of historical thinking from the three chapters, using the order presented in the Charap chapter for the AP history framework.

Table C3.1 shows that the three conceptions of historical thinking have much in common: cause and effect, continuity and change, comparison, context, appropriate use and interpretation of sources, and using evidence to offer historical arguments. While Eliasson and colleagues did not explicitly mention sequencing events or periodization, one might argue that this skill is implied in the use of a historical frame of reference and in the fact that the content of history education is organized chronologically (p. 175).

TABLE C3.1 Comparison of elements of historical thinking

Lazer—NAEP U.S. History	Charap—AP U.S. History	Eliasson, Alvén, Yngvéus, & Rosenlund—Swedish History
Historical thinking	**Historical thinking**	**Historical consciousness**
Establishing cause-and-effect relationships	Historical causation	Causes—Consequences
Identifying historical patterns	Patterns of continuity and change over time	Continuity—Change
Sequencing events	Periodization	
Recognizing multiple perspectives and seeing an era or movement through the eyes of different groups	Comparison	Similarities and differences
Knowing and understanding people, events, concepts, themes, movements, contexts, and historical sources	Contextualization	To use a historical frame of reference
Finding value statements; Establishing significance; Applying historical knowledge; Weighing evidence to draw sound conclusions; Making defensible generalizations	Historical argumentation	To reflect on the uses of history; To use a historical frame of reference; To use sources to create history
Knowing and understanding people, events, concepts, themes, movements, contexts, and historical sources	Appropriate use of relevant historical evidence	To use a historical frame of reference
Explaining issues; Establishing significance	Interpretation	Sources, interpretation
Developing a general conceptualization of U.S. history; Rendering insightful accounts of the past	Synthesis	To use sources to create history
		Identity

The major difference between what the U.S. assessment programs designated "historical thinking" and what the Swedish assessment program designated "historical consciousness" is the inclusion of identity as an element. From the chapter's emphasis on the students' experience, from the curriculum's emphasis on history's effects on students' current lives and future choices, and even from the term "historical consciousness," one may infer that "identity" in this framework means a student seeing himself or herself as a participant in history, who in some way shapes history and is shaped by it. ("Identity" is listed as a theme in the AP U.S. History curriculum [Charap, p. 165], but it means group identity, not personal identity.)

The lack of identity on a list of historical thinking skills for the U.S. assessment programs may not amount to a large difference in practice. A sense of oneself being a person in history becomes part of historical thinking in the classroom. A common way to have students engage in higher-order thinking with particular content is to ask them to relate to the material in some way. For example, students might be asked to look at a picture of a one-room schoolhouse from a century ago and compare what it must have been like to be a student then with the experience of being a student today.

Similarly, some conceptions of historical thinking add understanding that historical interpretations contain an ethical dimension (Ercikan & Seixas, 2011, pp. 254–255). However, the ethical dimension may well be subsumed in the definitions of historical thinking in Table C3.1. The NAEP U.S. History framework includes "finding value statements." The AP history framework calls for argumentation skills, which often are construed to include critical thinking skills including making judgments about values (Brookhart & Nitko, 2015, p. 253). The Swedish national history test framework includes "reflection," which implies incorporating one's personal point of view.

Clearly, history education is moving toward an emphasis on historical thinking and away from an emphasis on having students memorize a body of historical facts. Recently in the United States, fifteen professional organizations collaborated to produce *The College, Career, and Civic Life (C3) Framework for Social Studies State Standards: Guidance for Enhancing the Rigor of K-12 Civics, Economics, Geography, and History* (NCSS, 2013). The framework presents an inquiry arc with four dimensions: (1) developing questions and planning inquiries, (2) applying disciplinary concepts and tools, (3) evaluating sources and using evidence, and (4) communicating conclusions and taking informed action. The disciplinary concepts and tools identified for history include (a) change, continuity, and context; (b) perspectives; (c) historical sources and evidence; and (d) causation and argumentation. These dimensions and tools would line up nicely with the elements of historical thinking presented in the chapters in this section and summarized in Table C3.1.

If there is so much agreement about the elements of historical thinking that should be taught and assessed in schools, then what is the problem? As Charap (this volume) discusses in his chapter, the problem is that this view of historical thinking does not match with the content and teaching methods found in many history classes. If curricular aims feature historical thinking, then history instruction will need to teach students to think, and classroom learning activities will need to center on student thinking (Burenheide, 2007).

While there are teachers who excel at student-centered instructional practices and in cultivating student thinking, there are others who persist in a teacher-centered, knowledge-transmission model of teaching. However, most teachers exercise what Cuban (2009, p. 52) calls "pedagogical pragmatism," borrowing strategies from both student-centered and teacher-centered pedagogies and practicing a middle-ground teaching style Cuban (2009, p. 31) calls "teacher-centered progressivism." As its name implies, the main instrument of thinking in this sort of pedagogy is the teacher. Students are given small group work, oral reports, and projects to do, for example, but teacher thinking remains at the center of the lesson.

Cuban (2010) applies this concept to the teaching of history in particular. He notes that while history teachers practice a mix of teacher- and student-centered pedagogy in order to keep their lessons from being "boring," most history teachers still "engage in a variety of text-driven practices that tilt toward a *heritage* rather than *historical* pedagogy" (Cuban, 2010, italics in original). A heritage view of history-teaching inculcates students into a national identity by passing on selected facts and received interpretations (e.g., lessons on "the founding fathers"). An historical view of history-teaching aims for producing students who can deal with multiple accounts of the same events, analyze source documents, base historical arguments on evidence, and the like—in short, supporting the kind of historical thinking that underpins the assessments described in the three chapters in this section.

However, Cuban reminds his readers that professional historians since the late nineteenth century have tried to move teachers from a heritage pedagogy, typically dependent on a single textbook and emphasizing selected historical facts, toward making the study of history in schools more inquiry-oriented and thoughtful. "In light of the evidence, thus far, of how teachers teach, professional historians—given their erratic but episodically vigorous efforts since the 1920s—have succeeded in raising public and professional awareness of the importance of history as a school subject but failed in their mission to substantially alter how teachers teach history" (Cuban, 2010). The item-level data presented in the Lazer chapter suggests that U.S. fourth, eighth, and twelfth graders do indeed have difficulty with questions that require historical thinking. Eliasson and colleagues' data on students' sample task performance suggests a similar picture for ninth grade students in Sweden. For both, rates of successful performance are lower and failure is higher than one might hope.

Is it possible that the assessment programs described in this section, the new C3 Framework from the National Council for the Social Studies, and other efforts that encourage a focus on historical thinking can move the needle—as previous efforts have failed to do? Assessment programs can and do influence teaching and learning, partly by clearly defining valued outcomes and partly by exerting pressure on teachers and students to work toward those outcomes (National Research Council, 2001). The valued outcomes measured by each of the three assessment programs share a great deal in common. The purposes of the assessment programs, however, and the uses of results differ quite a bit.

The Purpose of the Assessment Program

For the NAEP U.S. History Assessment (Lazer, this volume), the main purpose is research. Stakes are low for students and relatively low for teachers. The framework describing historical thinking does not serve as the standards or goals to which teachers teach. National level reports are produced every four to six years and focus on what students across the country know and can do. The impact of the NAEP definition of historical thinking on classroom instruction and assessment is likely to be minimal.

For the Advanced Placement Program's U.S. History exam (Charap, this volume), the main purpose is certifying attainment of outcomes comparable to those in college-level survey courses in U.S. History. The AP definition of historical thinking forms the basis for a curriculum framework for AP U.S. History courses. Participation in AP courses is voluntary, as is taking the AP exam. Results are reported to individual students and their selected colleges, and teachers of AP courses can see the results for their students. Stakes are moderate to high for AP teachers and are high for AP students, if one considers that qualifying to receive credit for a college course gives a student much-desired flexibility in planning his or her college experience, but not for all teachers and students. The impact of the AP Program's definition of historical thinking on classroom instruction and assessment is likely to be high to the extent that AP teachers follow the curriculum and do not, as Charap's chapter notes, succumb to the pressure to cover as many topics and facts as possible.

The ninth grade national history test in Sweden (Eliasson et al., this volume) has several purposes. One is to provide data on the national history curriculum, and another is to contribute to students' course grades. Participation is not voluntary. Results are reported, it seems, to teachers, students, and parents, as well as school administrators and national researchers. The impact of the new curriculum and assessment program's definition of historical consciousness on classroom instruction and assessment should, therefore, be high.

What are the implications of these differing test purposes for teaching and assessing history in the classroom? While NAEP is expected to have little effect on classroom learning, the whole purpose of creating the curriculum and exams for AP U.S. History and ninth grade national history in Sweden was to have an impact on history learning in schools.

It is interesting, therefore, to read in both the Charap and Eliasson chapters that the realities of schooling seem to be at work to mitigate the effects of the new emphases on historical thinking. Charap (this volume) reports that AP teachers feel pressure to teach a wide variety of facts and topics, despite the curriculum's stress on historical thinking as the more important goal. Nevertheless, a study of the previous version of the AP U.S. History exam (before the redesign reported in Charap's chapter) found that for teachers of classes where the definition of "success" was a minimum score of 4 on the U.S. History exam, the amount of emphasis on development of historical research skills and techniques was weakly but positively related to success. This result differed by school type. Holding the teacher's amount of emphasis on historical research skills constant, non-public school students outperformed public school students (Paek et al., 2007).

The previous AP U.S. History exam was driven mainly by a list of 28 chronological topics rather than applying nine historical thinking skills across seven themes and nine chronological periods, as in the redesign. Therefore, one would predict that classroom emphasis on historical research skills and historical thinking should be even more related to success on the redesigned AP exam than on the previous version. Consequently, one would also predict that AP teachers' abilities to engage students in historical thinking in the classroom will mediate the effect of the new definition of historical thinking on students' learning of history.

Eliasson and colleagues (this volume) report that teachers in Sweden considered the test helpful in interpreting the curriculum and that it enhanced discussions with colleagues about learning. Nevertheless, the final course grades that teachers assigned to students were higher than their grades on the national test. Because the tests are part of the composite final grades, this must mean that teachers provided students other assessment opportunities that were, for whatever reason, easier overall than the national test. Whether this was intentional mitigation of low test grades, or the result of teachers' differential emphasis of the various historical knowledge and skill areas, or the result of classroom assessments being relatively easier than the national test, some combination of these things, or something else, the result was that students' final grades painted a rosier picture of students' achievement than did the national test.

The distribution of grades in Table 11.4 (Eliasson et al., this volume, p. 183) suggests that some intentional mitigation is indeed taking place. Many more students failed the national test than failed their history course (national test failures, 16.5%; history course failures, 4.7%). Differences in the rest of the grade distribution categories are much smaller, suggesting that classroom assessments were not so much easier overall as they were easier at the lower end of the distribution. Research on grading practices has shown that teachers treat the difference between failure and a passing grade differently than they treat other grade boundaries and make every effort not to fail a student who is trying (Brookhart, 1993). To the extent that intentional mitigation of failing grades on the national test is taking place in ninth grade history classrooms in Sweden, the curricular definition of historical consciousness is being mitigated as well, at the low end of the achievement spectrum, in favor of student effort.

It seems, then, that there is not a straight-line connection between large-scale assessment of historical thinking and classroom instruction and assessment in historical thinking. The remoteness of NAEP from the classroom means this conclusion is not a surprise in the case of the NAEP U.S. History test. However, for the AP U.S. History exam and the ninth grade national history test in Sweden, both of which have curricula associated with them, it also appears that the connection between the large-scale assessment and the classroom could be made stronger. The AP program addresses this issue in part by offering professional development to teachers (Charap, this volume; Paek et al., 2007). The Swedish national history test addresses this issue in part by involving teachers in test scoring (Eliasson et al., this volume). The long-term success of bringing classroom history learning in line with the vision of historical thinking or historical consciousness in the assessment programs should be monitored. Maybe the time is right, given the current move toward more rigorous standards and an emphasis on student thinking (NCSS, 2013), to make progress on this front.

Decisions About Test Construction

The three chapters discuss many decisions about test construction and administration, which differ according to the different purposes of each assessment program. This section will focus on only two aspects of test construction, both closely tied with the chapter's theme of connecting how the three assessments define and assess historical thinking with classroom learning. The first is the design decisions made about item types. The second is the interaction of classroom instruction and an item's ability to assess student thinking.

Each chapter describes the format of its respective assessment of historical thinking and gives a rationale for format decisions, including whether to include multiple-choice items. Because the historical thinking constructs to be measured were very similar among the programs, as Table C3.1 demonstrated, one must conclude that the reason for the differing format decisions lay not with the constructs but the different purposes for the assessments.

Lazer (this volume) shows that the NAEP U.S. History test uses a mixture of multiple-choice, short open-ended, and extended open-ended questions. At grades 8 and 12, some questions are gathered into thematic blocks. However, even the extended open-ended questions are not particularly long and ask students focused, scaffolded questions about small pieces of a topic area. The inclusion of some multiple-choice items and some open-ended items lessens the problems associated with greater omission rates for the open-ended items. In addition, the issue of having a representative sample of the domain is less of a problem for NAEP than for many assessment programs because NAEP uses matrix sampling and individual scores are not required. In Lazer's discussion of these format decisions, the overriding principle was to maximize the amount of information the assessment could collect about what students know and can do in the domain of U.S. history, maintaining the level of validity and reliability required for the research program.

Charap (this volume) describes very different task design decisions for a very different assessment program. The AP U.S. History exam is part of the "AP experience" (p. 162), which includes the *AP Course Description* and individual teachers' syllabi and which has as its goal giving high school students the opportunity to undertake and certify college-level course work. Therefore, document-based questions and short essay questions will remain on the redesigned exam. The written questions will feature writing well-supported historical arguments and interpreting primary and secondary source evidence. The exam will also have multiple-choice questions, although fewer of them and with less weight than in the previous U.S. History exam, organized into sets based on historical source material. In Charap's discussion of these format decisions, the overriding principles were to measure the new curricular objectives with their emphasis on historical thinking and to reflect the rigorous learning experience of a college-level survey course in the discipline, while maintaining the level of validity and reliability required for college faculty to take the results seriously.

Eliasson and colleagues (this volume) describe an assessment composed of several constructed response tasks. The national history test in Sweden does not contain any multiple-choice items, a design decision made in an effort to assess complex, discipline-based thinking. Curricular validity was the main principle behind this decision, although tasks were adjusted and given extra scaffolding in order to promote reliability.

In the scoring for all three assessments, weight is given to the quality of students' historical thinking, interpretation of sources, and explanations. Knowledge of content is still required for all three, but it is not possible to perform well on any of them without being able to apply knowledge, interpret sources, and construct arguments. The effects these design decisions should have on the classroom are considerable. Knowing students will take an exam on which they need to reason historically and express that reasoning in cogent written arguments should strengthen the focus on curricular goals that emphasize historical thinking. As the previous sections in this commentary have indicated, it is not clear yet whether this will be the case or whether the learning outcomes will be mitigated as intended rigor meets classroom realities.

A second issue of test construction was not mentioned in the chapters, but it is an important one for any assessment external to the classroom. Those who write questions and tasks designed to assess thinking evaluate the cognitive requirements of a question based on the definitions of historical thinking reviewed in the first section of this commentary, sometimes with the aid of a taxonomy of instructional objectives in the cognitive domain (e.g., Bloom's taxonomy, the SOLO taxonomy, or some other scheme). For a question or task to tap the intended level of thinking, its material needs to be new to the students. If a question asks students to interpret sources they have already interpreted in class, or analyze a document they have already processed as part of their instruction, the question or task is rendered a recall-level item.

For example, if ninth grade students in a particular class had analyzed Olof Palme's 1972 speech (Eliasson et al., this volume) as part of their class work and had discussed his use of historical examples and their rhetorical intent, then Sample Task 2 becomes a recall-level task ("What did we say in class about that?") instead of a task requiring the use of a historical event in the present, as intended.

Both the AP U.S. History exam and the ninth grade national history test in Sweden are tied to a curriculum that is taught, but not by the designers of the assessment. Only the teacher of each particular class, and her students, will know for sure which of the questions and tasks measure historical thinking and which measure memory and comprehension of historical conclusions drawn in the context of instruction. This problem affects the NAEP history test as well, but to a lesser degree because the content is not specifically designed to be taught. Therefore, the risk of prior lessons usurping on-the-floor thinking during assessment is lessened. To the extent that questions are interpreted to measure historical thinking when they in fact measure recall, the validity of score meaning is lessened. This is a case not of an assessment affecting classroom instruction, but of classroom instruction affecting the assessment.

Conclusion

The three chapters in this section described assessment of historical thinking in large-scale assessment programs, one tied to a national research agenda (NAEP) and two to curricular and instructional intentions (AP U.S. History and national history assessment in Sweden). This commentary highlighted three issues addressed in all three chapters where there is a clear relationship between large-scale assessment of historical thinking and classroom instruction and assessment. This connection is an important one to make. If students are to develop desired historical thinking skills and historical consciousness, it will happen in the classroom and manifest in performance on the assessments. Therefore, the treatment of historical thinking in classroom instruction and assessment is an important factor affecting the large-scale assessment programs described in this section. The validity of the assessment information depends in part on the coordination between classroom and large-scale assessment program.

References

Brookhart, S. M. (1993). Teachers' grading practices: Meaning and values. *Journal of Educational Measurement, 30*, 123–142.

Brookhart, S. M., & Nitko, A. J. (2015). *Educational assessment of students* (7th ed.). Boston, MA: Pearson.

Burenheide, B. (2007). I can do this: Revelations on teaching with historical thinking. *History Teacher, 41*(1), 55–61.

Cuban, L. (2009). *Hugging the middle: How teachers teach in an era of testing and accountability.* New York, NY: Teachers College Press.

Cuban, L. (2010, July 21). *How history is taught in schools.* Available: http://larrycuban. wordpress.com/2010/07/21/how-history-is-taught-in-schools/.

Ercikan, K., & Seixas, P. (2011). Assessment of higher order thinking: The case of historical thinking. In G. Schraw & D. R. Robinson (Eds.), *Assessment of higher order thinking skills* (pp. 245–261). Charlotte, NC: Information Age.

National Council for the Social Studies (NCSS). (2013). *The college, career, and civic life (C3) framework for social studies state standards: Guidance for enhancing the rigor of K-12 civics, economics, geography, and history.* Silver Spring, MD: NCSS.

National Research Council. (2001). *Knowing what students know: The science and design of educational assessment.* Committee on the Foundations of Assessment; J. Pellegrino, N. Chudowsky, & R. Glaser (Eds.). Washington, DC: National Academy Press.

Paek, P. L., Braun, H., Trapani, C., Ponte, E., & Powers, D. (2007). *The relationship of AP® teacher practices and student AP exam performance.* New York, NY: College Board.

PART IV

Validity of Score Interpretations

12

THE IMPORTANCE OF CONSTRUCT VALIDITY EVIDENCE IN HISTORY ASSESSMENT

What Is Often Overlooked or Misunderstood?

Pamela Kaliski, Kara Smith, and Kristen Huff

In assessment, the argument can be made that there is nothing more important than gathering validity evidence for the use or interpretation of the scores that are produced by the assessments. Put simply, it is the validity evidence that allows test score users to have confidence that the scores from the assessment are meaningful and that inferences made about examinees based on the scores are appropriate. This applies to any field that uses scores from assessments to make inferences about examinees; in this chapter, the focus will be on validity issues in the context of history assessment design.

The importance of gathering evidence to support the inferences made from the results of an assessment is not a new concept. Rather, researchers have touted the necessity of gathering construct validity evidence for years, with considerable debate as to its meaning and practical implications for assessment design (e.g., American Educational Research Association, American Psychological Association, & National Council on Measurement in Education, 1999; Cronbach, 1989; Cronbach & Meehl, 1955). The most comprehensive discussion of validity has been provided over the past couple of decades by Kane (e.g., 2006, 2013), and we have adopted this contemporary view of validity as a reference throughout our chapter. The cornerstone of Kane's (2013) validity framework is that there are two steps to formulating validity evidence: "(1) specify the claims inherent in a particular interpretation and/or use of test scores; and (2) provide an evaluation of the claims based on empirical evidence, logical arguments, etc." (Brennan, 2013, p. 74). This is known as an argument-based approach to validity, and is intended to "reflect the general principles of construct validity without requiring formal theories" (Kane, 2013, p. 9). For the purposes of this chapter, we use the argument-based approach to validity as a framework when we discuss two specific construct validity issues.

Purpose of the Chapter

Gathering construct validity evidence is critical when scores from assessments are being used to make some decision or inference about the examinee. The focus of this chapter is on construct validity evidence for history assessments. Among the various types of validity evidence that could be discussed, we focus our discussion on two components of history assessment construct validity evidence that are often overlooked and sometimes misunderstood—dimensionality and cognitive validity evidence. We then provide guidelines for history researchers and assessment designers with regard to how to gather these types of validity evidence. For the purposes of this chapter, dimensionality evidence is defined as evidence that all dimensions (e.g., historical thinking and historical knowledge) are assessed and cognitive validity evidence is defined as evidence of an item eliciting the intended cognitive processes (i.e., historical thinking) that the item was designed to assess. We selected these two types of validity evidence for two reasons. First, there continue to be different definitions of historical thinking as a construct (e.g., different number of dimensions, different interrelationships among these dimensions), therefore, dimensionality analyses play a critical role in examining if items relate to the target construct and in refining the construct definition. Second, due to the higher-order nature of emerging historical thinking constructs, determining whether or not items are measuring what they are intending to measure is difficult based on traditional content validity procedures that focus on domain coverage, and in turn necessitate that cognitive validity evidence be gathered through think-aloud protocols (TAPs). Although both types of validity evidence are empirically based, the sources of data and analytical approaches differ and contribute unique validity evidence. For example, conducting TAPs where students think aloud while completing and interacting with a task is an ideal approach for developing a cognitive model of task performance, whereas conducting factor analyses is an ideal approach for assessing dimensionality of history assessment test scores.

In the sections that follow, a thorough treatment of these two types of validity evidence for history assessment will be provided. The goal is to clearly describe these types of validity evidence, and illustrate best practices for conducting these types of validity studies, given that they are often overlooked or misunderstood. For each of the two types of validity evidence, relevant research will be presented as an example to assist the reader in conducting and implementing these approaches in their own practices. Throughout the chapter, we also describe the challenges of conducting these types of validity studies, and make recommendations for how to avoid said challenges.

Issue #1: Assessing Dimensionality of Historical Thinking

One of the reasons that assessments often fail to measure historical thinking is because practitioners and assessment developers are unclear of its various dimensions. The lack of clarity is not surprising given the many discussions of what students should know and be able to do in history. Dimensionality assessment is critical but challenging to measure, likely due to the complex nature of the construct. That is, the construct is made up of various components and authors often define the components differently (see, for example, Díaz, Middendorf, Pace, & Shopkow, 2008; Drake & McBride, 1997; Peck & Seixas, 2008; Wineburg, 2001). In order to specify the claims inherent in a particular interpretation of test scores as outlined in Kane's validity argument, it is important that a test developer take a position on the definition in building the assessments in order to assess dimensionality relative to that position appropriately.

Though the definition of the construct may vary, it is agreed that students need to know and understand both historical content knowledge and cognition. Historical thinking, though gaining great popularity, does not replace historical knowledge; rather the two are related and interdependent. Therefore, to cover all dimensions of historical knowledge, both historical thinking and factual knowledge should be assessed. The combination of themes is represented in the recent Common Core State Standards Initiative, where they discuss assessing both complex thinking in social studies and history learning (National Governors Association Center for Best Practices, Council of Chief State School Officers, 2010). For the purposes of this chapter, when discussing student learning in history we adopt a modified representation of that which Peck and Seixas (2008) presented, to use for illustrative purposes as we explain this dimensionality issue. We maintain that for students to be able to think historically they need to have mastered each of the dimensions presented (historical significance, using primary source evidence, continuity and change, cause and consequence, historical perspective, ethical dimension) in addition to a seventh dimension, factual knowledge.

The next section will discuss how to evaluate dimensionality empirically once a theoretical dimensionality approach is adopted. The methods for evaluating dimensionality and an example of studies that have utilized such methods are included as well.

The Importance of Gathering Evidence of Dimensionality

Gathering construct validity evidence allows a test user to empirically support that all dimensions are being assessed and are related to each other in expected ways. Construct validity requires the compilation of multiple sources of evidence to ensure that the test is measuring what it is intended to measure and not assessing unintended constructs.

No one study will prove the construct validity, and in turn the dimensionality, of an assessment; rather it is a fluid process with various iterations of evaluation and re-evaluation (Westen & Rosenthal, 2003). The goal is to gather as much evidence as possible to identify relationships between assessments that fit an expected pattern. A judgment is then made based on the strength of the relationships to understand whether the assessment is truly measuring the construct of interest. The following sections describe two general methods—correlation coefficients and factor analysis—for collecting information that will provide empirical evidence to inform the final judgment about the dimensionality of test scores.

Correlation Coefficients

If an assessment is measuring the construct that it is intending to measure, students' performance will be very similar to that on other tests that are measuring the same construct. Therefore, one method for gathering statistical evidence is to compare students' scores on them with other tests targeted for the same purpose. In this case, a new measure assessing historical thinking should have a strong relationship with other measures of historical thinking. To gather evidence of this, it is necessary to examine the correlation coefficients between the two assessments, which indicate the direction and the degree of the relationship between the two test scores. In terms of historical thinking, the newly developed assessment should have a "strong" correlation with other measures of "historical thinking." It should have "substantial" correlation with measures of "historical knowledge." It is expected to be correlated with measures of "reading" and "writing" given the reading and writing requirements in an assessment of historical thinking. However, these correlations should be lower than those with other assessments of historical thinking. This method helps history assessment test developers make an informed judgment about whether, and to what extent, they are measuring historical thinking and if the historical assessment is measuring any unintended skills as well. However, this is not the only method that is important for gathering evidence of dimensionality. Exploratory and confirmatory factor analyses can also support this effort.

Factor Analysis

There are two primary types of factor analyses, exploratory and confirmatory factor analyses (EFA and CFA). One uses an EFA when attempting to understand a data set and determine the number and type of factors (i.e., dimensions) that the items represent. If a historical thinking assessment has been carefully constructed and there is a theoretical hypothesis about what dimension each item is assessing, a CFA is most appropriate to provide further evidence that the construct of historical thinking is being measured.

When writing items, the historical assessment developer should first state which factor/dimension each item on the assessment is being designed to assess. Based on the definition of historical assessment we have adopted for the purposes of this chapter, it is assumed that seven factors are being measured. If the test were adequately covering each of the seven dimensions, we would expect seven factors to emerge. It would be expected, for example, that the items developed to measure historical significance would all load on the same factor. Once the factors have been identified, preliminary descriptive statistical analyses should be conducted to understand data quality and check model assumptions. Next, the test developer should estimate the parameters in the factor model and assess the model fit (see Hu & Bentler, 1999, and Marsh, Hau, & Wen, 2004, for a thorough treatment of assessing model fit). Parameter estimates should then be examined. If the test developer finds that the model produces a good "fit" and parameter estimates are appropriate, this provides further empirical evidence that the assessment is measuring historical thinking skills and is not measuring unintended skills. The second step in Kane's validity argument indicates that an evaluation of the claims based on the empirical evidence gathered should be provided. Therefore, once appropriate statistics have been identified, the results of the analysis should be compared to the hypothesized structure and evaluated for similarity. If the results of the analysis represent the structure, it lends itself to validity evidence.

An Example of Gathering Dimensionality Evidence

This section provides an example of construct validity evidence for history assessments. Gathering such construct validity allows a test developer to assess dimensionality of the construct. The example is provided to offer the reader concrete evidence of the benefits of collecting such evidence.

The National Assessment of Educational Progress (NAEP) administers a national assessment in U.S. History to gauge knowledge and skills of the nation's eighth-grade students. The NAEP Validity Studies Panel (NVS) developed an agenda for NAEP Validity Research in 2002 (U.S. Department of Education, National Center for Education Statistics, 2003). The work conducted by the NAEP validity panel serves as a good example of the procedures for measuring validity presented here. The panel defined the construct of interest, collected a variety of evidence to measure validity, and utilized factor analyses to empirically evaluate whether the assessment was covering the domain of interest. NAEP brought in a panel of content experts to evaluate the skills measured on the assessments and ensure that the construct of interest was being measured and that other skills were not "contaminating" the items.

The NAEP study also included empirical validation through correlational studies, and factor analyses were conducted following earlier administrations of this assessment to provide the evidence necessary to ensure that all dimensions of historical thinking were being measured. In this study, the NAEP intended to obtain evidence to support the claim that the construct of interest was being measured by the assessment.

Although conducting empirical construct validity studies are important, researchers and practitioners should be aware of the limitations and cautions about these approaches. Actually, the limitations might be a reason why these studies are often overlooked. Factor analytic methods require large sample sizes of item responses, which are not always available in test development situations. In addition, these analyses (both correlation studies and factor analyses) are always sample-dependent, and practitioners must be mindful of this when interpreting the results. In other words, results from one study using one sample do not necessarily generalize to other samples. Accordingly, it is best practice to conduct multiple dimensionality studies for the same assessment, using different samples, to ensure that the validity of the scores is applicable to all types of examinees. Further, if test developers draw a representative sample and use results gathered under the testing conditions one wants to make inferences in they can increase the generalizability of the results.

Issue #2: Gathering Cognitive Validity Evidence of Historical Thinking

The focus of the remainder of the chapter is on an additional form of validity evidence that is also critical and all too often overlooked. Specifically, *cognitive validity evidence* is defined as evidence of an item eliciting the intended cognitive processes (i.e., the problem solving and reasoning that examinees employ when interacting with test items is the same as what is included in the definition of the construct). In the context of this chapter, the intended cognitive processes of interest for history assessments are the components of historical thinking. Understanding the cognitive processes used by students while completing tasks is imperative to ensuring the validity of our inferences from test scores (e.g., American Educational Research Association, American Psychological Association, & National Council on Measurement in Education, 1999). Although test score validation includes gathering evidence after the test is developed and scores are generated, it is equally important to gather evidence for the validity argument in the early phases of assessment design before scores are generated. When an assessment is being developed, there is an underlying theoretical hypothesis about what each item or task is assessing (e.g., continuity and change). This can be thought of as part one of gathering validity evidence in Kane's argument-based validity framework (i.e., "Specify the claims inherent in a particular interpretation and/or use of test scores," [Brennan, 2013, p. 74]). However, without evidence that a student is interacting with the task in the intended manner, one cannot have great confidence that the test scores are truly representing the knowledge and skills that they should be. This additional evidence aligns with part two of gathering validity evidence in Kane's argument-based validity framework (i.e., ". . . provide an evaluation of the claims based on empirical evidence, logical arguments, etc.," [Brennan, 2013, p. 74]). The approach to gathering cognitive validity evidence that we discuss below is an example of how such evidence can be collected before test scores are generated.

Cognitive validity evidence is typically gathered using qualitative methodologies, making them distinct from the other types of empirically-based validity evidence, such as those based on dimensionality, described previously. An approach that is recommended for gathering cognitive validity evidence is to conduct TAPs with students. TAPs are tools for gathering verbal reports of students' thoughts while they are responding to a test item. For example, during a TAP session, students are instructed to freely "think aloud" as they engage in a task (e.g., responding to an item from an exam). In turn, this provides information about the cognitive processes used when performing a task. The students' verbal reports comprise the data source that is collected from TAPs. Thus, TAPs are useful for identifying the cognitive processes and knowledge structures students employ as they complete a task (e.g., Ercikan et al., 2010; Leighton, 2009). TAPs can be conducted early in the assessment design phase, when items are being developed, to begin gathering validity evidence as well as to inform the design of the tasks. The verbal reports from TAPs can reveal how students actually react and respond to tasks/items. The consequence of not gathering this type of evidence is that the validity argument for the scores produced by the assessment is threatened. For example, in the words of Leighton (2004), "If test items are being systematically misunderstood, this would mean that (a) the assessment is eliciting content understandings and processes other than what was intended, or (b) the inferences drawn from the scores are inaccurate, or both" (p. 8). With the current new directions of history assessment design that emphasize the assessment of historical thinking more than ever, it is critical for assessment designers to make the effort to gather cognitive validity evidence early in the assessment development phase in order to ensure that the intended components of historical thinking are indeed being elicited. This will be particularly helpful for newer item types that have not been traditionally used in history assessment and are currently limited in validity evidence, as well as for traditional multiple-choice assessment items that are being designed to elicit historical thinking in examinees.

How to Gather Cognitive Validity Evidence Using Think-Aloud Protocols

At least two types of TAPs exist (e.g., Ercikan et al., 2010; Ercikan, Seixas, Lyons-Thomas, & Gibson, this volume; Leighton, 2009): (1) concurrent think-aloud protocols, which focus on understanding cognitive processes that occur during the completion of a task (also known as protocol analysis) and (2) retrospective think-aloud protocols, which focus on identifying and evaluating knowledge structures (e.g., beliefs, attitudes about what an item is assessing; also known as verbal analysis). Determining which of these two types of think-aloud protocols to conduct should be driven by the research question. For example, a research question such as "What skills were being elicited while the student interacted with the item?" lends itself to a concurrent TAP, whereas a research question such as "Did the student find this item to be difficult, and if so, why?" lends itself to a retrospective TAP. These two approaches are not necessarily a dichotomy—both approaches can be incorporated into one study, if this best suits the purpose of the research.

Planning a cognitive validity study using TAPs entails many important steps (Ericson & Simon, 1993; Ferrara, 2008; Leighton, 2004). The order of the steps may vary from study to study. First, the purpose of the think-aloud protocols must be clearly articulated. Is the purpose to understand whether or not the intended components of historical thinking are being assessed (which would suggest conducting a concurrent TAP)? Is the purpose to understand what the sources of cognitive complexity are from a student's perspective (which would suggest conducting a retrospective TAP)? The purpose of the study is what will determine whether or not concurrent TAPs, retrospective TAPs, or a combination of both should be conducted.

After selecting what types of TAPs to conduct, the researchers must develop the items to be administered during the think-aloud interview. Avoiding items that are too easy and may result in automatic cognitive processing is encouraged; similarly, avoiding items that are too difficult and may result in cognitive overload is also encouraged. Also, consider the amount of time available for each TAP session. Plan to administer as many items as possible to get the greatest benefit, with the awareness that students cannot be rushed through the process. The amount of time spent on a TAP will vary from student to student; some students might think aloud for 18 items in 90 minutes, whereas others might only get through 10. If forms are spiraled to students who participate in the TAPs, some data will be collected on all items and running out of time is less of a concern.

When recruiting the students to participate, consider the population who will be completing the assessment operationally. Attempt to recruit as representative a sample as possible to participate in the TAPs. In addition, either during recruitment or as part of a survey completed by participants during the TAPs, facilitators should collect as much demographic and background information as possible about the participants. If there are other theoretically relevant variables, such as history course grade, that would be informative to associate with the verbal reports, collect this data.

A facilitator script should be written so that any researcher leading the TAPs has a standardized script of the process to walk through with the students. In this script, students are given some background information about the purpose of the study and why they are selected. They are also told that they are not being evaluated in any way, and there is no right or wrong answer to their thinking aloud; rather, it is the items that are being developed. Emphasizing this is important in order to encourage students to think aloud as accurately as possible.

Before the student begins the TAP, or the actual process of thinking aloud, the researcher should demonstrate this process for the student using an actual test item. Then, the student should be given the opportunity to practice thinking aloud with at least two items (more if necessary). Therefore, developing or finding items for the researcher demonstration, as well as the student practice, is also an important part of the advance item development.

Whenever possible, conducting a pilot study of the cognitive lab in advance of the actual study is ideal. This allows researchers to uncover any parts of the process that might be unclear before the actual study begins. Moreover, this allows the researcher to become familiar with the process of being a TAP facilitator.

An analysis plan for the verbal reports must be developed before conducting the TAPs, and revised and implemented after the verbal reports have been collected. Typically, the verbal reports obtained from students are transcribed, and then coded by a group of trained researchers. A coding framework should be developed before beginning coding. For example, when the purpose of the cognitive validity study is to gather evidence of components of historical thinking, the coding framework would include each of the components as potential codes. Other behavioral codes might be relevant to the purpose of the research study (e.g., misreading the question). After an initial coding framework is drafted, each researcher in the coding group should apply the framework to a couple of verbal reports. The research team should then meet and discuss the framework, making any necessary revisions. It is important for all coders to be using and internalizing the codes in the same manner. Ideally, each verbal report would be coded by at least two coders, to ensure rater reliability of codes. When discrepancies are identified, the two (or more) coders should meet to discuss the causes, and decide on a final code. Cognitive validity evidence is considered present when students' verbal reports demonstrate that the intended historical thinking skill is being elicited (see Ericson & Simon, 1993, and van Someren, Barnard, & Sandberg, 1994 for detailed coverage of how to design, conduct, and analyze data from TAPs). If there is no evidence of the intended cognitive processes, results should be shared with test developers, discussing how the items might be revised to achieve the desired evidence.

Practical Limitations and Cautions About Think-Aloud Protocols

There are some practical limitations and cautions about TAPs that must be noted. As evident from the above description, TAPs are a resource intensive methodology. The implementation of TAPs involves time of researchers and test developers in advance of, during, and after the TAP study takes place. The time that is required of these people in and of itself is costly. What's more, transcribing the verbal reports can also be very costly. Transcription services are available that can transcribe the verbal reports quickly; however, these services can be expensive. Once the transcriptions of the verbal reports are available, the coding can be very time consuming, especially if best research practices are followed and at least two coders code each verbal report. Finally, because of the cost associated with conducting TAPs, large sample sizes are often difficult to obtain. Perhaps the resource intensive nature of conducting TAPs is the reason why gathering cognitive validity evidence using this approach is often not conducted. However, we strongly believe the cost of conducting TAPs—especially as supplements to other construct validity studies, such as the ones described earlier in the chapter—is worth the benefit of having a strong evidentiary argument for the validity of history assessment test scores. The next chapter in this volume provides a detailed treatment of using TAPs during the development of an assessment called the Historical Thinking Assessment Tool (HTAT).

Conclusions

We hope that the readers of this chapter have gained a clear understanding of the importance of gathering construct validity evidence for history assessments, and particularly about the importance of dimensionality evidence and cognitive validity evidence. We believe these two forms of validity evidence are often overlooked or misunderstood, and hope that this chapter has shed light on not only what these forms of evidence are and why they are important, but has also pointed the reader to examples of how these studies can be conducted in their own practices. In regards to history assessments, where assessing multiple dimensions of historical thinking skills and knowledge is more important than ever, these two types of construct validity evidence are essential for large-scale high-stakes history assessment scores. When the stakes are high, good measurement is critical, and it is the responsibility of the test developers and the test users to understand what inferences are supported by the test scores.

References

American Educational Research Association, American Psychological Association, & National Council on Measurement in Education. (1999). *Standards for educational and psychological testing.* Washington, DC: American Educational Research Association.

Brennan, R. L. (2013). Commentary on "Validating the interpretations and uses of test scores." *Journal of Educational Measurement, 50,* 74–83.

Cronbach, L. J. (1989). Construct validation after thirty years. In R. E. Linn (Ed.), *Intelligence: Measurement, theory, and public policy* (pp. 147–171). Urbana, IL: University of Illinois Press.

Cronbach, L. J., & Meehl, P. E. (1955). Construct validity in psychological tests. *Psychological Bulletin, 52,* 281–302.

Díaz, A., Middendorf, J., Pace, D., & Shopkow, L. (2008). The history learning project: A department "decodes" its students. *Journal of American History, 94*(4), 1211–1224.

Drake, F. D., and McBride, L. W. (1997). Reinvigorating the teaching of history through alternative assessment. *The History Teacher, 30,* 145–173.

Ercikan, K., Arim, R. G., Law, D. M., Lacroix, S., Gagnon, F., & Domene, J. F. (2010). Application of think-aloud protocols in examining sources of differential item functioning. *Educational Measurement: Issues and Practice, 29,* 24–35.

Ericson, K. A., & Simon, H. A. (1993). *Protocol analysis: Verbal reports as data.* (rev. ed.). Cambridge, MA: MIT Press.

Ferrara, S. (2008, January). *Thinking about the think aloud method to guide development of assessments of modified achievement standards.* Paper presented at the OSEP GSEG Project Directors Conference, Washington, DC.

Hu, L., & Bentler, P. M. (1999). Cutoff criteria for fit indexes in covariance structure analysis: Conventional criteria versus new alternatives, *Structural Equation Modeling, 6*(1), 1–55.

Leighton, J. P. (2004). Avoiding misconception, misuse, and missed opportunities: The collection of verbal reports in educational achievement testing. *Educational Measurement: Issues and Practice, 23,* 6–15.

Leighton, J. P. (2009, April). *Two types of think aloud interviews for educational measurement: Protocol and verbal analysis.* Paper presented at the annual meeting of the National Council on Measurement in Education (NCME), San Diego, CA.

Kane, M. T. (2006). Validation. In R. Brennan (Ed.), *Educational measurement* (4th ed., pp. 17–64). Westport, CT: American Council on Education and Praeger.

Kane, M. T. (2013). Validating the interpretations and uses of test scores. *Journal of Educational Measurement, 50,* 1–73.

Marsh, H. W., Hau, K. T., & Wen, Z. (2004). In search of golden rules: Comment on hypothesis testing approaches to setting cutoff values for fit indexes and dangers in overgeneralizing Hu & Bentler's (1999) findings. *Structural Equation Modelling, 11,* 320–341.

National Governors Association Center for Best Practices, Council of Chief State School Officers (2010). *Common Core State Standards.* National Governors Association Center for Best Practices.

Peck, C., & Seixas, P. (2008). Benchmarks of historical thinking: First steps. *Canadian Journal of Education, 31*(4), 1015–1038.

U.S. Department of Education, National Center for Education Statistics. (2003). NAEP validity studies: An agenda for NAEP validity research, NCES 2003–07. Washington, DC.

van Someren, M. W., Barnard, Y. F., & Sandberg, J.A.C. (1994*). The think aloud method: A practical guide to modelling cognitive processes.* London, England: Academic Press.

Westen, D., & Rosenthal. R. (2003). Quantifying construct validity: Two simple measures. *Journal of Personality and Social Psychology, 84,* 608–618.

Wineburg, S. (2001). *Historical thinking and other unnatural acts: Charting the future of teaching the past.* Philadelphia, PA: Temple University Press.

13

COGNITIVE VALIDITY EVIDENCE FOR VALIDATING ASSESSMENTS OF HISTORICAL THINKING

Kadriye Ercikan, Peter Seixas, Juliette Lyons-Thomas, and Lindsay Gibson

Introduction

When assessments are targeted to measure recall or simple skills, obtaining evidence to support the claim that the assessments are measuring them is relatively easy. The main validity evidence to support the claim is often based on experts' judgment of whether the tasks align with the assessment framework and whether they require the knowledge and competencies targeted by the framework. However, when the assessment is intended to measure complex thinking such as historical thinking, expert reviews and judgments are not sufficient, as demonstrated by growing research on assessment tasks with targeted cognitive components and difficulty levels (Ferrara & Chen, 2011; Gorin & Embretson, 2006; Huff & Ferrara, 2010; Sato, 2011). This research has demonstrated limitations of expert judgments about what the tasks capture and has exposed challenges in designing assessments that actually engage students in complex thinking. Curriculum experts' judgments about what assessment tasks are measuring are hypotheses about what the tasks may assess. Research investigating cognitive processes captured by tasks has demonstrated that such hypotheses are often contradicted by empirical data. This research found mismatches between targeted and actual cognitive processes captured by tasks (e.g., Ferrara & Duncan, 2011; Ferrara et al., 2004). Even predicting a simpler characteristic of tasks, such as difficulty based on task features evaluated by experts, could account for only 25% to 50% of the variance (Ferrara, Svetina, Skucha, & Davidson, 2011). All of this research highlights the importance of empirical evidence that can be used to support experts' judgments about what tasks are measuring. Such empirical evidence is based on students' reporting of their thinking and response processes and is referred to as cognitive evidence. The purpose of this chapter is to describe and discuss creation and use of cognitive evidence in the validity investigation of an assessment of historical thinking. We describe a think-aloud protocol (TAP) approach to gather data on students' response processes, present a three-step approach to analyzing data from TAPs, and examine the degree to which student verbalizations provide evidence of students' historical thinking.

Cognitive Data for Validating Assessments of Historical Thinking

The importance of validity evidence based on examinee response processes has been highlighted in the Standards for Educational and Psychological Testing (AERA, APA, & NCME, 1999) and emphasized by measurement researchers (Ercikan, 2006; Haertel, 1999; Pellegrino, Chudowsky, & Glaser, 2001) for a long time. Response process data can be used to understand how item format, content, and context affect examinee thought processes and are very important for creating tests that assess constructs such as those that comprise historical thinking.

One of the key methods used for gathering student response data is TAPs. TAPs require participants to verbalize their thoughts while they engage in an educational activity (Ericsson & Simon, 1993). They have been used for gathering data about student thinking while they engage in tasks such as solving a problem, interpreting a chart, or completing an activity (Leighton & Gierl, 2007). These studies have focused on describing why and how students do what they do while engaged in solving a problem or completing an activity. Student verbalizations may be collected *concurrently*, as the student is engaged in the activity, or *retrospectively*, after the student completes the activity. Data gathered using TAPs are then used to develop models of student thinking processes, or to test hypotheses regarding such models (Pottier et al., 2010).

In validity investigations, TAPs provide student verbalizations that can be used for examining how students understand test questions, and whether elements of test items (such as words, phrases, sentence structures, or graphics) cause confusion or difficulty for them (Ercikan et al., 2010). TAPs have also been used to examine the constructs measured by tasks (Baxter & Glaser, 1998; Ercikan et al., 2012; Ferrara & Chen, 2011; Kaliski, France, Huff, & Thurber, 2010; Magone, Cai, Silver, & Wang, 1994; Messick, 1989); to examine whether different item types such as multiple-choice (MC) versus constructed-response (CR) capture similar constructs (e.g., Kaliski et al., 2010 and Ercikan et al., 2012); to examine features of items that are related to difficulty levels of items (Ferrara & Chen, 2011); to examine how these features affect special student populations such as English Language Learners and Students With Disabilities (Sato, 2011); and for identifying or testing hypotheses about sources of differential item functioning (Ercikan et al., 2010).

Use of TAPs in Validating an Assessment of Historical Thinking

Our insights about use of TAPs in validation are based on research described in the Seixas, Gibson, and Ercikan chapter in Part II of the book. Here we provide further details about the assessment tool used in that research, the procedure we followed in administering TAPs, the sample of students who participated in the research, and our analyses and findings.

Historical Thinking Assessment Tool

Several definitions of historical thinking have been provided in different chapters in this book. The assessment tool our research focused on followed a conceptualization of historical thinking developed by Peter Seixas and his colleagues (Peck & Seixas, 2008; Seixas, 2009). These researchers define historical thinking as the ability to establish historical significance, to use primary source evidence, to identify continuity and change, to analyze cause and consequence, to take historical perspectives, and to understand the ethical dimension of historical interpretations.

The assessment tool was developed using an evidence centered design (ECD) approach. ECD is a model-based approach to assessment design with three components (Ercikan, 2006; Ercikan & Seixas, 2011; Mislevy, Steinberg, & Almond, 2002; National Research Council, 2001). The *cognition and learning model* includes the definition of the target construct and its development, the *task model* identifies how tasks need to be designed to assess different construct components and progression of the construct, and the *evidence model* specifies how student performance should be interpreted and evaluated in relation to the targeted construct (see Fig. 13.1). The key difference between ECD and typical assessment design approaches is a requirement in ECD for clear and explicit description of how tasks and the interpretation and evaluation of performance on tasks should be related to the construct. This requirement provides opportunities for designing tasks and assessments that are coherent with intended target inferences in assessing complex constructs such as historical thinking. Student response process data provide information about student cognitive processes and can help evaluate the connection between what the tasks are measuring and the targeted constructs.

To limit the time of the assessment to one hour, the cognition and learning model in our assessment consisted of three of the six historical thinking concepts: (1) using primary source evidence (*Evidence*); (2) taking historical perspectives (*Perspective*); and (3) understanding the ethical dimension of historical interpretations (*Ethical*). Using primary source evidence refers to finding, selecting, contextualizing, and interpreting sources for a historical argument. Taking historical perspectives involves (a) understanding that the "past is a foreign country," with its different social, cultural, intellectual, and even emotional contexts that shaped

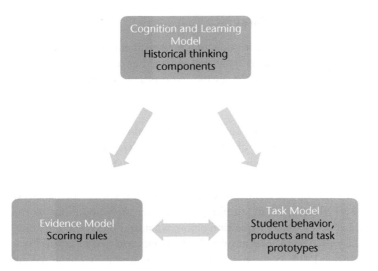

FIGURE 13.1 Cognition and learning, task, and evidence models

people's lives and actions and (b) reading sources in view of the conditions and worldviews at the time when they were created. Understanding the ethical dimension of historical interpretations requires understanding how we, in the present, judge actors in different circumstances in the past, when and how crimes and sacrifices of the past bear consequences today, and what obligations we have today in relation to those consequences.[1] The selection of three concepts was based on the limited number of tasks we could include in a single assessment that could be administered at schools.

The assessment tool focused on assessing historical thinking in Grade 11 students and in particular on the internment of Ukrainians in Canada during World War I. All the factual knowledge students needed for answering questions on the assessment was presented to them in a six-point "background information" page and five excerpts from original source documents related to the Ukrainian internment. In order to capture historical thinking independent of factual knowledge, providing this background was necessary.

One to three questions asked students to interpret the views presented in each document, how they themselves or historians might use the source document, compare views presented in the documents, and explain why they differed. Students were expected to demonstrate understanding of how to make justifiable inferences about primary source evidence, present explanations for the different perspectives, and make inferences about authors' motivations after considering their positions, purposes, and contexts. The final two questions asked students to consider the different documents they read before making ethical judgments about Ukrainian internment.

Think-Aloud Protocol Procedures

TAPs involved individual administration of the assessment to students. They were asked to think aloud concurrently as they engaged in responding to each of the questions. At the beginning of the testing session the test administrator read the following instructions to the student:

> I would like you to start reading the questions aloud and tell me what you are thinking as you read the questions. After you have read the question, interpret the question in your own words. Think aloud and tell me what you are doing. What is the question asking you to do? What did you have to do to answer the question? How did you come up with your answer? Tell me everything you are thinking while you are responding to the question. Let's try a practice question before we start. I'll go first. I'm going to read the passage and then answer the first question. (After administrator models the TAP): Now you read the passage and answer the second question.

When the students were responding to questions, the test administrator noted (1) the start and end time for each question; (2) where the student was stumbling, and if the student misinterpreted the question, how the student misinterpreted the question; (3) if the student slowed down on a particular word, graphic, or part of the question; and (4) a brief version of the student's answer. If the student stopped verbalizing during a question, they were prompted to *"Remember to think aloud."* If the students' verbalizations did not include their interpretation of the question and how they came up with their response, the students were asked *"In your own words, tell me what the question asks"* and *"How did you come up with your answer to this question?"* which provide information about their understanding and thinking retrospectively. TAP administration took 48 to 118 minutes and took place in empty classrooms after the end of a school day.[2]

Sample

The TAPs and accompanying assessment were administered to a total of 35 (11 male, 24 female) students in grade 11 (10 fifteen year old students and 25 sixteen year old students). Most students (n=30) reported that they had lived in British Columbia all their lives or had moved there before elementary school. However, 34% (n=12) of students reported that Mandarin or Cantonese was the most frequently used language in their home, while 37% (n=13) indicated that English was used most commonly. With respect to previous performance in history, students were asked to report the mark that they usually get on social studies tests and projects. Almost half of the students (n=17) reported getting an A, 12 said that they usually get a B, two said C+, and another two said C. None of the students reported getting lower than a C, however two students provided multiple marks. Ten of the students were part of an enriched academic program offered by the municipal school board, while the other 25 students attended a mainstream high school.

Coding of Student Verbalizations

Student verbalizations were transcribed verbatim. These transcripts were then analyzed to examine (1) whether the student understood and interpreted the tasks as intended; and (2) the extent to which the students engaged in targeted historical thinking. Both of these issues are relevant to the validity of interpreting scores as indicators of students' historical thinking. Two sets of codes were developed to interpret student verbalization in relation to these validation issues. An initial set of codes were tested with a sample of five student verbalizations and refined to make sure that the codes were clear and captured the intended meaning in verbalizations accurately. For each question, the research team defined a set of codes, which the coders used to analyze the student verbalizations. Two coders independently coded each student verbalization and recorded their codes in Excel spreadsheets prepared by the research team. After each question was completed, the coders compared codes, discussed disagreements, and reached a consensus code. The initial independent codes were recorded for examining coder agreement.

Code Set 1: Understanding of Tasks

Code Set 1 included two codes that captured understanding of the tasks. The first was the degree to which the student had a clear understanding of the question, rated as 0 to 2 for different degrees of understanding. The second was whether there were any vocabulary in the task the student did not understand, indicated by Yes or No.

Code Set 2: Historical Thinking in Student Verbalizations

For each task, we identified key historical thinking competencies and cognitive demands we expected students to engage in. These competencies and cognitive demands guided our identification of evidence of students' engagement in historical thinking in their verbalizations. For *Evidence* and *Perspective,* we identified the following types of verbalizations as evidence of or lack of historical thinking:

- *Source*: student comments on the author's identity, experience, date, or nature of the document;
- *Perspective*: student comments on the perspective of the source or its author;

- *Purpose*: student comments on the authors' purposes;
- *Comparison*: student corroborates with or contrasts to *other* documents or texts;
- *Document as Fact*: student interprets a document as fact (evidence of lack of historical thinking);
- *Traces*: student interprets sources as traces.

As evidence of *Ethical Dimension* we looked for the following in student verbalizations:

- *Fair*: student states principles of ethics or fairness (potentially, but not necessarily evidence of historical thinking);
- *Distance*: student comments on temporal distance between the time of the document and now;
- *Collective*: student builds an argument for or against the imposition of reparations (or other measures) for a historical injustice, based on considerations of collective responsibility;
- *Descendant*: student builds an argument for or against the imposition of reparations (or other measures) for a historical injustice, based on considerations of benefits and deficits to respective present-day descendants.

Analyzing Student Verbalizations

Coder Agreement

Inter-coder agreement Kappa (Cohen, 1960) for Code Set 1, which focused on student understanding of the questions, was very high, ranging between 80% and 100% for all codes across the 11 tasks, except for Tasks 2 and 8 for coding Understanding of the Question (UN), which were 68% and 54% respectively. Code Set 2, which required coders to make judgments about evidence of students' historical thinking, was highly challenging. Inter-coder agreement for Code Set 2 was lower than that for Code Set 1 but tended to be moderate for most of the tasks, ranging between 60% and 70%, though for some tasks it was as high as 100%, and in a handful of cases around the 30% to 40% range. These tended to be the codes that required greater interpretation of verbalizations rather than direct observations of evidence of historical thinking.

Understanding of Tasks

The student verbalizations indicated that the great majority of the students understood what the questions were asking them to do or respond to. On all tasks, except for Tasks 2 and 8, student verbalizations indicated full understanding of questions for over 70% of the students. On Task 2, 68% and on Task 8, 51% of students' verbalizations indicated full understanding of the questions. Further examination indicated that poor understanding of Tasks 2 and 8 was not caused by confusion about the wording in the question. Instead it was caused by either a lack of knowledge about how primary sources are used in history, or confusion about whether the question was asking about the author's perspective versus the student's own perspective.

Evidence of Historical Thinking

Once the verbalizations are coded, using these codes as evidence of historical thinking requires a systematic analysis of the codes. There were three steps in this process. The first step was to determine whether student verbalizations included codes identified as evidence of either *Evidence* and *Perspective* or *Ethical Dimension*. This information is valuable in understanding what types of evidence verbalizations included. Since each task may include evidence of more than one code, for example by commenting on the perspective of the source or its author (*Perspective*) as well as interpreting sources as traces (*Traces*), evidence of both of these would provide supporting validity evidence that the task measures historical thinking. Therefore, as part of a validity investigation, the second step is to determine to what extent *any* of the relevant codes were included in the verbalizations. For example, if *Perspective* and *Traces* were the relevant codes, the second step would determine what percentage of the students included evidence of either or both of these aspects of historical thinking. This additional level of summary would therefore reflect the students who included evidence of *Perspective*, evidence of *Traces*, and those that included both aspects of historical thinking.

In order for particular verbalizations to be interpreted as evidence of historical thinking, such verbalizations should be observed for students who have higher historical thinking scores, and they should not be observed for those students who did not score well on these tasks. The consistency of inferences from verbalizations and student responses to tasks is necessary for meaningful interpretation of scores. To verify this relationship between verbalizations and scores, the third step involved comparing historical thinking scores of students who included the relevant codes of historical thinking in their verbalizations and those who did not. Each of these three steps in our research are summarized below.

Step 1: Evidence of Historical Thinking in Verbalizations Separately by Code

Evidence and Perspective

In our research, evidence of historical thinking demanded by each task was first summarized by the percentage of students who included the relevant verbalizations in their TAPs. Table 13.1 summarizes evidence of historical thinking in student verbalizations for each code in each task. Greater percentages for each code indicate that higher proportions of students included these codes in their verbalizations and therefore constitute stronger evidence of historical thinking demanded by these tasks compared to the other tasks.

Students were expected to demonstrate *Evidence* and *Perspective* competencies on Tasks 1 to 9. There was a great degree of variability of evidence across the nine tasks. Evidence of sourcing varied from question to question, with 6% to 89% of students commenting on the author's identity, experience, date, or nature of the document (*Source*) in their verbalizations. On most of the *Evidence* and *Perspective* tasks, students commented on the perspective of the source or its author (*Perspective*) with 43% to 91% students making such comments in their verbalization of these tasks, except for three of the tasks in which only a small proportion of students made such comments. On one question, 29% of the students commented on historical worldviews or contexts of the events and information presented to them in the documents (*Context*). Only small proportions of students commented on authors' purposes (*Purpose*: 2% to 17%).

Students were expected to corroborate with or contrast documents on only three of the tasks (*Compare*). On two of these tasks, the great majority of students (100% and 74%) corroborated and contrasted documents, and on one task, only 20% verbalized corroboration or contrasting.

For evidence of historical thinking, students were expected to interpret sources as traces (*Traces*) and not read documents as fact (*Document as Fact*). Larger proportions (31% to 71%) of students provided evidence that they were aware of sources as traces, than students who read documents as facts (14% to 44%) across the nine tasks.

Ethical Dimension

In responding to questions about ethical judgment (Tasks 10 and 11), students stating general principles of ethics or fairness (*Fair*) to justify their responses could not *prima facie* be considered evidence of historical thinking or lack thereof. In question 10, if students used such statements while remarking on the historical context, or in question 11, if they used such statements qualified by recognition of the temporal distance between now and World War I, then they were interpreted as providing evidence of historical thinking. If these two qualifiers were absent in their responses to the two questions, respectively, then general principles of fairness were not considered to be evidence of historical thinking. In the two questions assessing ethical judgment, 37% and 49% demonstrated such reasoning. As evidence of understanding the ethical dimension of historical interpretations, students were expected to comment on the temporal distance between now and then (*Distance*). While more than half of the students (54%) made such comments on one of the questions, only a small proportion (6%) verbalized such comments when responding to the other question. In responding

TABLE 13.1 Evidence of historical thinking in student verbalizations by code

Task	Codes	Percentage expressed in verbalization	Task	Codes	Percentage expressed in verbalization
1 (MC)	Perspective*	65	10 (CR)	Comparison**	74
	Traces*	71		Context*	29
2 (MC)	Purpose*	3		Document as Fact	34
	Perspective*	44		Traces**	57
	Document as Fact*	44		Fair	37
	Traces*	32		Distance**	6
3 (MC)	Source**	77	11(CR)	Fair*	49
4 (CR)	Source**	89		Distance*	54
	Perspective*	91		Collective*	37
	Purpose*	17		Descendants**	46
	Comparison	100			
5 (CR)	Source*	6			
	Perspective*	43			
	Purpose*	9			
	Comparison**	20			
6 (MC)	Source*	20			
	Perspective*	3			
	Document as Fact*	29			
	Traces*	31			
7 (MC)	Source*	26			
	Perspective*	9			
	Purpose*	14			
	Document as Fact*	14			
8 (CR)	Perspective**	4			
	Purpose*	11			
9 (MC)	Source*	66			
	Perspective*	43			
	Purpose*	2			

*indicates that the scores were higher for students who included evidence of historical thinking in their verbalizations; **indicates statistically significant mean differences at alpha = 0.05 level for two student groups who included evidence of historical thinking and those who did not.

to the last question on reparations for Ukrainian internment in Canada, students were expected to build an argument for or against the imposition of reparations (or other measures) for a historical injustice, based on considerations of (1) collective responsibility (*Collective*); and (2) benefits and deficits to respective present-day descendants (*Descendants*). Fewer than half of the students (37% *Collective*, 46% *Descendants*) made arguments using these considerations.

Step 2: Evidence of Historical Thinking in Verbalizations Combined Across Codes

The previous section summarized evidence of historical thinking separately by code for each task. In this section, such evidence is combined across codes for each task resulting in the percentage of students who included at least one relevant aspect of historical thinking for each task (though it could also consist of students whose verbalizations included multiple relevant aspects of historical thinking). The percentage of students who provided evidence of historical thinking varied between 32% (for Task 7) to 100% (for Task 4). The Task 7 with the lowest evidence of historical thinking asked students to choose one of four options that answered "**Whom did the newspaper editors think was to blame for the situation they describe?**" based on a brief excerpt from a letter signed by six Ukrainian Canadian newspaper editors. On a closer look, answering this item correctly required students to read and understand what was presented in the excerpt without necessarily exercising historical thinking. The task with the highest evidence of historical thinking, Task 4, asked students to provide an explanation for differences in perspectives between an American government official and a religious leader presented in two separate documents: "**Mr. Willrich describes the Ukrainian prisoners as good, law abiding residents. In one sentence explain why Mr. Willrich describes Ukrainians so differently from Father Moris.**" In this task, students were explicitly required to compare perspectives in two documents and, not surprisingly, all students included comparisons of perspectives in their verbalizations.

Tasks 4, 5, 8, 10, and 11 are CR items. Even though two of these five tasks (4 and 11) had the highest percentage of students demonstrating evidence of historical thinking, some of the MC items, e.g., tasks 1, 2, 3, and 9, also had strong evidence of historical thinking and were stronger than three of the CR tasks (5, 8, and 10) (See Figure 13.2). Based on this step of the analyses, there was not consistently stronger evidence of historical thinking on CR items.

Step 3: Correspondence Between Evidence of Verbalization and Performance

If the verbalizations indicated evidence of historical thinking, then students who demonstrated historical thinking in their verbalizations would be expected to have

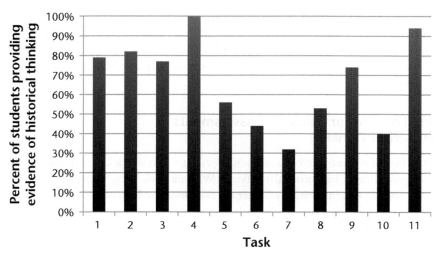

FIGURE 13.2 Percentage of students providing evidence of historical thinking in their verbalizations for each of the eleven tasks

higher scores on their written responses to those tasks. In Table 13.1, '*' indicates that the scores were higher for students who included evidence of historical thinking in their verbalizations and '**' indicates that the differences in score means were between high and low scoring students statistically significant at alpha = 0.05 level. On 36 codes, across 11 tasks, there were statistically significantly different score differences on six codes. In 25 of the comparisons, the differences were in the direction supporting historical thinking but were not statistically significant. This was not surprising given the low sample size of 35. In all, there were 2 codes (*Comparison* on task 4 and *Fair* on Task 10) for which either there were no score differences between students who provided evidence of historical thinking in their verbalizations and those who did not or they were not in the expected direction. Corroborating or contrasting (*Comparison*) on Task 4 was included in all the student verbalizations because the question specifically asked them to compare information presented in two documents. Therefore, no relationship between this evidence of historical thinking and historical thinking scores could be established because everyone, whether they were employing good or poor levels of historical thinking, included it in their verbalizations. Stating general principles of fairness (*Fair*) on Task 10 could be considered as evidence of lack of historical thinking. Task 10 asked students to discuss whether the Canadian government was justified in their policies toward Ukrainians. If students discussed contrasting perspectives in the documents and accurately explained how each is relevant to the justifiability or unjustifiability of the policies, then they would have obtained the maximum score of 3 even if their verbalizations indicated they referred to broad fairness principles. In other words, verbalizations classified as *Fair* was not clear evidence of lack of historical thinking.

Based on the analyses in this step, there was stronger evidence of historical thinking from student verbalizations for CR tasks than for MC tasks. While on all of the five CR tasks at least one code had a statistically significant association with scores based on students' written responses, only one MC task had such a relationship.

Implications for Validating Assessments of Historical Thinking

Data from TAPs provided clear cognitive evidence that the tasks in the assessment engaged students in historical thinking. Without such data, it would not have been possible to demonstrate whether the tasks measured the intended constructs. The first step of the analyses of verbalizations determined what types of historical evidence each task elucidated. This is a necessary step to understand the constructs captured by the tasks. The second step of the analyses provided information about which tasks required historical thinking from students more consistently. Such information is useful in the assessment design stage for revising or selecting tasks so that tasks with strong and consistent historical thinking requirements can be included in the assessment. In the third step, examining the relationship between evidence of historical thinking in student verbalizations and historical thinking scores demonstrated a consistent pattern for the great majority of codes across the tasks (except for three). Even when relatively small proportions of students expressed particular evidence of historical thinking in some questions, these were associated with higher scores on these tasks. On three tasks, these differences were statistically significant. Overall, the three steps of analyses provided complementary information about what the tasks were measuring.

The TAP methodology has several limitations that one needs to be aware of in using it in validation research. The first, as noted by Kaliski et al. (this volume), is that due to the labor-intensive nature of the procedure, the sample size that can be included in this type of research is limited. The small sample size also limits the strengths of inferences that can be made. For example, statistical significance may not be obtained even when there are strong systematic relationships, and moderate or weak associations may not be observed. Secondly, there is not a one to one relationship between student verbalization and evidence of competency. There are many reasons why students may or may not verbalize, including their willingness and ability to communicate their thinking, their metacognitive ability to be aware of their thinking, and the extent to which the task lends itself to the type of verbalization needed, among others (Leighton, 2011). Another issue to consider is that the tasks with the highest percentage of students including evidence of historical thinking cannot be considered as the best tasks for measuring historical thinking. In our research, Task 4 had 100% of students including comparing and contrasting perspectives in their verbalizations. This item can be considered as capturing the most basic levels of historical thinking students demonstrated by following specific instructions in the task. Other more difficult tasks which are targeted to capture higher levels of historical thinking may not include evidence of historical thinking in verbalizations by students whose historical thinking levels may not be sufficiently high to manage the task. The third step in our analyses, which connects verbalization evidence with performance, provides better evaluation of the degree to which verbalizations were good indicators of historical thinking. Based on the findings from our research, TAPs provide necessary validity evidence for assessments of historical thinking. Without such evidence, any assessment of historical thinking will have a major gap in supporting claims about what the assessment is truly measuring.

Notes

1 www.historicalthinking.ca
2 This time includes administration of a short test with 15 multiple-choice factual knowledge questions on World War I.

References

American Educational Research Association, American Psychological Association, & National Council on Measurement in Education. (1999). *Standards for educational and psychological testing*. Washington, DC: American Educational Research Association.

Baxter, G., & Glaser, R. (1998). Investigating the cognitive complexity of science assessments. *Educational Measurement: Issues and Practices, 17*, 37–45.

Cohen, J. (1960). A coefficient of agreement for nominal scales. *Educational and Psychological Measurement, 20*, 37–46.

Ercikan, K. (2006). Developments in assessment of student learning and achievement. In P. A. Alexander and P. H. Winne (Eds.), *American Psychological Association, Division 15, Handbook of educational psychology, 2nd edition* (pp. 929–953). Mahwah, NJ: Lawrence Erlbaum.

Ercikan, K., Arim, R., Law, D., Domene, J., Gagnon, F., & Lacroix, S. (2010). Application of think aloud protocols for examining and confirming sources of differential item functioning identified by expert reviews. *Educational Measurement: Issues and Practice, 29*(2), 24–35.

Ercikan, K., & Seixas, P. (2011). Assessment of higher order thinking: The case of historical thinking. In G. Scraw and D. H. Robinson (Eds.), *Assessment of higher order thinking skills* (pp. 245–261). Charlotte, NC: Information Age Publishing.

Ercikan, K., Seixas, P., Lyons-Thomas, J., & Gibson, L. (2012, March). *Designing and validating an assessment of historical thinking using evidence centered assessment design*. Paper presented at the annual meeting of the American Educational Research Association, Vancouver, BC.

Ericsson, K. A., & Simon, H. A. (1993). *Protocol analysis: Verbal reports as data* (rev. ed.). Cambridge, MA: MIT Press.

Ferrara, S., & Chen, J. (2011, April). *Evidence for the accuracy of item response demand coding categories in think aloud verbal transcripts*. Paper presented at the annual meeting of the American Educational Research Association, New Orleans, LA.

Ferrara, S., & Duncan, T. (2011). Comparing science achievement constructs: Targeted and achieved. *Education Forum, 75*, 143–156.

Ferrara, S., Duncan, T. G., Freed, R., Velez-Paschke, A., McGivern, J., Mushlin, S., Mattessich, A., Rogers, A., & Westphalen, K. (2004, April). *Examining test score validity by examining item construct validity: Preliminary analysis of evidence of the alignment of targeted and observed content, skills, and cognitive processes in a middle school science assessment.* Paper presented at the annual meeting of the American Educational Research Association, San Diego, CA.

Ferrara, S., Svetina, D., Skucha, S., & Davidson, A. H. (2011). Test development with performance standards and achievement growth in mind. *Educational Measurement: Issues and Practice, 30*(4), 3–15.

Gorin, J. S., & Embretson, S. E. (2006). Item difficulty modeling of paragraph comprehension items. *Applied Psychological Measurement, 30*(5), 394–411.

Haertel, E. H. (1999). Validity arguments for high-stakes testing: In search of the evidence. *Educational Measurement: Issues and Practice, 18*(4), 5–9.

Huff, K., & Ferrara, S. (2010, June). *Frameworks for considering item response demands and item difficulty.* Presentation at the Council of Chief State School Officers National Conference on Large-Scale Assessment, Detroit, MI.

Kaliski, P., France, M., Huff, K., & Thurber, A. (2010, April). *Using think aloud interviews in evidence-centered assessment design for the AP World History exam.* Paper presented at the annual conference of the American Educational Research Association, Denver, CO.

Leighton, J. P. (2011). *Item difficulty and interviewer knowledge effects on the accuracy and consistency of examinee response processes in verbal reports.* Paper presented at the annual meeting of the American Educational Research Association, New Orleans, LA.

Leighton, J. P., & Gierl, M. J. (2007). Verbal reports as data for Cognitive Diagnostic Assessment. In J. P. Leighton and M. J. Gierl (Eds.), *Cognitive diagnostic assessment for education: Theory and applications* (pp. 146–172). New York, NY: Cambridge University Press.

Magone, M. E., Cai, J., Silver, E. A., & Wang, N. (1994). Validating the cognitive complexity and content validity of a mathematics performance assessment. *International Journal of Educational Research, 21,* 317–340.

Messick, S. (1989). Meaning and values in test validation: The science and ethics of assessment. *Educational Researcher, 18*(2), 5–11.

Mislevy, R. J., Steinberg, L. S., & Almond, R. G. (2002). On the structure of educational assessments. *Measurement: Interdisciplinary Research and Perspectives, 1,* 3–63.

National Research Council. (2001). *Knowing what students know: The science and design of educational assessment.* Pellegrino, J., Chudowsky, N., & Glaser, R. (Eds). Washington, DC: National Academies Press.

Peck, C., & Seixas, P. (2008). Benchmarks of historical thinking: First steps. *Canadian Journal of Education, 31*(4), 1015–1038.

Pellegrino, J. W., Chudowsky, N., & Glaser, R. (Eds.). (2001). *Knowing what students know: The science and design of educational assessment.* Washington, DC: National Academies Press.

Pottier P., Hardouin, J.-B., Hodges, B. D., Pistorius, M.-A., Connault, J., Durant, C., . . . Planchon, B. (2010). Exploring how students think: a new method combining think-aloud and concept mapping protocols. *Medical Education, 44*(9), 926–935.

Sato, E. (2011, March). *Cognitive interviews of English language learners and students with disabilities and features contributing to item difficulty: Implications for item and test design.* Paper presented at the annual meeting of the American Educational Research Association, New Orleans, LA.

Seixas, P. (2009). A modest proposal for change in Canadian history education. *Teaching History, 137,* 26–31.

14

MEASURING UP?

Multiple-Choice Questions

Gabriel A. Reich

Models of Achievement in History

In history education, there are several competing theoretical models of disciplinary achievement. Within the scholarly community, a loose consensus exists about some key disciplinary concepts that can enhance students' abilities to achieve a more nuanced understanding of history (cf. Lee, 2005; Lévesque, 2008; Seixas, 1996; Wineburg, 2001). Although grounded in empirical research, this theory has only a tangential relationship with another theoretical model of disciplinary achievement, official content standards.

Official content standards are produced by education bureaucracies. They may be influenced by the history education community, but they are developed in a different institutional context, with different imperatives, mandates, and political considerations (Broadfoot, 1996; Wineburg, 1991). Far from being merely technocratic, defining content standards is a political process, one that must contend with public anxiety about the transmission of heritage and culture to the next generation (VanSledright, 2008). As institutions that are accountable to the public, education bureaucracies tend to be careful not to violate the expectations of citizens, especially in the case of history (Nash, Crabtree, & Dunn, 1997; Zimmerman, 2002).

The research reported in this chapter took place in New York State. At the time data was collected for this study, The New York State Education Department (NYSED) had published two key documents that served as the guideposts for what students were expected to know and do upon completion of the global history and geography course: the "Core Curriculum" (NYSED, 1999a) and the "Standards and Performance Indicators" (NYSED, 1999b). The "Core Curriculum" (NYSED, 1999a) is a list of content that teachers are supposed to cover in the first two years of high school. The historical information that appears on this list varies from factual material, such as "the Marshall Plan" or the "Truman doctrine" (NYSED, 1999a, p. 113), to concepts, such as "surrogate superpower rivalries" (p. 113), and terms that denote larger narratives, such as "emergence of the superpowers" (p. 113). The "Standards and Performance Indicators" (NYSED, 1999b) present a model of achievement in history that consists of the conceptual understandings and historical thinking skills that history education should foster.

The primary purpose of state-sponsored examinations is to collect evidence that can be used to inform an argument about whether or not learning standards have been mastered by a population of students at a particular point in their education careers. To observe whether or not test-takers have met a set of standards, a task must be designed that elicits a performance that can be reasonably interpreted as an indication that the material was indeed learned (Pellegrino et al., 2001). Multiple-choice tests produce data collected under standardized conditions that can be used to make inferences about large populations of students. Stakeholders interpret test performances and use test scores to inform judgments about the effectiveness of teaching and learning (Linn, 2003; Pellegrino et al., 2001). However, the multiple-choice format includes no evidence of test-taker reasoning. Thus, a teacher may observe that students performed poorly on an exam, but the nature of the task occluded the possibility of more nuanced interpretations of what misunderstandings, for example, persist.

In New York, the state defines what it believes it is measuring when testing with multiple-choice questions in a document called the "Test Sampler Draft" (NYSED, 1999c). In it, the test developers explain that the multiple-choice questions sample from the list of content in the Core Curriculum (NYSED, 1999a). They explain further that

> the multiple-choice items are designed to assess students' understanding of content and their ability to apply this content understanding to the interpretation and analysis of graphs, cartoons, maps, charts, and diagrams.
> (NYSED, 1999c, p. 1)

The report also says that achievement of the more conceptual and skills-based standards (NYSED, 1999b) are measured by the thematic and document-based essays on the exam. The multiple-choice section of the exam is worth 55% of the final scaled score, and the two essays are worth 45% of the final scaled score (NYSED, 1999c).

The Study

The study described below was designed to collect evidence that informs an argument about the kinds of performances that multiple-choice history questions elicit. Scholars with an interest in test-score interpretation, or validity, have called for such research (Black, 2000; Hamilton, Nussbaum, & Snow, 1997;

Messick, 1989; Moss, 1996). The *think-aloud* (Ericsson & Simon, 1992) is a cognitive research method that asks study participants to vocalize their thoughts as they complete a task. Another useful data collection tool is the post-test interview. In this method, participants are asked to explain how they chose particular answers (Hamilton et al., 1997; Tamir, 1990). The data that these methods collect is then analyzed and interpreted to construct an argument about the extent to which test-takers made use of the knowledge, concepts, and skills that the task was designed to elicit.

Method

In order to collect data on test-taker reasoning on a history multiple-choice exam, I selected a small, diverse school in a large urban district. The school was chosen because test performance was judged to be better than the average for schools of a similar size and demographic profile. I observed the tenth-grade global history and geography teacher for one month as he taught material that covered the end of World War I through the beginning of the Cold War. The test used in the study was created by sampling multiple-choice test questions that covered the material listed in the NYSED Core Curriculum (1999a) for the time periods taught during my observation period. The questions were collected from published Global History and Geography Regents exams. Items were organized by theme and by item style into categories and a random selection was made to create a 15-item test.

Thirteen students elected to participate in the study. Data collection began following completion of the unit. Each participant was administered the 15-item test individually and asked to think aloud when answering the questions. Once they had completed the test, participants were asked to explain why they selected particular answers to questions (see Reich, 2009, 2013 for a more detailed description). The answers participants chose, as well as their think-aloud and post-test interview transcripts, were analyzed in two ways. First, the statements of fact in the think-aloud and interview transcripts were compared with the fact that the test question was designed to measure (Reich, 2013). Each participant (n=13) answering each question (n=15) totaled 195 such comparisons, or *events*. Second, the reasoning and knowledge of factual, conceptual, and narrative material that was brought to bear on the reasoning was analyzed qualitatively for each participant's response to each question (Reich, 2009). This analysis was iterative and had two steps: (a) a description of the cognitive processes used when answering the questions (Anderson et al., 2001); and (b) coding using a system developed from the verbs used in the NYSED (1999b) standards that describe competent performance. Those codes were used to test whether participants employed their "conceptual understanding to the interpretation of historical representations such as graphs, cartoons, maps and other texts" (NYSED, 1999c, p. 1) when answering the questions.

Findings

The findings discussed below include descriptions of the extent to which the items in this study measured the historical knowledge of test-takers and the cognitive domains evoked when participants attempted to answer the questions.

Test-Taker Knowledge

The think-aloud and post-test interview transcripts were analyzed to ascertain if the evidence suggests that each participant knew the key fact in each question. There were 13 participants, and 15 test items, so the study comprised 195 separate events. The results of this analysis were then classified into three groups: (1) consistent with expectations, (2) inconsistent with expectations, and (3) impossible to discern. Responses that were consistent with expectations were those in which the correct answer choice was selected and there was evidence of test-taker knowledge of the tested content, and those in which an incorrect answer was selected and there was no evidence of test-taker knowledge of the tested content. Responses categorized as inconsistent with expectations were those in which the correctness of the response *did not* match evidence of test-taker content knowledge. There were 10 events for which the data were not clear enough to infer whether the participant knew the key information or not. These are not included in the report of findings below. Table 14.1 displays the overall number of events that were consistent and inconsistent with these expectations.

The results of this study confirm those of other similar studies (Hamilton et al., 1997; Tamir, 1990) that found that test-takers were more likely to select the correct answer when they did not know the key fact—32 (17.3%) of the 185 coded events—than they were to select the wrong answer when they did know the key fact—16 (8.6%) of the 185 events.

TABLE 14.1 A comparison of evidence of test-taker knowledge and the selection of the "correct" answer choice

	Percentage of events in which the participant knew key information	Percentage of events in which the participants did not know the key information	Total
Percentage of events in which the correct answer choice was selected	38.9%	17.3%	56.2%
Percentage of events in which the incorrect answer choice was selected	8.6%	35.1%	43.7%
Total	47.5%	52.4%	99.9%[1]

[1] The total does not add up to 100% due to rounding.

Knowledge and Competency Domains

The Test Sampler Draft (NYSED, 1999c) explains that multiple-choice questions, specifically, are designed to measure the extent to which test-takers apply conceptual understanding to the interpretation of historical representations such as graphs, cartoons, maps, and other texts (NYSED 1999c, p. 1). There was evidence that some of the participants used the information given in maps, charts, and text to answer questions. At a more abstract level, however, the analysis indicated that students applied knowledge and competencies from three domains: content knowledge, literacy, and test-wiseness.

Content Knowledge

Content knowledge was operationally defined as knowledge of the factual and narrative material included in the "Core Curriculum" (NYSED, 1999a) for the world history and geography course. As discussed above, factual knowledge was not a prerequisite for selecting the correct answer. Nevertheless, knowledge of content was a significant factor in the success, or lack thereof, of participants who attempted to answer these questions. For example, the first question students responded to was the following:

1   A major result of the Nuremburg trials after World War II was that

    a)   Germany was divided into four zones of occupation.
    b)   the United Nations was formed to prevent further acts of genocide.
    c)   the North Atlantic Treaty Organization (NATO) was established to stop the spread of communism.
    d)   Nazi political and military leaders were held accountable for their actions.

This item asks test-takers to remember that the Nuremburg trials were established to hold Nazi political and military leaders accountable for their actions. The *distracters*—the wrong answer choices—are all factually correct, appear in the standards, and are likely to have been covered in class. The think-aloud and post-test interview transcripts of two participants—Claude and Franklin— illustrate the importance of factual knowledge.

When faced with this question, Claude read the stem and the answer choices. When reading them for the second time, he remarked

> A major result of the Nuremburg Trials after World War II was that the Nuremberg Trials—Nuremburg, sound like Germany. I don't know. Into four zones of occupation. Four zones . . . Military leaders held . . . I'll put um . . . I don't know, damn. This is hard. I can't remember all of this. Results the results! Germany was divided.

Claude was able to identify Nuremburg as "sound[ing] like Germany," but did not remember specifically what the Nuremburg trials were for. This led him to select a factual answer choice that did not answer the specific question. Claude performed poorly on the test, answering only four of the 15 items correctly. The excerpt from his think-aloud transcript above is evidence that poor content knowledge was a salient reason for his poor performance.

Franklin performed better than Claude, answering nine of the 15 questions correctly, a result that is a fairly accurate measure of his content knowledge. After reading through the question and answer choices, Franklin remarked "I think it is that Nazi political and military leaders were held accountable for their actions, because there were Nuremberg trials after the war." When he was asked why he selected this answer in his post-test interview, Franklin responded, "because I just remember, like,—that some of them are guilty. And that [trying war criminals] was possible."

These two responses to the question about the Nuremburg trials illustrate the importance of content knowledge when answering test items. In Franklin's case, it also appears that when a test-taker is confident of their knowledge, they do not engage in much explicit reasoning when responding to questions. A connection is made between related facts, or schema, and an answer is selected (Reich, 2009). This is consistent with what researchers have found about experts in other domains (Bransford, 2000).

Literacy

Literacy is defined here in a narrow sense as the command of relevant vocabulary and the ability to read and manipulate the ideas presented in printed text. Literacy could be used as an umbrella term to encapsulate all the sociocognitive processes discussed in answering multiple-choice history questions (Gee, 2012). Nevertheless, it was useful to define literacy in this narrow way in order to talk specifically about issues of decoding and as an orientation towards language that went beyond seeing words as a set of predetermined meanings to approaching them as a tool that could be manipulated by the user (Gee, 2012). In the following example, Roman and Francine illustrate the difference between these two orientations towards language and how that played out when answering question 12, shown in Figure 14.1.

When Roman first encountered this question, he skipped it saying, "What is appeasement? Appeasement. I don't know. Let me continue." He returned to question 12 after completing the rest of the test. This time, after rereading the question he said, "Let's see. The clearest example of the policy of appeasement in the statement made by speaker . . . I would say C, because that's something pleasing, I guess." When asked to explain his answer in the post-test interview, Roman replied that when he read "appeasement" he

> was kind of thinking about 'pleasing' and stuff like that . . . You know, if the Munich Pact saved it [Europe], you know, that's kind of pleasing,

Base your answers to questions 11 and 12 on the statements below and on your knowledge of social studies

Speaker A: "What was actually happening on the battlefield was all secret then, but I thought that the Greater East Asia Co-Prosperity Sphere would be of crucial importance to backward races."

Speaker B: "We Nazis must hold to our aim in foreign policy, namely to secure for the German people the land and soil which they are entitled..."

Speaker C: "The Munich Pact saved Czechoslovakia from destruction and Europe from Armegeddon."

Speaker D: "We shall defend our island, whatever the cost shall be. We shall fight on the beaches, we shall fight on the landing grounds, we shall fight in the fields and in the streets ... We shall never surrender."

12. The clearest example of the policy of appeasement is in the statement made by Speaker
A
B
C
D

FIGURE 14.1 Question 12

> and Speaker D, it doesn't say anything about like, any pleasing thing. Or Speaker B . . . so yeah, I picked C. . . . And yeah, I was thinking about that, because appeasement, I was thinking pleasement (sic). I mean, they both sound kind of like you're trying to please somebody.

Although Roman incorrectly connects appeasement with pleasing (the root of the term is peace not pleasure), it is important to note that Roman approaches language as a malleable tool, and has a sense of agency in using that tool.

Roman's response can be contrasted with that of Francine, who also did not remember what appeasement meant, but did not have the literacy skills, nor the dispositional orientation towards language, that Roman had. Francine read the quotes and the question and responded:

> I forgot what appeasement means, man. I have a guess for that one. If I knew what appeasement meant, I wouldn't have a problem with this. Probably appeasement mean, a treaty? I don't know.

In the post-test interview, Francine was reminded about a story her teacher told that was meant to illustrate the meaning of appeasement using a parable about a child throwing a tantrum in a store to convince her mother to buy her more and more candy. Francine had great difficulty making connections between the meaning of the word appeasement as expressed through the parable, and the situations described in the short quotes in the question. Although she read the words on the page quite well, there is something she is not getting. One could argue that her failure to respond to this question correctly illustrates the success of the item in discriminating those who can and cannot apply content understanding to the interpretation of (an unsourced) historical text. Roman also fails to remember the meaning of appeasement but has deeper literacy resources to draw upon, and has a disposition towards language as a malleable tool. The teacher who marks the response wrong, however, has little idea about why Francine failed to select the correct answer.

Test-Wiseness

Test-wiseness is defined as the knowledge of strategies that are "logically independent of the trait being measured" (Smith, 1982, p. 211) and are used to increase the likelihood of selecting the correct answer choice (Millman, Bishop, & Ebel, 1965). In other words, test-wiseness refers to the heuristics, or—less graciously—tricks, used by test-takers to raise their score that have nothing to do with the domain the test was designed to measure. One could describe this phenomenon as test-literacy, or familiarity with the discourse, logic, and opportunities presented to test-takers in exams. Participants who were test-wise were better able to make use of the information given in the test, even on different questions, to increase the probability that they were selecting the correct answer choice. Participants who were less test-wise struggled to do so; sometimes they even appeared to not understand what was being asked of them in this genre of assessment, and used heuristics that may have been appropriate in other genres but were not effective on multiple-choice history tests (see Reich, 2009).

Test-wiseness goes beyond the elimination of answers believed to be incorrect in order to increase the chances of guessing the correct answer. Although this particular strategy is employed by many, savvy test-takers will also look to see if information in subsequent questions verifies, casts doubt upon, or suggests other possibilities in previous questions whose content is related. For example, Lawrence attempts to answer question 8, is unsure of his answer, and when he encounters confirmatory information in question 10, goes back and changes his answer to question 8 from the incorrect answer to the correct one (see Figure 14.2). He is able to do so using information in question 10, even though he did not select the correct answer to question 10. Thus, rather than selecting the incorrect answer to two questions, he gets only one of them wrong. One could, though it would be a stretch, argue that Lawrence's move is an example of Lawrence's understanding of the content being evoked, as well as his "ability to apply this content understanding to the interpretation of and analysis of graphs, cartoons, maps, charts, and diagrams" (NYSED, 1999c, p. 1). I would argue, rather, that he has learned a set of test-wise skills that he can employ to boost his score when he fails to remember the content.

Discussion

Assessment results are interpreted based on particular assumptions and models set out in the design process (Pellegrino et al., 2001; Mislevy, 2009). In the case of this particular study, achievement in history is indicated when test-takers are able to select correct answers to multiple-choice questions at least 65% of the time. New York State claims that choosing correct answers indicates student mastery of content knowledge and the ability to employ that knowledge to interpret graphs, quotes, maps, and other historical texts. So, what can we learn about student achievement in a world history unit from their performance on a multiple-choice test?

First, it is important to note that this study interprets results at a very small scale—13 students, 15 questions, one curricular unit—using a technology that is vetted for large-scale use. It is, thus, difficult to generalize beyond this sample. As far as this group of students is concerned, the findings reported above indicate that they did remember some of the curricular material they were taught. The findings further suggest that when memory of content knowledge fails them, more skilled test-takers will employ other intellectual strengths, such as literacy and test-wise skills to select correct answers. Test-takers who are less test-wise may construct an understanding of a multiple-choice question that does not conform to that of the test designer, making connections in "unsystematic ways depending on idiosyncratic features of the tasks and how they match up with the student's prior experiences" (Mislevy, 2009, p. 6; see also Reich, 2009).

When considering the adequacy of a particular format for measuring achievement in a discipline, one must first consider to what extent the model of competence that informs the construction of the assessment is based on that of the target discipline. Multiple-choice history test scores indicate something about what Bell and McCollum (in Wineburg, 2004) called "the narrowest, . . . and least important type of historical ability," factual recall, as well as literacy and test-wiseness. Unlike laboratory research, tests are not given in a low-stakes environment. The high stakes that surround K–12 testing imbues exams with the power to define the criteria for success, and thus the power to affect *how* a discipline is taught. This creates a somewhat closed system in which student success is measured using a format that they have been prepared to be successful on. If we attempt to judge whether the multiple-choice format is adequate for measuring achievement in history under current conditions using technical tools, the answer is likely to be positive. If we permit ourselves the space to apply different moral and philosophical ends to history education, such as the sophisticated historical reasoning skills found in standards documents, then the evidence no longer suggests that multiple-choice questions measure up.

Text	Lawrence's Think Aloud
8. Which event occurred *first* and led to the other three? a. rise of fascism in Europe b. Bolshevik Revolution **c. World War I** d. signing of the treaty of Versailles	Which event occurred first and led to the other three? One—rise of fascism in Europe. Two—Bolshevik Revolution. Three—World War I. Four—signing of the Treaty of Versailles. Okay, fascism came quite close to World War II, so that can't be it. Bolshevik Revolution was in Russia. Signing of the Treaty of Versailles and World War I. Lets see, I don't know, but I'll go with four because I'm guessing.
Question 10 asks: 10. The Treaty of Versailles punished Germany for its role in World War I by **a. forcing Germany to accept blame for the war and to pay reparations** b. dividing Germany into four occupied areas c. supporting economic sanctions by the United Nations d. taking away German territory in the Balkans and Spain 8. Which event occurred *first* and led to the other three? a. rise of fascism in Europe b. Bolshevik Revolution **c. World War I** d. signing of the treaty of Versailles	The Treaty of Versailles punished Germany for its role in World War I by— Uh oh—I got number eight wrong, The Treaty of Versailles by forcing Germany to accept blame for the war and to pay reparations, dividing Germany into four occupied zones, supporting economic sanctions by the United Nations, or taking away German territory in the Balkans and Spain. I know it has to do something with taking off, taking away Germany's land and stuff, but it's either between dividing Germany into four occupied zones or taking away German territory in the Balkans and Spain. I don't really know what it has to do with Spain, but OK, I don't think that's it. So I'm going to go with number two—dividing Germany into four occupied zones. *Goes Back To Question 8 After Completing Question 10* The Treaty of Versailles Uh oh—I got number eight wrong, so I'm going to take that one off and I'm going to go with number three, World War I came first.

FIGURE 14.2 Text of questions 8 and 10 alongside Lawrence's think-aloud protocol

References

Anderson, L. W., Krathwohl, D. R., Airasian, P. W., Cruikshank, K. A., Mayer, R. E., Pintrich, P. R., Raths, J., & Wittrock, M. C. (2001). *A taxonomy for learning, teaching and assessing: A revision of Bloom's taxonomy of educational objectives.* New York, NY: Longman.

Black, P. (2000). Research and the development of educational assessment. *Oxford Review of Education, 26*(3), 407–419.

Bransford J. (Ed.). (2000). *How people learn: Brain, mind, experience, and school* (expand ed.). Washington, DC: National Academy Press.

Broadfoot, P. M. (1996). *Education, assessment and society.* Philadelphia, PA: Open University Press.

Ericsson, K. A., & Simon, H. A. (1992). *Protocol analysis: Verbal reports as data* (rev. ed.). Cambridge, MA: MIT Press.

Gee, J. P. (2012). *Social linguistics and literacies: Ideology in discourses* (4th ed.). New York, NY: Routledge.

Hamilton, L. S., Nussbaum, E. M., & Snow, R. E. (1997). Interview procedures for validating science assessments. *Applied Measurement in Education, 10*(2), 181–200.

Lee, P. J. (2005). Putting principals into practice: Understanding history. In M. S. Donovan & J. D. Bransford (Eds.), *How students learn* (pp. 31–78). Washington, DC: National Academies Press.

Lévesque, S. (2008). *Thinking historically: Educating students for the twenty-first century.* Toronto, ON: University of Toronto Press.

Linn, R. L. (2003). Accountability: Responsibility and reasonable expectations. *Educational Researcher, 32*(7), 3–13.

Messick, S. (1989). Meaning and values in test validation: The science and ethics of assessment. *Educational Researcher, 18*(2), 5–11.

Millman, J., Bishop, C. H., & Ebel, R. (1965). An analysis of test-wiseness. *Educational and Psychological Measurement, 25,* 707–726.

Mislevy, R. J. (2009). *Validity from the perspective of model-based reasoning* (CRESST Report No. 752). Los Angeles, CA: National Center for Research on Evaluation, Standards, and Student Testing.

Moss, P. A. (1996). Enlarging the dialogue in educational measurement: Voices from interpretive traditions. *Educational Researcher, 25*(1), 20–28.

Nash, G., Crabtree, C., & Dunn, R. E. (1997). *History on trial: The culture wars and the teaching of the past.* New York, NY: Knopf.

New York State Education Department (NYSED). (1999a). *Resource guide with core curriculum.* Albany, NY: The State University of New York.

New York State Education Department (NYSED). (1999b). *Social studies resource guide: The standards and performance indicators.* Albany, NY: Author.

New York State Education Department (NYSED). (1999c). *Test sampler draft.* Albany, NY: Author.

Pellegrino, J. W., Chudowsky, N., & Glaser, R. (Eds.). (2001). *Knowing what students know: The science and design of educational assessment.* Washington, DC: National Academy Press.

Reich, G. A. (2009). Testing historical knowledge: Standards, multiple-choice questions and student reasoning. *Theory and Research in Social Education, 37*(3), 298–316.

Reich, G. A. (2013). Imperfect models, imperfect conclusions: An exploratory study of multiple-choice tests and historical knowledge. *The Journal of Social Studies Research, 37,* 3–16.

Seixas, P. (1996). Conceptualizing the growth of historical understanding. In D. R. Olson & N. Torrance (Eds.), *Handbook of education and human development: New models of learning, teaching and schooling* (pp. 775–783). Cambridge, MA: Blackwell Publishers.

Smith, J. K. (1982). Converging on correct answers: A peculiarity of multiple choice tests. *Journal of Educational Measurement, 19*(3), 211–220.

Tamir, P. (1990). Justifying the selection of answers in multiple choice items. *International Journal of Science Education, 12*(5), 563–573.

VanSledright, B. A. (2008). Narratives of nation-state, historical knowledge and school history education. *Review of Research in Education, 32*, 109–146.

Wineburg, S. S. (1991). Historical problem solving: A study of the cognitive processes used in the evaluation of documentary and pictorial evidence. *Journal of Educational Psychology, 83*(1), 73–87.

Wineburg, S. S. (2001). *Historical thinking and other unnatural acts.* Philadelphia, PA: Temple University Press.

Wineburg, S. S. (2004). Crazy for history. *Journal of American History, 12*(29), 1401–1414.

Zimmerman, J. (2002). *Whose America?: Culture wars in the public schools.* Cambridge, MA: Harvard University Press.

15

HISTORY ASSESSMENTS OF THINKING

An Investigation of Cognitive Validity

Mark Smith and Joel Breakstone

Introduction

The United States is in the midst of a testing gold rush. The federal government has committed hundreds of millions of dollars to the creation of tests to correspond to new national standards (Gewertz, 2011). Simultaneously, test-makers and publishing companies have produced scores of new assessment tools to capitalize on the demand for resources that address these new standards. A search of Amazon.com for such assessments yields no fewer than 500 results. Despite the plethora of assessment materials for sale, history teachers have few options. Multiple-choice questions and essay prompts predominate (Martin, Maldonado, Schneider, & Smith 2011). Document-based questions (DBQs), which require students to use a series of historical documents to write an analytic essay, have become particularly popular. Although multiple-choice questions and DBQs can both help in assessing students' historical understanding, these two disparate item types leave teachers shorthanded when it comes to assessment. We don't expect a chef to make a gourmet meal with only a paring knife and a stockpot. Expert cooking requires a range of tools from colanders to sauté pans to food processors. Why would we expect history teachers to effectively monitor students' progress and adjust instruction with the limited tools currently available? History teachers need a broader range of assessment instruments at their disposal.

This need for new assessments is even more pronounced given the demands of the United States' new Common Core State Standards. These standards, which have been adopted by 43 states, call for students to engage in a wide array of historical thinking. The new standards ask students to compare multiple historical accounts, consider source information, use evidence in discussions, and mount written historical arguments (Common Core State Standards Initiative, 2010). Despite their prominent role in the new standards, historical documents have not been routinely analyzed in American classrooms. Instead, history courses have traditionally been structured around the passive learning of textbook narratives (Paxton, 1999; Ravitch & Finn, 1987; Wineburg, 2007). To meet the Common Core's ambitious goals, teachers will need more than discrete multiple-choice questions and lengthy DBQs. New types of history assessments need to be created and research is needed to better understand how these new tools work.

Assessments of Historical Thinking

The most readily available history assessment options exist at opposite ends of the assessment spectrum. Multiple-choice questions are widely used, but they are imprecise tools for gathering information about students' grasp of specific dimensions of historical thinking. Scholars have argued that these questions primarily demand recall and recognition of facts (Reich, 2009; Wineburg, 2004) and students often use ahistorical test-taking strategies to answer them (Smith, 2011). Multiple-choice questions also provide limited information to teachers because they do not reveal the student thinking that led to answers (Haney & Scott, 1987; Madaus, Russell, & Higgins, 2009). Darkened circles on an answer sheet are the only indications of student thinking.

At the other end of the spectrum, DBQs are complex tasks. Each DBQ poses a historical question that students answer using a set of documents. Students must interpret the question, read through the documents, generate a thesis statement, decide how to use the documents to support their argument, and write an essay. The DBQ's emphasis on historical argumentation aligns with the Common Core, but it also has limitations. Young and Leinhardt (1998) found that when completing DBQs, Advanced Placement students often raided documents for appropriate quotes or facts instead of analyzing them as historical sources. In some cases, students could mount solid historical arguments without having carefully interrogated the documents. The complexity of the task can also make it difficult to tell what it measures. Is it students' ability to develop a historical argument? Or is it their ability to quickly process original sources? Or perhaps it is their ability to produce an analytic essay under serious time constraints? Given the task's various components, it's hard to know for certain. The lengthy essays that students compose also make it difficult for teachers to quickly identify particular skills or concepts that need further attention. Teachers with classes of more than 30 students have to wade through hundreds of pages of student writing to determine next steps for teaching. It is unrealistic to expect teachers to frequently assign DBQs to all of their students or to use them to make quick adjustments to classroom instruction. Given the limitations of the most readily available assessment options, history teachers would benefit from manageable tasks that yield better information about student thinking.

In response, we began to construct, pilot, and revise tasks to fill the void between the simple recall of multiple-choice questions and the complexity of

DBQs. As part of our development process, we explicitly defined components of historical thinking for the secondary history curriculum (cf. Ercikan & Seixas, 2011; Holt, 1990; Lévesque, 2008; Wineburg, 1991). This was an attempt to remedy Stake's (2007) critique of the impoverished conception of the domain that guides current psychometric practice. In our definition, the components of historical thinking include historical knowledge, evaluation of evidence, and use of evidence/argumentation (see Table 15.1).

We further defined the sub-processes that comprise the three pillars of historical thinking. For example, *evaluation of evidence* includes three sub-processes identified by Wineburg (1991): *sourcing, contextualization,* and *corroboration.* We then delineated the specific facets of each of these sub-processes. For example, sourcing, the understanding that a document's provenance is crucial in determining its value as historical evidence, can take many forms. Sourcing entails not only considering who wrote a document, but also where, when, and for what purpose. These facets identify specific processes that can be directly observed through assessment. This definitional work yielded a framework for the processes that secondary students should develop and guided our development of new types of assessments.

TABLE 15.1 Domain of historical thinking for the high school history curriculum

Component	Sub-Component	Types of Sub-Components
Historical knowledge	Significance	Consequential, exemplar, and point of view
	Periodization	Grouping, sequence, and location in time
	Narrative	Framework, connections, and point of view
	Historical info	Recall, recognition, and evaluation of fact
Evaluation of evidence	Sourcing	Date, perspective of author, interest/motivation of author, circumstances, credibility of author, genre, and knowledge of missing information
	Corroboration	Comparison, verification, and articulation of need
	Contextualization	Socio-political, biographical, context of entire document, intellectual, environmental/geo-spatial, zeitgeist, and linguistic
Use of evidence/argumentation	Claims	Legitimate question, generalization, causality, counterfactual, and comparison
	Evidence	Selecting appropriate evidence, sufficient evidence, and evaluating claims
	Coherence	Evidence follows claim, appropriate evidence for claim, and address counter-argument

After we created our map of historical thinking, we drafted short tasks that addressed specific aspects of it. Each item required students to analyze primary sources and to write short responses that provided insight to underlying reasoning. Each of our tasks, which we call History Assessments of Thinking (HATs), can be completed in less than ten minutes. Consider one of our assessments that seeks to gauge whether students attend to a document's date of creation. The task features a painting from 1932 titled *The First Thanksgiving, 1621* (see Figure 15.1).

Directions: Use the painting to answer the question below.

FIGURE 15.1A Sample task 1

Title: *The First Thanksgiving 1621*
By: J.L.G. Ferris
Date: 1932

Question: The painting *The First Thanksgiving 1621* helps historians understand the relationship between the Wampanoag Indians and the Pilgrim settlers in 1621.

Do you agree or disagree? (Circle one.)

Briefly support your answer:

_____
_____
_____
_____
_____
_____
_____

FIGURE 15.1B Sample task 1

The prompt asks students to explain whether the painting would be useful to historians trying to understand the relationship between the Pilgrims and the Wampanoag Indians in 1621. More than three centuries separate the painting from the event it depicts. Yet, when we piloted the HAT, many students ignored the document's attribution entirely.

Rather than weighing the limitations of a painting created three centuries later, many students focused solely on the content of the painting and ignored the source information. One student argued that it would be helpful for historians and explained, "You can see how they are interacting with each other. Without any picture, you couldn't really see how Wampanoag Indians and the Pilgrims acted." Other students challenged the painting's depiction of the interaction between the Pilgrims and the Wampanoag. This student rejected the source and wrote, "As soon as the settlers arrived, there was mass curiosity, which turned into violence and hatred. There was never such a 'party' between the two peoples. They couldn't even understand each other." Although these students had very different interpretations of the painting, they both ignored the most salient detail: the painting's date. Some students, however, demonstrated a firm understanding of the importance of a document's date. One astute eighth-grader wrote,

> This painting was drawn 311 years after the actual event happened. There is no evidence of historical accuracy, as we do not know if the artist did research before painting this, or if he just drew what is a stereotypical Pilgrim and Indian painting

The student identified the problems associated with a document created so long after the event it depicts and explained that additional information about the artist would allow for a more nuanced evaluation of the document. In each case, the students' written responses provide teachers with information that could inform future instruction.

Other assessments address historical content more directly. Consider a HAT that seeks to measure how well students understand the narrative arc of the Civil Rights Movement (see Figure 15.2), and presents students with two letters drawn from the archives of the NAACP (cf. Bates, 1957; Roosevelt, 1936). Letter A, written by the First Lady to the Executive Director of the NAACP, references the President's reluctance to intervene at the state level to stop the brutal lynching of African Americans. Letter B describes the challenges faced by African American children in a previously all-white school and mentions that the President of the United States was concerned. The dates are removed from both letters, leaving students to answer a key question: which was written first? Instead of emphasizing the rote memorization of dates, this task taps students' chronological reasoning. Specifically, whether they can understand these documents in the broader context of the Civil Rights Movement.

Directions: The following two letters are both from the archives of the National Association for the Advancement of Colored People (NAACP) and were written over <u>20 years apart</u>. Read the letters and determine the order in which the documents were most likely written. Then explain your answers using evidence from the letters and your knowledge of history.

Letter A: From First Lady of the United States to Walter White, Executive Secretary of the NAACP.

Before I received your letter today I had been in to the President . . . and he said the difficulty is that it is unconstitutional apparently for the Federal Government to step in in the lynching situation . . . The President feels that lynching is a question of education in the states, rallying good citizens, and creating public opinion so that the localities themselves will wipe it out. However, if it were done by a Northerner, it will have an antagonistic effect . . . I am deeply troubled about the whole situation as it seems to be a terrible thing to stand by and let it continue.

Letter B: Daisy Bates to Roy Wilkins, Executive Secretary of the NAACP, on conditions of black children in a previously all-white school.

Conditions are yet pretty rough in the school for the children . . . The treatment of the children had been getting steadily worse for the last two weeks in the form of kicking, spitting, and general abuse. As a result of our visit, stronger measures are being taken against the white students who are guilty of committing these offenses . . . [The President of the United States] was very much concerned about the crisis . . . Last Friday, the 13th, I was asked to call Washington and see if we could get FBI men placed in the school.

Letter_____ was likely written <u>first</u> because _____

_____

_____

_____

Letter_____ was likely written <u>later</u> because _____

_____

_____

_____

FIGURE 15.2 Sample task 2

Short written responses provide a window into student thinking. One student wrote, "Letter B was likely written first because letter B is addressing the unsegregation [sic] of schools and letter A is about the response to the issue." The student, like many others, believed that the integration of previously all-white schools prompted the lynching of African Americans. Such a claim has a certain logical appeal. But it is wrong. This student lacked a basic understanding of the narrative arc of the struggle for equal rights. By the time the Supreme Court ruled to desegregate schools in the 1950s, lynching had been virtually eradicated. Moreover, federal intervention increased as the Civil Rights Movement progressed. This student's response about lynchings incited by school desegregation provides teachers information about a crucial gap in student understanding. Although we were pleased with results like these from piloting, further work was needed to explore aspects of item validity.

Validity

Responsible test development requires a rigorous and systematic evaluation of validity of test score interpretation and use. Today, the field of educational measurement adheres to an argument-based approach to the evaluation of validity. Under this approach, validity is not a property of a test, but rather is a logical argument about the intended uses and interpretations of test results (AERA et al., 1999; Cronbach, 1988; Kane, 2006, 2013). According to Kane (2013): "To validate a proposed interpretation or use of test scores is to evaluate the plausibility of the claims based on the scores" (p. 1). HATs are designed to support inferences about student proficiency in key aspects of historical thinking. This means that a validity argument requires evidence of the soundness of the inferences about student thinking drawn from these items. To explore the plausibility of these inferences, we gathered a variety of evidence for a validity argument.

The remainder of this chapter considers one aspect of validity that we have studied: cognitive validity. This aspect of validity considers whether a given assessment actually elicits the kinds of things it is designed to measure. A sound validity argument about the use of HATs requires evidence that they actually elicit historical thinking among students. According to Pellegrino, Chudowsky, and Glaser (2001), an evaluation of cognitive validity "should rest in part on empirical evidence that the assessment tasks actually tap the intended processes" (p. 207). Our challenge was to gather the necessary evidence.

Concurrent and retrospective think-aloud protocols have been central to our efforts to collect evidence about cognitive validity. Research across disciplines has shown that think-aloud protocols, in which participants report their cognitive processes aloud as they solve problems, are effective tools for revealing cognitive processes (Ericsson & Simon, 1993; Leighton, 2004). Although recognized as an essential source of validity evidence, think-alouds are often neglected in the test development process. In developing HATs, we were determined to elicit this critical evidence to ensure that HATs were gauging the historical thinking skills they were designed to measure.

Methods

Think-aloud interviews are time intensive. Given this reality, we only used items in think-aloud interviews that had already withstood a rigorous item development process that included expert review and extensive classroom piloting. Each of the items that we used in think-aloud interviews had been piloted with hundreds of high school history students around the United States. Moreover, they had shown promise for measuring important aspects of historical thinking. Student answers appeared to reflect proficiency in the aspects of historical thinking that the assessments were designed to measure.

Participants

We carefully selected participants for think-aloud interviews. We strategically sampled high school seniors from an urban public school district in the Midwest. Each of the students had completed a one-year Advanced Placement United States History course and had scored a 3 or better (on a five-point scale) on the national exam, which would have earned the students college credit at two of the three public universities in their home state. These parameters ensured that students had been given the opportunity to learn the material that was tested and that literacy demands would not impose unnecessary barriers. If students struggled to read the items, it would be difficult to discern their grasp of the targeted historical thinking constructs. If students answered incorrectly, was it because they lacked the requisite historical thinking skills? Or did they possess the necessary historical thinking skills but lacked the literacy skills to understand the questions? Thus, data from high-ability students allowed us to draw better conclusions about whether the items were tapping the intended constructs. In the future, we will gather cognitive validity evidence from more representative samples of high school students, which will provide additional evidence that the items elicit the targeted processes among students with a broader range of prior achievement.

Procedures

Before interviews were conducted, we developed a protocol that specified all research procedures and all researchers received training on it. All interviews began with an introduction to thinking aloud, which can be somewhat strange at first. Warm-up items, such as thinking aloud as students loaded lead into a mechanical pencil, provided an opportunity to practice thinking aloud while solving problems and allowed researchers to help students hone their think-aloud technique. Warm-up items then built up to tasks that were similar to HATs so that researchers could ensure students were comfortable with thinking aloud on tasks like those under investigation.

After completing the warm-up items, students completed HATs one-at-a time. We first asked students to engage in concurrent think-alouds, in which they thought aloud without interruption while solving the problem. Researchers only interjected reminders to "think aloud" if students fell silent for more than three seconds. In these instances, the research script specified that researchers would prompt students to think aloud by saying, "What are you thinking?" After students had completed the problem, researchers engaged students in retrospective think-alouds. Researchers first asked students to clarify statements made during the concurrent interview (if needed) and then asked a series of scripted questions to further probe student thinking. For purposes of analysis, we focused on data from the concurrent interviews. Retrospective data were used only to clarify statements made in the concurrent interviews.

Analysis

Interviews were audio recorded and the recordings were transcribed verbatim (Afflerbach & Johnston, 1984; Taylor & Dionne, 2000). The transcripts were coded on the alignment between the thinking processes elicited by the items and the constructs that the items were designed to measure. Alignment between the processes and the targeted constructs provided evidence that student performance on the HATs supported valid inferences about student proficiency in the targeted construct. Similarly, a validity argument was supported if students who missed the item committed errors that showed a lack of mastery of the construct or failed to engage in the targeted construct altogether. Conversely, think-aloud evidence undermined a validity argument if students arrived at the correct answer but made critical errors in thinking, or if students showed proficiency in the targeted construct but did not answer the HAT correctly.

Results

Our analyses revealed that HATs did indeed tap critical aspects of historical thinking. For example, the Thanksgiving HAT consistently provided indicators of student proficiency in a critical aspect of sourcing—whether students can consider a document's date and use that information to reflect on the document's usefulness as evidence of what happened in the past. Consider a response from a student named Susan:

> It was painted a long time after this event was supposed to happen, so I don't know. Maybe . . . I just don't feel that it would be too relevant. I mean it is three hundred years later. They probably just painted what they thought from that time.

Susan's response is an indication that the Thanksgiving HAT tapped the targeted construct of sourcing a document's date and provided rich information about her ability to do so. She identified the magnitude of the breach in time between when the painting was created and the event that it depicts. She also understood that the painting was perhaps a better reflection of the time period in which it was created than the event that it depicted. Susan then appropriately discounted the usefulness of the source as evidence about an event that occurred more than 300 years earlier. In short, the task elicited evidence that Susan could consider the importance of the date when evaluating a particular historical document.

Susan's written response also yielded important validity evidence. In rejecting the source, she wrote:

> I disagree [that the image is useful to historians] because there is a three-hundred year disparity between the painting of the picture and the actual

event that the picture is supposed to portray. Because of this disparity, it is unlikely that this is a relevant primary source because information from the picture will have come from what the artist knows about the First Thanksgiving.

Susan's written response mirrored the sophistication of her thinking. This degree of alignment between the cognitive process used to solve a problem and the evidence of thinking provided by the written answer bolstered a validity argument about the use of HATs to gauge students' historical thinking.

Susan's verbal and written answers clearly indicated that the task supports inferences about her ability to engage in a key aspect of sourcing. As expected, Susan also engaged in other aspects of historical thinking. Rich historical tasks typically require an orchestration of multiple historical thinking skills. In addition to sourcing, students often considered the context in which the Thanksgiving document was created and used evidence to craft responses. However, for purposes of analysis, we focused on whether the assessment yielded evidence of students' ability to consider the date of the document, the targeted construct.

The validity argument was further bolstered by the fact that, like Susan, each of the students in this think-aloud study who answered the assessment correctly used the targeted skill of sourcing. The same pattern held with other HATs, too. Students who answered assessments correctly used the targeted aspects of historical thinking. If educators aim to measure complex cognitive processes, then it is critical that the tools used to measure these processes provide sufficient evidence to evaluate student thinking. Think-aloud protocols revealed that both verbal and written responses consistently provided sound evidence of student thinking.

Our analysis also showed that HATs detected key misconceptions. Consider a response to the Thanksgiving HAT from Jonathan, who had earned a 4 on the Advanced Placement United States History exam just a few months earlier. When asked by the prompt if he agreed or disagreed that the painting would provide useful evidence for a historian, Jonathan reasoned: "I agree [that the painting is useful] because it accurately shows the interaction between Puritans and the Native Americans. I say yes, because the painting shows them interacting in friendly ways." Jonathan didn't question the source information and never considered how the date of production might affect the usefulness of the document as evidence. Instead, he viewed the 1932 painting as a direct window into the past. The think-aloud interview revealed a critical error in Jonathan's thinking about the source. Across think-aloud studies, HATs have consistently provided clear signals about critical errors in students' historical reasoning. Like the correct response described above, these types of inaccurate answers provided evidence in support of a validity argument about the use of HATs to measure historical thinking among secondary students.

In contrast to HATs, multiple-choice items often obscure student reasoning behind darkened bubbles or circled letters. Our think-aloud studies have consistently revealed that the types of standardized multiple-choice items used to measure historical thinking in the United States rarely tap the intended higher-order thinking processes. For example, the National Assessment of Educational Progress (NAEP) is a national exam used to measure American students' knowledge in various academic disciplines, including history. Another of our think-aloud studies examined multiple-choice questions drawn from the 2010 NAEP Grade 12 United States History exam. One NAEP item designed to gauge "historical analysis and interpretation" shows depression-era homes enveloped in a cloud of dust and asks students to identify a famous book written about conditions like those in the photo. Julia, a senior who earned a 4 on the AP exam, said:

> The picture shows a bunch of houses. You know it's a dust storm. The options are: (A) The Great Gatsby by F. Scott Fitzgerald, which I have to admit I've never read; (B) The Scarlet Letter by Nathaniel Hawthorne, which I know is a book about cheating—I have actually not yet read any of these—so, that one can be eliminated off the bat. (C) The Grapes of Wrath by John Steinbeck, and; (D) For Whom the Bell Tolls, which I've never even heard of. I just know Grapes of Wrath because it was something we talked about in history. This is almost a rote memory question.

In the retrospective interview, we asked Julia if she had ever read *The Grapes of Wrath*. "No," she responded. "I have yet to read any of these. I want to read the top three. I haven't even heard of that bottom one." To answer the question, she drew on surface knowledge to select a book from the list—a far cry from the aspects of historical thinking identified under the umbrella definition of "historical analysis and interpretation." None of the 27 students in the sample used the targeted skills of "historical analysis and interpretation" to answer the question. Our data also showed that some students got the answer right even when they focused on irrelevant features of the question, such as when a word in the prompt matched one in the answer. In some instances, the multiple-choice format allowed students to simply guess a letter and land on the right answer, something we have never observed with HATs.

Conclusion

Historical thinking has played a prominent role in discussions about history education reform in the United States. Aspects of historical thinking are central to the new Common Core State Standards and the College Board has made historical thinking a focus in its United States and world history Advanced Placement curricula. If reformers hope to create classrooms that foster students' ability to think historically, then assessments that gauge whether students have learned these skills are crucial. Research has shown that tests shape classroom instruction and without valid tests of historical thinking, it is unlikely that the teaching of historical thinking will become part of classroom practice (Frederiksen, 1984; Koretz, 2008; Madaus, West, Harmon, Lomax, & Viator, 1992). Unfortunately, the types of tests that are currently used to measure student learning may not adequately gauge these skills. HATs were developed to meet the need for assessments that elicit the kind of thinking we seek to develop among twenty-first century citizens.

References

Afflerbach, P., & Johnston, P. (1984). On the use of verbal reports in reading research. *Journal of Literacy Research*, *16*(4), 307–322.

American Education Research Association, American Psychological Association, & National Council on Measurement in Education. (1999). *Standards for educational and psychological testing*. Washington, DC: American Educational Research Association.

Bates, D. (1957, December 17). *Daisy Bates to NAACP Executive Secretary Roy Wilkins on the treatment of the Little Rock Nine*. National Association for the Advancement of Colored People Records. Retrieved from www.loc.gov/exhibits/naacp/the-civil-rights-era.html#obj16

Common Core State Standards Initiative. (2010). Common Core State Standards for English Language Arts & Literacy in History/Social Studies, Science, and Technical Subjects. www.corestandards.org/the-standards

Cronbach, L. J. (1988). Five perspectives on validity argument. In H. Wainer & H. I. Braun (Eds.), *Test validity* (pp. 3–17). Hillsdale, NJ: Erlbaum.

Ercikan, K., & Seixas, P. (2011). Assessment of higher order thinking: The case of historical thinking. In G. Schraw (Ed.), *Assessment of higher order thinking skills* (pp. 245–261). Scottsdale, AZ: Information Age Publishing.

Ericsson, K. A., & Simon, H. A. (1993). *Protocol analysis: Verbal reports as data*. Cambridge, MA: MIT Press.

Frederiksen, N. (1984). The real test bias: Influences of testing on teaching and learning. *American Psychologist*, *39*(3), 193–202.

Gewertz, C. (2011). Common-assessment consortia add resources to plans. *Education Week*, *30*(21), 8.

Haney, W., & Scott, L. (1987). Talking with children about tests: An exploratory study of test ambiguity. In R. Freedle (Ed.), *Cognitive and linguistic analysis of test performance* (pp. 69–87). Norwood, NJ: Ablex Publishing.

Holt, T. (1990). *Thinking historically: Narrative, imagination, and understanding*. New York, NY: College Entrance Examination Board.

Kane, M. T. (2006). Validation. In R. L. Brennan (Ed.), *Educational Measurement* (4th ed.). Westport, CT: Praeger.

Kane, M. T. (2013). Validating the interpretations and uses of test scores. *Journal of Educational Measurement, 50*, 1–73.

Koretz, D. (2008). *Measuring up*. Boston, MA: Harvard University Press.

Leighton, J. P. (2004). Avoiding misconception, misuse, and missed opportunities: The collection of verbal reports in educational achievement testing. *Educational Measurement: Issues and Practice*, *23*(4), 6–15.

Lévesque, S. (2008). *Thinking historically: Educating students for the twenty-first century*. Toronto, ON: University of Toronto Press.

Madaus, G., Russell, M., & Higgins, J. (2009). *The paradoxes of high stakes testing*. Charlotte, NC: Information Age Publishing.

Madaus, G., West, M., Harmon, M., Lomax, R., & Viator, K. (1992). *The influence of testing on teaching math and science in grades 4–12*. Boston, MA: Boston College, Center for the Study of Testing, Evaluation, and Educational Policy.

Martin, D., Maldonado, S. I., Schneider, J., & Smith, M. (2011). *A report on the state of history education: State policies and national programs*. National History Education Clearinghouse. http://teachinghistory.org/system/files/teachinghistory_special_report_2011.pdf

Paxton, R. J. (1999). A deafening silence: History textbooks and the students who read them. *Review of Educational Research, 69*(3), 315–339.

Pellegrino, J. W., Chudowsky, N., & Glaser, R. (2001). *Knowing what students know: The science and design of educational assessment*. Washington, DC: National Academy Press.

Ravitch, D., & Finn, C. (1987). *What do our 17-year-olds know?* New York, NY: Harper & Row.

Reich, G. (2009). Testing historical knowledge: Standards, multiple-choice questions and student reasoning. *Theory and Research in Social Education, 37*(3), 325–360.

Roosevelt, E. (1936, March 21). *Letter, Eleanor Roosevelt to Walter White detailing the First Lady's lobbying efforts for federal action against lynchings*. National Association for the Advancement of Colored People Records. Retrieved from www.loc.gov/teachers/classroommaterials/presentationsandactivities/presentations/timeline/depwwii/race/letter.html

Smith, M. (2011). *Measuring historical thinking with multiple-choice questions: A validity study*. Unpublished doctoral qualifying paper. Stanford University.

Stake, R. E. (2007). NAEP, report cards and education: A review essay. *Education Review, 10*(1), 1–22.

Taylor, K. L., & Dionne, J. P. (2000). Accessing problem-solving strategy knowledge: The complementary use of concurrent verbal protocols and retrospective debriefing. *Journal of Educational Psychology, 92*(3), 413–425.

Wineburg, S. (1991). On the reading of historical texts: Notes on the breach between school and academy. *American Educational Research Journal, 28*(3), 495–520.

Wineburg, S. (2004). Crazy for history. *Journal of American History, 90*(4), 1401–1414.

Wineburg, S. (2007, June 6). Opening up the textbook. *Education Week*, 36–37.

Young, K. M., & Leinhardt, G. (1998). Writing from primary documents: A way of knowing history. *Written Communication, 15*(1), 25–68.

COMMENTARY

The Validity of Historical Thinking Assessments

Denis Shemilt

"What we think we ought to think is bad enough, God knows. If people knew what we really do think it would ruin the whole show."

(George Bernard Shaw)

When assessing historical thinking (HT) it is fairly easy to determine what students "think they ought to think" about the past since, in the quest for marketable grades, teachers train them how to decode questions and write what examiners wish to read. What and how students actually think is harder to establish. Indeed, many students may be unsure where lines between recalling what they were taught and thinking about the past should be drawn. Locating boundaries between assessments of HT, knowledge of course content, general intelligence, literacy, and data-handling skills may prove even more difficult. In attempting to fix such boundaries, the four contributors to this section address issues noted by Messick (1995) when articulating his unified theory of construct validity.

Kaliski, Smith, and Huff argue that, with respect to assessments of HT, attention should focus primarily, though not exclusively, on ascertaining the cognitive validity and "dimensionality" of inferences from test data. By "dimensionality," Kaliski et al. draw attention to what Messick refers to as structural validity. The three following chapters say little about structural validity, or "dimensionality," but much about how cognitive validity may be determined. In this connection, all four chapters evaluate the merits of "think-aloud" protocols and, in the case of the three empirical chapters, offer persuasive case studies as to how protocols may be used and resultant data analyzed to refine test instruments and inform coding schedules.

Comments on the achievements of and issues arising from the four chapters will address both shared and diverging assumptions about construct validity, the methods used to obtain and evaluate evidence thereof, the sorts of test items most likely to yield information about HT and, last but not least, how HT might be defined as an assessable learning construct.

The Many Faces of Construct Validity

Throughout the academic literature, entities carrying the "validity" label continue to proliferate. Messick (1995) attempted to rationalize this ongoing speciation by arguing that content validity, structural validity, substantive validity, and so on are neither distinct types nor aspects of validity but approaches to the measurement of a single concept, that of construct validity. Very loosely, inferences from test data have construct validity to the extent that score variance accurately reflects the distribution of the target construct, the whole construct, and nothing but the construct, across the population assessed. All four chapters in this section focus upon cognitive validity as a means of determining the extent to which interpretations of written responses to test items and tasks are congruent with theoretical models of HT. Cognitive validity differs from what Messick (1995) terms substantive validity in that the former pertains to individual items and tasks while the latter signifies for whole assessments. Inferences about the cognitive processes deemed to account for similarities and differences in written responses to a given item or task exhibit cognitive validity to the extent that they match one or more mental processes specified in the HT construct of interest and other constructs and factors account for no significant fractions of score variance. It follows that demonstrating the cognitive validity of inferences from responses to individual items and tasks is a necessary first step toward establishing the substantive validity of inferences from performance on a test as a whole. It is not, however, a sufficient step. Inferences from an entire assessment have substantive validity if and only if (a) inferences derived from an assessment correspond with the totality of processes in the HT construct specification and (b) the distribution of scores across written responses is congruent with construct scaling.

The priority afforded cognitive validity over other beasts in the validity zoo demands explanation. For example, content validity is a major issue for assessments of historical knowledge (HK) but evidence of cognitive and/or substantive validity is rarely, if ever, sought. So why is cognitive validity such a big deal for contributors to this section? The simple answer is that the inference chain from evidence to measurement is longer for HT than for knowledge or skills. Assuming that HK tests are reliable and responses uncontaminated by guesswork, literacy problems, and inadvertent cues, direct evidence of students' HK and skills is exposed to view. In contrast, written HT tests and tasks elicit the indirect "products" of what may or may not be HT from which we must, first, infer the cognitive "processes" connecting each task stimulus to each written response; and second, determine whether or not—for the generality of students—these processes may be deemed particular manifestations of more general strategies and operations described in the theoretical HT construct. In short, it is necessary to show how cognitive processes may be inferred from written responses *and* from the HT construct. In order to check the cognitive validity of this "bottom-up plus top-down" inferential chain, all four contributors rightly assert the need for corroborating and, if possible, direct evidence of what and how students think while completing tasks.

One other approach to the measurement of construct validity is deemed essential by Kaliski and colleagues: demonstration of "dimensionality" or structural validity. Kaliski et al. argue for the design of tests that ensure measurement of student attainment on all dimensions of an HT construct. As a minimum, evidence for the structural validity of inferences about HT should include: (1) the emergence of factors that account for the bulk of test data variance and correspond in number and contents to the dimensions theorized; and (2) demonstration of non-orthogonal relationships between all or most factor pairs. Were the second requirement not to be met, it would be more reasonable to interpret factors as evidence for the existence of two or more HT constructs rather than as dimensions of a single HT construct. Although such an eventuality might complicate theoretical exegeses of HT, its measurement would be rendered neither more nor less difficult thereby.

The failure of the other three chapters to seek evidence of the structural validity (or "dimensionality") of inferences from test responses may indicate disagreement about the nature of construct validity. As previously noted, potentially more problematic is the failure of all four contributors to consider, or even mention other approaches to construct validity—content validity, generalizability, external validity, and consequential validity—discussed in Messick's unified theory. This could be because Messick's theory is less unified than sometimes supposed. One species of construct validity, which decomposes into substantive and structural validity, focuses upon the integrity of inferences about what is measured and seeks to establish whether or not we are justified in inferring that something is a duck if it looks and sounds like one. A second species, inclusive of content validity, consequential validity, external validity, and generalizability relates to the uses and applications of test scores not to inferences about their meaning. Here we are less concerned with the ontological integrity of a duck than with whether it walks like one, tastes like one, and lays eggs in season. The substantive and structural validity of inferences about HK are rarely questioned because, unlike HT, we feel we can recognize knowledge when we see it. It follows that we are more concerned with establishing the content validity of HK applications to particular bodies and kinds of information about the past, to determine whether or not the contents of specified domains have been sampled in ways that permit valid inferences about knowledge of an entire domain to be made.

It may be objected that the content validity of HK applications is a special case, that were HT as transparent a construct as HK (perhaps wrongly) is assumed to be we would focus on the content validity of HT about Icelandic history, world history, demographic history, counterfactual histories, and so on without troubling to first establish the structural, cognitive, and then substantive validities of inferences about the nature and meaning of test measurements. This may be true. It is possible that measures of HT are vacuous unless the objects of thought are specified and, in turn, the content validity of inferences from samples to universes of objects established. The problem is that understanding of HT is, as yet, too uncertain and contested for interactions with different kinds and bodies of content to be investigated.

Theories of validity have suffered from a surfeit of fine distinctions but the divide between validation of assessment meanings and validation of uses is both real and significant. Construct validity is about the justification of meanings attributed to data with reference to some theoretical construct. The boundary between construct validity and invalidity shifts according to the rigor of justification demanded in principle or for intended applications. It follows that the validation of assessment meanings, via cognitive, substantive, and structural validity approaches, can be made to connect with the validation of assessment uses. However, this connection does not obtain in the nature of the case; it is contingent upon our purposes and standards. For example, use of HT scores to select students for enrollment into history degree courses may be said to possess external validity when coefficients of determination between HT and degree scores consistently exceed 0.50. It is, however, possible for HT scores to meet this criterion even were student work-rates, literacy, data handling, and generic cognitive skills tested to a greater extent than HT. It is also possible that HT scores could fail to predict degree success because the kinds of HT measured are not prerequisite for degree success. But if scores work as intended, and in consequence exhibit external validity, does it matter if they don't mean what they're supposed to mean? And what is the use of scores that mean what they claim to mean but don't work as we'd like? What is true beyond a peradventure is that valid inferences about score meanings (construct validity) and valid inferences about score uses (what we might term "functional validity") can exhibit null, negative, and positive relationships. They are complementary but distinct approaches to validation and should be treated as such.

In conclusion, since contributors to this section focus on the validity of meanings attributed to assessment scores without reference to potential uses and applications thereof, they are justified in ignoring most beasts in Messick's construct validity zoo. The same cannot be said, however, for overlooking the concept of reliability. The composite R coefficient sets the upper limit for all measures of validity, whether construct or "functional." The validity of meanings attributed or uses made of perfectly reliable data—all signal and no noise—can, in theory, range from zero to unity; but the validity of inferences from perfectly unreliable data—all noise and no signal—is necessarily zero. Ercikan et al. report procedures for establishing, and enhancing, the inter-coder reliability of "think-aloud" data, but reliability coefficients for written test data are not reported in any of the four chapters. Given the sample sizes of experiments reported—35 cases for Ercikan et al., 13 for Reich, and an unreported but apparently small number for Smith & Breakstone—and, in consequence, their vulnerability to errors arising from "small numbers syndrome," this is understandable, but the significance of score reliability for any investigation of validity is worth acknowledging nonetheless.

The Construct Validity of Inferences About Historical Thinking

As previously noted, all four chapters address a problem particular to the assessment of mental processes for which direct evidence is unobtainable. All four chapters advocate the same basic methodology: the use of think-aloud protocols (TAPs) to check measures of HT inferred from written responses to tasks and items. Respondents may be required to "think aloud" while responding to tasks (concurrent TAPs) and/or to recapitulate their thought processes after the event (retrospective TAPs). The three research chapters offer valuable examples of how TAPs may be used to interpret and evaluate individual test responses. Examples are given of false negatives where ignorance of assumed facts or word meanings pre-empts opportunities for HT, and of false positives where tasks are successfully completed by following instructions or using data culled from other test items to eliminate distractors. Above and beyond this, Ercikan et al. explain how TAPs data may contribute to the development of (a) assessment instruments and coding schemes, and (b) "models of student thinking processes" as well as helping "to test hypotheses regarding such models."

Less certain is the extent to which TAPs data can be used to determine the cognitive, and ultimately the substantive, validity of assessment data. Metacognitive introspection is likely to prove more intellectually challenging than most HT tasks and, in consequence, to exceed the capabilities of many students offering reasonable answers to written tasks. It may be no accident that the most impressive instances of TAPs data come from the 15 high-ability students interviewed by Smith & Breakstone! A more serious question is whether TAPs data yield more direct evidence of HT "processes" than do written task responses—in particular than do tasks set by Smith and Breakstone in which students asked to make Yes/No or Before/After decisions are then required to "support" or explain the decisions made. The logic of these two-stage tasks (which may also be termed "extended objective items") is similar to that of a Multiple Choice (MC) item plus retrospective TAPs combination and, for estimating the cognitive validity of inferences derived from MC items, should perhaps be used as such.

Whether evidence obtained from concurrent TAPs is as useful as that from retrospective TAPs is questionable. It may be argued that "thinking-aloud" in real time opens a direct window onto the cognitive processes used to produce written responses to items and tasks, but why "thinking-on-paper" should be deemed an indirect product and "thinking-aloud" a direct expression of cognitive processes is unclear. We are just as likely to "think-before-we-speak," to rehearse statements prior to utterance as before writing them down. In which case, spoken and written statements are both products of thought processes and more might be learned by asking students to explain and evaluate what they wrote (or said) after the event. In this connection, it is significant that researchers sometimes supplemented concurrent think-aloud responses with retrospective TAPs material. As Ercikan et al. explain, when "students' verbalizations did not include their interpretation of the question and how they came up with their response, the students were asked *'In your own words, tell me what the question asks'* and *'How did you come up with your answer to this question?'* which provide information about their understanding and thinking retrospectively."

A final issue is the difficulty of making inferences about thinking processes from written and oral products. In order to minimize disagreements between coders about what may legitimately be inferred from TAPs data it is necessary to formalize indicators of HT. Ercikan et al. do so with economy and precision. Unfortunately, what is gained on coding swings can be lost on hermeneutic roundabouts. For example, one indicator is coded thus: *"Comparison*: student corroborates with or contrasts to *other* documents or texts." This guidance is as close to being coder-proof as we are likely to get and, in conjunction with comparably precise descriptions of other indicators, should guarantee acceptable inter-coder reliability. It can, however, be difficult to determine exactly what is going on in a student's head when comparisons are made: Is X being compared "with" or "to" Y? What points of similarity and contrast are identified? Does one source corroborate the other or do they corroborate each other? And what implications for truth are taken from source contrast or corroboration? Investigations of what British students think they are doing when using multiple sources of evidence to adjudicate between contested propositions about the past (Shemilt, 1979), reveal that many students fail to distinguish between statements that genuinely corroborate each other (i.e. are both true or both false) and statements which are merely consistent (i.e. the truth or falsity of the one fails to signify the truth or falsity of the other). Worse still, many students struggle to distinguish between contradictory statements (in which the truth of either entails the falsity of the other and vice versa) and contrary statements (in which one and only one can be true but both can be false). All too often students construe agreement (or the absence of palpable disagreement) between sources as corroboration and corroboration as proof of truth. Likewise, they often leap from perceiving disagreement between sources to concluding that one source reports the truth and the other falsehood.

More information and, it may be argued, greater precision in the analysis and coding of HT may be gained by allowing interviewers to augment fixed-schedule questions with "free-range" explorations and probes extemporized in response to

TAPs data. Enhanced hermeneutics, however, is likely to come at a price paid in the time, effort, and ingenuity necessary to ensure inter-coder consistency.

How Should Historical Thinking Be Assessed?

If replicated with larger samples and longer instruments, Gabriel Reich's analysis of the construct validity of inferences from MC items sounds their death-knell in HT tests. Reich's critique is devastating. He argues that MC items designed to assess "conceptual understanding" measure little more than "content knowledge, literacy, and test-wiseness" in practice. The possibility of designing multiple-choice and other objective tests that genuinely assess higher-order learning outcomes has long been disputed, but Reich also suggests that attempts to do so may compromise judgements about students' HK. In his study, factually ignorant test-takers are twice as likely to select the correct (key) option as an incorrect distractor. Ercikan et al. shrewdly controlled for variations in students' HK by selecting a topic unfamiliar to all and, in addition to primary sources, by providing all background information necessary to complete both MC items and constructed response (CR) tasks. Although less stark than those offered by Reich, the findings of Ercikan et al. support the conclusion that MC items yield less persuasive measures of HT than do CR tasks.

Persistence with MC items testifies to the manifest deficiencies of essay and long document-based questions (DBQs) more than to confidence in their intrinsic merits. As Smith & Breakstone opine, "the complexity" of the DBQ makes "it difficult to tell what it measures." Indeed, we may suspect assessments of time-management skills and prose style to be the only constant outcomes of essays and DBQs. The limited number of extended-writing tasks that can be accommodated in a practicable examination system, and difficulties in ensuring inter-marker reliability, are concomitant weaknesses of such tasks. This is where MC tests impress: it is possible to eliminate scoring error and, by using large numbers of items, to effectively sample low-level content domains.

While HT is normally considered to be multi-dimensional, it is not a domain—at least not in the sense that bodies of desirable HK can be represented as content domains. Each of the six dimensions of HT specified by Ercikan et al., e.g. "Taking historical perspectives," has extension reflecting differences in the quality (and hence learning difficulty) of students' perspective-taking. Unlike content domains, however, HT dimensions are not specific to time, place, or subject. It follow that although students may well find it easier to "take the perspectives" of early twentieth-century Canadians regarding treatment of alien internees than of Palaeolithic hunter gatherers regarding initiation rites, the HT dimension is assumed to extend through scale-points having the same meanings. Such assumptions, of course, need to be tested.

Provided that dimensions are few in number—the six specified by Ercikan et al. are probably close to the practicable limit for public examinations—it should be possible to deploy a sufficient number of tasks intermediate in length between MC items and long essays (or DBQs) to determine variations in HT quality along each dimension. With good luck and a following wind it might even be possible to build redundancy into sets of instruments such that the full extension of each dimension is assessed several times by different kinds of tasks and, thereby, facilitate checks on the reliability, substantive, and structural validity of test data. In this connection, examples of CR items and HATs offered by Ercikan et al. and by Smith & Breakstone provide grounds for optimism.

Is Historical Thinking a Valid Learning Construct?

The chapters in this section offer four definitions of HT. Ercikan et al., following Peck and Seixas (2008) and Seixas (2009), identify six HT dimensions of which three are operationalized for research purposes. Kaliski et al. accept the six dimensions described by Peck and Seixas (2008) and add a seventh: HK. Reich draws upon two NYSED (1999) standards to define HT in two dimensions: "conceptual understandings" used to make sense of past developments and "historical thinking skills." For operational purposes, Smith and Breakstone define three dimensions of HT: "historical knowledge, evaluation of evidence, and use of evidence/argumentation." Some differences have more to do with semantics than substance. For instance, "historical knowledge" usually refers to the material upon which HT operates not to the cognitive processes giving effect to such operations but, as defined by Smith & Breakstone, "historical knowledge" includes "evaluation of fact," "consequential, exemplar, and point of view" and much else besides. Clearly, we need to standardize terminology, if only to keep our metaphysics dry.

Stripping operational definitions of HT down to bare essentials may facilitate standardization of terminology. More important still, it should increase the practicability of HT assessments. Inferences from assessments spread thinly across multiple targets have little chance of demonstrating construct validity. Inferences from assessments with built-in redundancy that concentrated on a few austerely specified dimensions have a fighting chance of doing so. A useful first step towards a bonfire of HT entities would be professional agreement as to how, for assessment purposes, HT should be specified. Cognitive *processes* are almost certainly generic, not particular to individual disciplines. Arguing about the past could make kids smarter but other disciplines might prove as effective for this purpose. *Skills* of data processing, sorting, and matching are usually measured in terms of the speeds and inverse error rates with which tasks of known difficulty can be completed. Of the skills in which historians excel, it is difficult to pinpoint those in which the general population needs to become more proficient. A third approach focuses upon the *conceptual tools*—concepts of source and evidence, change and development, cause and consequence, and so on—used to make sense of the past (Lee, 2005). Of course, cognate concepts are used in everyday life and other empirical disciplines but differences in meaning and use signify as much, if not more, for concept learning than do similarities. For example, because historical sources differ from live testimonies and direct observations different rules of evidence from those used day-to-day or in science lessons must be learned. Likewise, the status of historical accounts is not equivalent to those reporting events within living memory or with cultures and societies capable of being revisited. To be practicable, an operational specification of HT may need to focus on *processes* **or** *skills* **or** *conceptual tools*. All other things being equal, it would make sense to specify processes or skills or conceptual tools peculiar to history and which students are unlikely to acquire without sustained and intellectually challenging study of the past. Unfortunately, the equality of "all other things" is improbable.

Before considering the philosophical, political, or educational desirability of different HT constructs we must be confident that HT is a valid learning construct. In short, we must have good reason to believe that it is possible, not only to teach students to think in the ways or with the conceptual tools intended, but also to identify and scale differences and progress in the kinds of learning intended. This can be tricky. Researchers usually find instantiated in assessment data the brands of HT different than other people are looking for, raising thereby suspicions that new names are being given to old learning. This is not to deny that researchers in this section have identified and illustrated instances where students are clearly "thinking about history." Some written and oral examples have considerable formative value for teachers wishing to remediate false-steps and misconceptions. Other responses testify to the sophistication of what intelligent adolescents can be taught to do and understand. Thinking about the past and, in particular, about what we are and are not entitled to say about it on the basis of surviving sources—or "traces" in the words of Ercikan et al.—suffuses examples given in the research chapters, but does so without validating any of the three HT constructs used. Indeed, it is possible that we may always be able to see and feel instances of HT without ever being able to arbitrate between competing descriptions of what we're seeing and feeling nor, in consequence, to measure differences and changes in its quality across populations of interest.

Some challenges are ontological: students may learn to think historically in ways so various and idiosyncratic that common threads and themes prove elusive. More likely, is that the quality of HT is inherently unstable as adolescents seek to justify what they would like to be true and how they would prefer history to work. Perhaps, indeed, HT only becomes sufficiently stable to be measured when the disposition to accept uncomfortable truths and rational argument gets the better of us. Insistence on teaching students that some bits of the past constitutes "our history" while the rest belongs to other national, ethnic, religious, social, or gender groups may prove as antithetical to HT as it is to peace, good will, and fair shares of apple pie.

Other challenges are technical. Demonstration that tasks load significantly on and only on the dimensions predicted is necessary but not sufficient for a construct to be adjudged operationally valid. Each dimension must also be scalable in the sense that (a) tasks are sensitive to various extension points of the dimension on which they load; and (b) extension (or scale) points have qualitative as well as quantitative meaning, i.e. in addition to signifying "better than 2," scale-point 3 must indicate what "better" means: for example, while scale 2 "perspective-taking" might indicate a student's ability to imagine how s/he would think and feel were s/he a hand-loom weaver in the situation described, a scale 3 might signify understanding that and why s/he would have thought and felt very differently in the eighteenth century than they do now. It is theoretically possible to test and verify the ordinal progression of scale points by various means, but the size of intervals between them is operationally meaningless and should not be assumed. In this connection, differences between HK domain and HT dimensional scaling should be noted. In knowledge domains it is reasonable to ascribe the same value to each unit of knowledge assessed, to award one mark for each correct answer and to treat summed marks as measures of HK without reference to the facility and discrimination indices of correctly and incorrectly answered MC items. When dealing with HT tasks however, facility refers not to the phenomenal difficulty of a task in terms of average scale-point achieved but to its stimulus difficulty defined as the range of continuous scale points achievable by at least 90% of any target population. A qualitative description, not numerical value, should attach to each scale-point on an HT dimension and individual scores should be determined by "goodness-of-fit" procedures, not through accumulation of numerical marks. It follows that once defined with reference to two or more dimensions the reporting of summative marks or grades for HT becomes risible and profiling necessary.

Conclusion

Before measures of HT can have educational value, three conditions must be met: (1) the operational validity of an HT construct is demonstrable; (2) for given student samples, distributions of scores must actually mean what we claim them to mean with respect to the HT construct, i.e. inferences from scores are construct valid; and (3) the uses to which scores are put are congruent with their meanings, i.e. contexts and purposes of use exhibit functional validity.

As the four chapters in this section demonstrate, significant progress is being made in answering the second of these questions.

References

Lee, P. J. (2005). Putting principles into practice: Understanding history. In M. S. Donovan & J. D. Bransford (Eds.), *How students learn* (pp. 31–78). Washington, DC: National Academies Press.

Messick, S. (1995). Validity of psychological assessment: Validation of inferences from persons' responses and performances as scientific enquiry into score meaning. *American Psychologist, 50*(9), 741–749.

New York State Education Department (NYSED). (1999). *Social studies resource guide: The standards and performance indicators.* Albany, NY: Author.

Peck, C., & Seixas, P. (2008). Benchmarks of historical thinking: First steps. *Canadian Journal of Education, 31*(4), 1015–1038.

Seixas, P. (2009). A modest proposal for change in Canadian history education. *Teaching History, 137,* 26–31.

Shemilt, D. J. (1979). *The evaluation of schools council project: History 13–16. Final report submitted to the History Committee of Schools Council.* Held by the Council for Educational Technology following the dissolution of Schools Council.

INDEX

★ 9 7 8 1 1 3 8 0 1 8 2 6 6 ★

An environmentally friendly book printed and bound in England by www.printondemand-worldwide.com

PEFC Certified

This product is
from sustainably
managed forests
and controlled
sources

www.pefc.org

PEFC/16-33-415

This book is made of chain-of-custody materials; FSC materials for the cover and PEFC materials for the text pages.

#0069 - 070116 - C0 - 229/152/15 [17] - CB - 9781138018266